PELICAN BOOKS

PERICLEAN ATHENS

C. M. Bowra was Warden of Wadham College, Oxford, until 1970. He was Professor of Poetry at Oxford from 1946 to 1951, when he was knighted, and Vice-Chancellor of the University from 1951 to 1954. He was made a Companion of Honour in 1971 for services to literature. His numerous and distinguished publications include *The Creative Experiment*, *The Romantic Imagination*, *Heroic Poetry*, *The Greek Experience*, *Primitive Song* and *In General and Particular*.

PERICLEAN ATHENS

C. M. BOWRA

PENGUIN BOOKS

Penguin Books Ltd, Harmondsworth, Middlesex, England
Penguin Books Australia Ltd, Ringwood, Victoria, Australia

—

First published by Weidenfeld & Nicolson 1971
Published in Pelican Books 1974

—

Grateful acknowledgement is made to the following for per-
mission to use copyright material:
The Bodley Head for excerpts from *Thucydides: The Pelo-
ponnesian War* translated by Rex Warner, Penguin Books
Ltd. Cambridge University Press for excerpts from *The
Oresteia of Aeschylus*, Vol. I by George Thomson. The
Clarendon Press for excerpts from *The Oxford Book of Greek
Verse in Translation* edited by T. F. Higham and C. M.
Bowra. Macmillan and Co. Ltd for the map from *History of
Greece* by J. B. Bury.

—

Copyright © C. M. Bowra, 1971

—

Made and printed in Great Britain by
Richard Clay (The Chaucer Press) Ltd
Bungay, Suffolk
Set in Linotype Pilgrim

TO W. G. FORREST

PREFACE

THE history of Athens in the fifth century B.C., especially the central part which we associate with Pericles, has been studied by countless scholars from every kind of angle, and we may feel that it is unnecessary to write yet another book on it. Yet every generation feels impelled to see the past in its own way and to find in it something relevant to its own needs and experience. This constant change of approach keeps the past alive. Periclean Athens has still much to reveal and much to teach, and I hope that this justifies my writing about it. There is no doubt of its pre-eminent importance, both for its actual achievements and for its influence on the whole course of history. I have tried to discern some leading characteristics of this period and to make them less abstract by illustrating them with facts and quotations. Though this period contains a great deal more than war, war determined its course and has to be treated in some detail if only to show by what unexpected factors the course of events is decided. My subject is Periclean Athens, but I have tried to set it in a right perspective by saying something about what preceded and what followed it. Nor have I confined myself to political history, since this is a period in which every kind of achievement contributes to a rich and complex result.

In this task I have been enormously helped by Professor A. Andrewes and Mr W. G. Forrest, each of whom has read my typescript and removed many errors of fact and judgement. I could only wish that what remains were in some degree worthy of their high standards in scholarship and understanding.

It remains for me to express thanks to Messrs Macmillan & Company for allowing me to reproduce a map of Greece at the outbreak of the Peloponnesian War, and to certain authors and publishers for permission to quote from their texts, notably Rex Warner and Penguin Books from *Thucydides: the Pelopon-*

PREFACE

nesian War; Professor George Thomson and the Cambridge University Press from *The Oresteia of Aeschylus*; T. F. Higham and the Clarendon Press for two quotations from *The Oxford Book of Greek Verse in Translation*, and to the same Press for some lines by G. M. Cookson.

C. M. BOWRA

CONTENTS

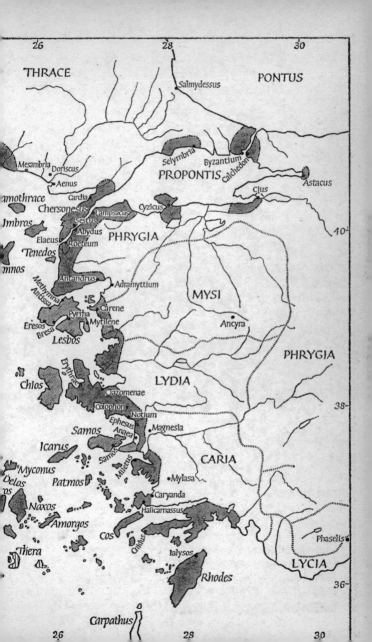

I

INTRODUCTION

SOME periods of the past stand out with a glowing distinction in the width and wealth of their achievements. Though they were not golden ages in any Utopian sense, we can hardly fail to be fascinated by them. They may be as different from each other as Augustan Rome, the Byzantium of Justinian, Elizabethan England, and the France of Louis XIV, but each in its own way exhibits a range of accomplishment outstanding alike in quantity and quality. Though success in war usually plays some part, it is not always the chief part, and the most triumphant conquerors, Attila, Genghis Khan, Tamerlane, Napoleon, and Hitler, have done little to enrich the human consciousness or its understanding of the world. Equally, though some dominating personality may impose his name on an age, this is not the case, for instance, with Islam in the eighth century or with Florence in the fifteenth or with Spain in the sixteenth. Even when such figures emerge, they are as much the products of their time as an inspiration to it. They give voice and effect to what lurks less articulately in the minds of their countrymen. What such ages have in common, what stirs our curiosity and admiration, is a prolonged outburst of vigour alike in action and spirit, which transforms the whole character of a society and leaves enduring monuments not only in the arts but in human habits. Why such ages come into existence is a matter for inconclusive speculation. There is no reason to think that they are all governed by the same laws of birth, accomplishment, and decay, but they enforce our respect for them and provide standards of comparison for assessing ups and downs in the history of mankind.

Of such ages a classic case is that of Athens in the fifth century B.C. Its pre-eminence is the more remarkable because many of its works and even the evidence for them have disappeared, and we must form our opinions on a small selection made as much by chance as by choice. We might argue that we are guided, almost unconsciously, by the Roman conception of Athens and that the pursuit of antiquity in both Classicism and Romanticism is a Roman vision adapted to later times. But in fact we know Athens much less from its admirers and imitators than from its own authentic relics. Many of these are fragmentary or ruinous, but they still make an overwhelming impact and excite a passionate curiosity. The great age of Athens has left visible records in the ruined buildings on the Acropolis, in many carved stones and painted pots, in figures and figurines of bronze and marble, in administrative records beautifully registered on stone. All this is enough to stir our delighted wonder, but it is supported by an inestimable counterpart in Athenian literature, of which a reckonable portion, both in prose and in verse, survives. This gives an articulate commentary on what we surmise vaguely from visible objects. From our strangely and happily assorted evidence a picture emerges, which reveals a most unusual exuberance and originality, a range of accomplishment equally notable in political action, poetry, history, the fine arts, architecture, science, and philosophy. Each separate success discloses a large variety in its own field, and when we try to form an inclusive notion of the Athenian genius, we are amazed to see how rich it was and how easily it accommodated different ideas and ideals. No great age quite equals that of Athens in the breadth of its performance or the sustained level of its surviving works. They impel us to ask what kind of society fostered them. In such an inquiry even small scraps of evidence may shed a revealing light and uncover not only the foundations on which noble structures are built but the practical workings of a community, which from a fundamental simplicity was capable of producing fine and complex results.

The chronological boundaries of the great age of Athens are not precise but they are easier to settle than with similar ages elsewhere. It starts with the defeat of the Persian invaders in 480–479. In the battle of Salamis the Athenian navy took a leading part in the victory, and by their own heroic efforts the Athenians, who had abandoned their city and their homeland to the enemy, were able to occupy them again, though the Persians had destroyed the city walls, houses, temples, and monuments. This brought Athens to the forefront of Greek politics and confirmed her in her high opinion of herself. If Sparta inspired the Greeks to victory on land, Athens inspired them on sea. Thenceforward she was eager to assert and extend her strength and became increasingly feared by other cities. This situation set the pattern for Greek history through the rest of the fifth century. From 479 to 462 there was an uneasy equilibrium between Athens and her allies on one side and Sparta and hers on the other; then, without any long respite, for the rest of the century Athens struggled to increase her power and was met by formidable opposition. From 462 to 454 a new policy was formed in which Pericles played a part but not the leading part. In 454 he was elected general and thence until his death in 429 he dominated Athenian affairs more and more, and this is the truly Periclean age, but the preceding years shaped issues for him, and after his death, at least until the peace with Sparta in 421, the ambitions of Athens still bore his mark.

The period after this, which ends with the surrender of Athens to Sparta in 404, shows new phases both in national temper and in strategy. Though Athens is sometimes thought to have deteriorated morally and intellectually at this time, her people kept up the struggle against Sparta with indomitable persistence, and her writers and artists lost little of their creative zest. Even after Athens lost her army and navy in Sicily in 413, she still continued to fight for another eight years.

The fifth century is the heyday of Athenian greatness and, though the fourth century brought new triumphs in other fields, the fifth is the time of unprecedented advance. In it the most active years are those which coincide with the rise and predominance of Pericles. Into it are crowded a series of parallel developments in action and mind. Each supplemented the other, but each advanced by its own inner compulsions. The various elements form a rich and complex whole which presents many problems for analysis.

The evidence for this age is all the better for being mixed. The indispensable stuff of history appears in the many inscriptions on stone with which the Athenians recorded their major administrative decisions on finance and public policy. From them we can fashion a trustworthy account of the machinery of government. But to understand what impelled the Athenians to act as they did, and the spirit and motives that guided them, we need the support of historians, and in this we are indeed fortunate. The Greeks invented history in the modern sense, and both Herodotus 'the father of history' (c.485–c.429) and his successor Thucydides (c.460–c.400) wrote about Athens. Herodotus, whose lively and eager curiosity peered into many odd corners of the world, centred his attention on the Persian Wars and had only incidental comments to make on what happened after them. This fell to Thucydides, whose account of the second war between Athens and Sparta is enriched by invaluable comments on what preceded it and throughout by many moments of insight into the forces which made Athens what she was. To him we owe above all what we think of Athenian character and temper and conduct. We cannot fail to see the heyday of Athens through his eyes, and even when we are on guard against his persuasive and dominating influence, he nonetheless affects our thinking because he is our fullest, most critical, and most conscientious witness.

Thucydides was a second father of history because he insisted that every possible care must be taken to find the truth. He knew how quickly and how easily it is distorted, how difficult it is to decide between contradictory witnesses, how even those who tell the same story may all be wrong. He understood the importance of chronology, topography, seafaring, epidemics, armour, and weapons, but unlike Herodotus, whose eager mind scoured the world for new topics of every kind, Thucydides concentrated his attention on political history and particularly on the war between Athens and Sparta from 431 to 404, which he watched from the beginning to the end. His primary concern was power, its acquisition and its maintenance, and he examined the war from this point of view. He had completed its story as far as the events of 411, but though he had lived through the final stages of the war, his death prevented him from recording them. His History illustrated, as almost nothing else could, the exercise of power, its claims, and its pressures. He judged politicians by their use of it, and cities by their ability to acquire it and keep it. Yet this severe and restricted outlook was informed by an imaginative and passionate spirit. Though Thucydides came from an aristocratic family, which owned gold mines in Thrace and was traditionally opposed to Pericles and his policies both at home and abroad, he became, with all a convert's zeal, his devoted admirer and made him a pivotal figure in his History. He felt the grandeur and the danger of Pericles' vision of Athens and applied to it his brilliant gift of analysis, diagnosed what went wrong, and decided that the fault lay not in Pericles' policy or his conduct of it, but in the men who succeeded him in office and governed Athens after his death. Despite his air of austere detachment and impartiality Thucydides was swayed by powerful forces, and, despite his unflinching realism in assessing political action, he had strong moral principles and was deeply shocked by the corruption in behaviour which came with the war. Beneath the impressive, impassive surface there are conflicts and contradictions which should warn us that Thucydides, despite his brilliant insight and his incorruptible integrity, may not have said the last word about Athens, nor need we see her only through his eyes.

In 424 Thucydides was a general in command of troops and ships in the northern Aegean. The Spartans had arrived under Brasidas, and for failing to succour Amphipolis from them Thucydides was deprived of his command and sentenced to exile which lasted for twenty years until the general amnesty after the war. Like Machiavelli, he took advantage of his exile to think about politics, especially those of the war, and to record his conclusions in a History which he had begun at its start. He found out much that he would have missed if he had held busy posts on active service. His information, gathered from both sides in many places, is beyond price, and though he failed to finish his History, it was largely because he took enormous care with it and was so fine an artist in narrative and analysis that he carries his readers with him and almost inhibits them from questioning his judgements. He began the History early and made substantial corrections and additions after the surrender of Athens in 404, when he returned under a general amnesty, but though he drew on many sources and may have got private information from Alcibiades, who also was in exile for part of the time, he could not attend the debates at Athens which settled the course of the war after 424 or see at work the personalities which guided the city in the later and the last years of her struggle. Thucydides' knowledge of Athens from 424 to 404 was secondhand and cannot have failed to be influenced by the emotional stresses from which even the most impartial of exiles may suffer.

Thucydides had seen Pericles in the ascendant, and this shaped his loyalty and his thinking. If the death of Pericles in 429 consecrated his memory for Thucydides, the passage of years confirmed his reverence for the man and his policies. He admired Pericles as a man and as a statesman, particularly for the skill with which he managed Athens. But emotionally he was committed far beyond this. When early in the war he quotes a Funeral Speech by Pericles he must have known that many of his readers would respond with all their natures to the ideal so presented. But this did not mean that the historian liked and admired democracy at all times and in all forms. Though he did not like the oligarchic government by four hundred which was set up in Athens in 411, he praises the limited democratic system of government by five thousand which soon superseded it. The politicians whom he liked were those who showed a clear judgement on men and events, and these were not all democrats. In Periclean Athens he saw a democracy which, so far from repressing outstanding talents as democracy was said to do, actually encouraged them. This won his devotion, but the devotion was more emotional and more imaginative than we should expect from this severely intellectual man. The artist in him need not always have been in full accord with the thinker, and what caught his imagination may have prompted doubts in the sharp, critical analyst.

If Thucydides himself was capable of shifting his point of view, others may have done it more blatantly, and thus it is difficult to form any single conception of Athens. From our diverse sources we must try to extract a notion of the main forces at work and to see how closely they come together in the whole picture.

The prodigious eruption of Athens could not easily have been foreseen in the sixth century. In that period Athens was in many respects very like other Greek city-states and even lagged behind some in the scale of her enterprises. Her literature compared poorly with that of the Greek cities of Ionia or with the early choral songs of Sparta; she had no scientists or philosophers worth speaking of. But there were nonetheless signs that she was in some ways different and beginning to move in unusual directions. It is true that she had not sent large bodies of self-governing colonists overseas as Corinth much earlier had sent them to Syracuse and Corcyra, which grew into rich and formidable states, but early in the century she had seized Sigeum in the Troad and in the fifties the elder Miltiades settled a colony on the western shore of the Dardanelles. The abundant remains of early Athenian sculpture have indeed affinities with other Greek work, but show a new insight and delicacy in their treatment of women and women's drapery. Her painted pots found a large market, and she was fortunate in having a soil which baked into excellent shapes, while her artists excelled in the firm, confident line which is indispensable to any fine design. In politics Athens might seem to be more backward than some other places, notably the island of Chios which had already a moderate form of democracy in the sixth century. But Athens began that century well with Solon's reforms, which curbed the rapacity of the rich and gave some security to the poor. Even when power was seized by Pisistratus, a tyrant in the sense that he was a military despot, he looked after the populace in his own way for his own uses, and did indeed keep the existing laws even if he was their chief executant, and paid his tribute to regular government by building a new council chamber. He and his family, off and on, stayed in power until 510, when his eldest son, Hippias, was driven out not by Athenian rebels but by a Spartan army under King Cleomenes, who evidently thought that under a tyrant Athens was more dangerous than under its old nobles. Pisistratus projected and sometimes finished large buildings and encouraged sculpture on a full scale for their decoration. It is true that Athens had nothing to compare with the advance of science and mathematics among the Greeks of Ionia, but at least she showed signs of life which in retrospect we see to have contained great promise.

Though hardly any Greek states were richly endowed by nature, Attica was no worse off than most. If she lacked truly well-watered and fertile districts such as existed in Laconia and Thessaly or on islands like Corcyra and Rhodes, yet she had advantages. She was larger than most city-states. The light and not too abundant soil was suitable for olive trees; the rough scrub on the mountain slopes sustained the omnivorous goat; on three sides the sea added variety to diet and provided a few much-valued delicacies. Athenians were slow to take to maritime trade, but they were well placed for it. Attica had a number of small harbours which were useful for local commerce, and in the Piraeus she had the safest and largest harbour on the Greek mainland. Though for many years the Athenians preferred to beach their ships on the exposed strand of Phaleron, that was but another indication of their early lack of enterprise. For building purposes Attica contained inexhaustible supplies of first-class marble, which clamoured for sculptors to carve it into expressive shapes; but other places had marble equally good or could import it from the island quarries of Paros and Naxos. Strategically Attica was not disadvantageously placed. Her northern frontier with Boeotia did not forbid invasion but at least discouraged it, while to the south the narrow road along the mountainous strip north of the Isthmus of Corinth, held by the small but tough state of Megara, presented a boundary which could be guarded quickly in time of danger. Moreover, Attica was a conscious unity. No part of it was held on terms of serfdom or near-serfdom as the Messenians held large parts of Spartan territory. The inhabitants of Attica were proud of their country and claimed to have lived as a single unit for many centuries since the legendary Theseus united them. The villages had their separate lives but were held by loyalty to Athens. Athens had the potentiality of increasing its power and developing its arts, and in the fifth century it proceeded to do so with an unprecedented energy. It was this release of force which drove Periclean Athens forward on new and adventurous paths.

It was not until the fifth century that Athens took full advantage of her natural resources and made herself a leading power in Greece. The driving impetus in this process was her democratic system and the energies which it liberated and set to work. This was given a special direction by her control, from 477 onwards, of a large alliance of Greek cities, which she was, in due course, to transform into an empire. Such a combination of democracy and empire was unique in Greek history and entirely altered the pattern of Greek politics. Its full results were not at first obvious, nor perhaps did most Athenians real-

ize what possibilities lay in their grasp. Between 477 and 462
Athens fitted into the Greek balance of power and excited envy
but no fatal hostility; her leading figures were content that she
should leave Greece alone while she continued to harass Persia.
Even at home the democracy which had begun with such brilliance was kept in order and not allowed to extend its powers.
This was natural enough after the strain of the Persian Wars,
but it did not last. The new spirit might be contained for a few
years, but it was eager for fresh fields and soon enough found
them. The period which began about 462 saw an accumulation
of strength and the growth of a new spirit through the responsibilities of the alliance. To appreciate Athens in her
highest glory we must first look at the preliminaries.

2

ATHENIAN DEMOCRACY
BEFORE PERICLES

ATHENIAN democracy existed before Pericles and revealed much of its nature from the start. It emerged soon after the expulsion of the last tyrant, Hippias, in 510, and attained a remarkable new shape in 508–507. When the tyranny was abolished, it looked as if power would revert to the rich families who had opposed the tyrants and were ready to take over Athens and run it as an oligarchy based on a property qualification. But such a scheme had flaws which led to unforeseen consequences. The rich families were not on good terms with one another, and unwilling to cooperate. Among them the Alcmaeonids had pursued unsuccessfully a policy of resistance to the tyrants and now wanted power as a recompense for their sacrifices. To succeed they needed more support than they had. One of them, Clisthenes, solved the problem with a stroke of genius. In the words of Herodotus, 'he took the people into partnership'.[1] The 'people' was the unprivileged populace, whose poverty kept it out of account and out of power. Under the tyrants they had been better treated than before, but now their prospects again looked bad. The rich would do nothing for them, and they had nothing to gain from the oligarchic leader Isagoras. Clisthenes took command of these masses and made effective a franchise which they had long claimed but had been prevented from enjoying. By this means Clisthenes established a real democracy. Isagoras called in the Spartans, who expelled 700 families hostile to Isagoras and tried to restore the oligarchy. But the Athenian people went into action. The Spartan king, Cleomenes, was surrounded on the Acropolis and forced to surrender, and Clisthenes repaid his popular supporters by creating a new system of democratic government. There was nothing else for him to do. He had called the populace to his aid, and with it he had triumphed over Sparta and the Athenian oligarchs. Clisthenes may not have been indulging the unpolitical virtue of gratitude, but he saw where the strength of Athens lay, and was prepared to do his best with it.

The reforms of Clisthenes were ingenious, complex, and far-reaching. The people of Attica were traditionally divided into four tribes, each of which had its own internal pyramidal structure. Politically this might not have been very important if the division into tribes did not reflect local attachments and loyalties. But it did, and thereby promoted strife and trouble, not on strict lines of class but on regional differences which were no less difficult to control and were largely determined by the power and prestige of landlords. Clisthenes abolished this system and created ten new tribes, each of which contained elements from quite distinct areas of the country. This destroyed the importance of local feeling as a political force, since it no longer made itself felt in the operations of the several tribes. The disappearance of the old tribal boundaries meant that Attica responded more easily to the call of a national unity transcending particular attachments, and that the influence of the landowners was seriously diminished. Athens was not only a true democracy but well organized against internal disruption.

At the same time Clisthenes reformed the old Council, which had been instituted by the law-giver Solon, about 594, and increased its membership from four hundred to five hundred, to suit his increase of tribes to ten. The Council, in which every part of Attica was represented, was the supreme administrative authority of the state. It ran finances through special officers, had certain judicial powers, and could fine officials. It dealt with public works and even with the conduct of war, though it could not declare war nor make peace. The Council was a deliberative body and had the initiative in law-making. It prepared business for the Assembly, to which all free adult male citizens belonged, and which could not meet without it. In plenary session the Council sat with the same members all the year round, but for immediate decisions the year was divided into ten parts, and the representatives of each tribe acted in turn to carry out business for a tenth of the year. The Council thus became a popular representative body, but its powers were controlled and modified by the Assembly, which decided all important matters.

The Athenian constitution could afford to leave final decisions to the Assembly of all citizens, because the total population was not too big to prevent a mass gathering. If the Council was extremely influential because it prepared the way, the Assembly had the last word. The power of the Court of the Areopagus, as the protector of the laws, was reduced but not abolished and, though it might seem to have been superseded, it could still intervene in public affairs and was a potential instrument against the democracy. But for the moment democracy was triumphant. Those who wanted power could get it by their own efforts. Athens was transformed into a democracy such as almost no other Greek state, with equality for all before the laws, freedom of speech, and freedom to vote on all public issues. The populace, faced by this astonishing revolution, may have been slow to realize how much power it could win if it tried, but for the moment it was content with what it had got. The birth had been swift and successful; it was up to the new democracy and its leaders to see that the enormous gains were not lost. They set to work with speed. As Herodotus comments, 'Athens, which had been great before, on being rid of its tyrants, became greater,'[2] and greatness was sought in more than one direction. The first was through the extension of Athenian territories at the expense of neighbours. Despite the formidable aggression of Sparta, Thebes, and Chalcis, Athens seized a rich plain in Euboea and settled it with Athenian colonists. This first success strengthened the Athenians' belief in themselves, but also reflected that belief and owed much to it. Like all Greeks, they were proud to show their superiority to other states, but now they felt that they were superior in a very special sense; that, when they defended their homeland, they defended a way of life which other Greeks did not share or understand. Like the first armies of the French Revolution, they 'knew for what they fought', and this gave them a magnificent impetus which was all the stronger because they saw that they were distrusted and feared by such reactionary powers as Sparta and Thebes.

The unusual circumstances in which democracy was established at Athens exerted a lasting influence on its subsequent career. First, though the unprivileged were largely responsible for the first successes, their leaders were aristocrats. Clisthenes was an Alcmaeonid, and though not all Alcmaeonids shared his views, he provided a precedent which later Pericles, related to him through his mother, followed with passionate conviction. This meant that democratic Athens maintained an aristocratic style and lost nothing of the refinement and distinction which it had developed under the tyrants. Secondly, though Athens continued to have sharp party politics and was not for long united in democratic views, its different sections were led by men of very similar origins, and when the social level of politicians sank, the doctrines, if not the manners, of the popular nobles were largely maintained. Thirdly, democratic Athens from the start showed its appetite for power and expansion. It was not content with its old boundaries or with playing a modest part in Hellenic politics. It wanted influence and dominion and was confident of getting them. Fourthly, whatever Clisthenes' motives may have been for establishing democracy, there was no doubt of his thoroughness in it, and of its acceptance as a formidable fact by his political successors. If his original motive was the need for support against rivals, he saw that to keep this he must make democracy a reality. Nor need we assume that he was unaware of the large principles involved in such a change. Once he had made it, he must have seen how vigorously it set a large number of Athenians to work and infused a new spirit into a whole people. Lastly, the emergence of Athenian democracy was strongly opposed by Sparta and Thebes. In defeating them Athens ceased to be afraid of them. But, realizing the depth of their distrust for her, she also knew she must rely on her own efforts, and not repeat the sad experience of Isagoras, who put his trust in Sparta and was painfully humiliated. These were important lessons, and the more active Athenian democrats took them to heart. All the lessons shaped in one way or another the system which Clisthenes founded and others were to strengthen, control, and proclaim to the Greek world.

It was not long before Athens, remodelled and embattled, was put to tests of extreme severity and passed them with glory. In 490 she was invaded by an amphibious Persian force in revenge for helping, not very effectively, the Ionian Greeks when they revolted from Persia in 498. The Persians landed at Marathon and there, between the mountains and the sea, they were driven back to their ships by a combination of skilful tactics, high morale, and physical fitness. For ten years thereafter Athens was free to look to her defences and plot the future of Greece and herself.

Though Marathon set the seal on Greek democracy, the general, Miltiades, who was responsible for the victory, was an aristocrat who had owned and lost large estates outside Attica and was the centre of a rich and cultivated circle. Very soon after the victory his political opponents prosecuted him for raising false expectations when he met with an accident in an ill-judged attack on Paros, and he died soon afterwards. In coming years the myth of Marathon was used to counter overtly democratic causes. It was exalted to a heroic magnificence and honoured as a modern equivalent to the legendary achievements of heroes in the distant past. In the Portico of Frescoes in the market-place at Athens Micon painted a large-scale picture of the battle in its different stages with recognizable portraits of the chief soldiers. On Athenian coins an olive wreath, symbol of victory, was placed on the goddess' head. To have fought at Marathon was the acme of a man's pursuit of honour, and it is significant that when the great poet Aeschylus died in Sicily, his epitaph, thought to have been written by himself, says not a word about his poetry but boasts that 'his glorious valour will be spoken of by the wood of Marathon and by the long-haired Mede who knows'.[3] The dead were buried in a single mound which still stands on the battlefield, and the anniversary of the battle was celebrated by the sacrifice of three hundred goats to Artemis.

Marathon was a national victory over a formidable enemy. As such it was the pride of every Athenian, but since Miltiades was a rich aristocrat, the battle was honoured with a proprietary satisfaction in those circles which held his views. In later years Athenians who did not share the ideals of a complete democracy looked back to the battle as a golden age. The men who fought in it were honoured as models of what Athenians ought to be, and critics of the innovating present saw in them the finest exemplars of Athenian manhood. As late as 425, Aristophanes, obsessed by another war, marked his own hardy villagers as the kind of men to play a tough part in it:

> Acharnians, men of Marathon, hard in grain,
> As their own oak and maple, rough and tough.[4]

This manner of thought was not exactly anti-democratic, but it acted as a corrective to more advanced democratic thinking. Marathon was a national but not a democratic myth. It might transcend party divisions, and it was in fact a justification of the new democracy, but it was not seen in that light. A parallel, even a rival tradition, was needed to emphasize the strength of Athenian democracy, and this came with the next wave of Persian invasion in 480–479. Here the victories of Salamis and Plataea were shared by the Athenian people as a whole, and their leaders were prominent men on the democratic side.

Marathon for the moment put political controversies into the shade, but they were not forgotten. After it the leaders of various groups manoeuvred for power and exploited the new and ingenious device of ostracism. This was called after the *ostrakon*, or potsherd, on which the voter wrote the name of some man of whom for political reasons he wished to be rid. Many such shards have been found in Athens with famous names written on them. Ostracism was the means to send a man into exile, without loss of property, for ten years, and was perhaps intended to control the violence of factional and personal hatreds. It was more generous and more humane than most punishments or revenges inflicted by newly born democracies. The whole Assembly voted, and the decision was not valid unless six thousand votes were cast. Athenian politicians thus got rid of their opponents by using the populace against them. From 486 to 482 it was turned successfully against Megacles, the leader of the Alcmaeonids; Xanthippus, the father of Pericles; Aristides, later called 'the just'. Fortunately all three were allowed to return to Athens before the Persian invasion of 480. National peril closed for the moment rifts between political groups.

At this period Athenian democracy was struggling into a second phase. For a few years the most powerful man in Athens was not a member of any large party or social group but an individual who made his way to the top by sheer genius, grasp of political issues, and clear understanding of where the advantages and the dangers of Athens lay. Themistocles, son of Neocles, came of a good but not rich family. He was already archon, or chief magistrate, in 492 and later fought at Marathon, and played a large part after that. It was his foresight and determination which saved Athens when the Persians returned to the attack in 480. He saw that if Athens was to take full advantage of her geographical position, she must have a navy to protect her long sea coast and transport her soldiers expeditiously to other fronts. Themistocles had drawn a lesson when the Athenians took Chalcis in 506 and captured twenty ships, but, not knowing what to do with them, burned them. Athens must have her own fleet, for which she had a splendid harbour waiting, and he had a strong argument in the presence at the Piraeus of Aeginetan sea power a few miles away across the Saronic Gulf. Athens was intermittently at war with Aegina and made very little headway, since without a fleet she could never subdue Aegina any more than Sparta could – Sparta who had tried and failed. Then in 483 a rich new vein of silver was found at Laurion in Attica. Themistocles resisted the demand that it should be divided among the public and persuaded the Assembly, very much to its credit, that the money should be used to build at least one hundred warships. These were ready just in time for the Persian invasion of 480 and by their action at Salamis changed the whole course of Athenian, Greek, and European history. The future of Athens lay upon the water. This was the second stage in the growth of Athens as a democracy, and we may identify it with the name of Themistocles. He was to meet with considerable opposition in these years, but for the present he was victorious.

The construction of a navy had repercussions in Athens far beyond any immediate target. The ships must be manned, and the crews must be trained to a high efficiency. Men could most easily be found among the poorer sections of the population, who were not tied too closely to the land or to the workshop of some skilled handicraft. Slaves could be used for the more menial or more mechanical services, but the essence of the new seafaring class was that it consisted of free men who had little to lose and much to gain by adopting a new manner of life. They need not all come from the coastal regions of Attica, for most Athenians would know something about sailing. Among them many were drawn from the underprivileged classes to whom Pisistratus had given security and whom Clisthenes had taken into partnership. In the urgent national call for men these were given a splendid chance, while most seafaring men seem to have found a new solidarity in their profession. The creation of a fleet meant the creation of a class which depended largely on the state for its pay and subsistence. As it became more conscious of itself, it could exert more influence in the Assembly. As yet it was probably too inexperienced to grasp what its full powers were, but we may assume that Themistocles taught it to use its votes to counter his opponents. As seamen they differed socially and economically from the old class of heavily armed soldiers, or hoplites, who paid for their own equipment, and from the cavalry, who kept horses, both claiming a high position in the state for their services. In effect this meant that soldiers and sailors were divided not merely by their tasks but by social considerations and distinctions. For a few years the bold and farsighted policy of Themistocles caught the popular imagination and won overwhelming support. When war came in 480, he was ready just in time and was appropriately elected general.

In the actual war Themistocles dealt boldly with an appalling situation on land by transferring the population of Athens to Salamis and elsewhere. He placed his hopes of victory on the fleet, but he had first to overcome the fears of his allies, who wished to leave the enclosed waters between Salamis and the mainland for somewhere off the Peloponnese. Themistocles frustrated them by tricking the Persians into blocking the entrances to this enclosed water and so forcing the Greeks to fight. In this he used his family tutor, Sicinnus, to act as a double agent with the Persians. In the battle the Greeks' ships, helped by the wind, had the advantage over their opponents, who were drawn from Phoenician ports. The surviving enemy ships retired from Greece across the Aegean, where they were routed at Mycale in the next year. At this period Themistocles was a national hero and on good enough terms with the other Greek leaders. This lasted through the immediately post-war period, when Themistocles, knowing that the Spartans opposed the rebuilding of the Athenians' walls, which the Persians had destroyed, fooled the Spartans by spinning out negotiations at Sparta until the walls were completed with splendid haste at home. In this he was abetted by Aristides and supported by most of his countrymen.

The supporters of Themistocles came largely from the socially underprivileged and politically inexperienced, and it was perhaps inevitable that they should be outwitted by the merchants and landowners who were the most important class at Athens. Themistocles was not as rich as some of his rivals, and this made him an easy target for hostile propaganda. It was said that he took bribes and, having taken them, did not keep his side of a bargain. A Rhodian poet called Timocreon, who had collaborated with the Persians, claimed that he had given Themistocles three talents of silver to restore him to Rhodes but Themistocles, perhaps because he was summoned to a meeting of the allies at the Isthmus of Corinth, did not carry out his part of the deal. Timocreon was furious and, when a little later Themistocles had some setback to his ambitions, Timocreon reviled him in drinking songs, of which one says:

> Rogue, blackguard, traitor, he
> From crooked bribery
> Refused to take his friend
> Timocreon or send
> Him to his island home.
> He pocketed the pay,
> And then he sailed away
> To the devil and to doom.[5]

In his lack of ample private resources and of an organized party, Themistocles may have improved his financial position by taking bribes, and anyhow the accusation of corruption stuck.

Themistocles was well aware of his natural gifts and not ashamed to say so. This won him the reputation of being too clever, which could be tolerated so long as Greece was in danger but, when she was safe again, was turned against him. His personal faults provided ammunition for a deeper dislike and distrust. The wealthy families of Athens, notably Miltiades', represented by his son Cimon, and the Alcmaeonids, who had hitherto been on bad terms with the former, had but recently been reconciled by the marriage of Cimon to the Alcmaeonid

Isodice. These families now joined forces against Themistocles and about 470 secured his ostracism. A little later, about 466–465, when he was in Argos, he was accused of treachery, no doubt because he had alienated Sparta by having his own ideas about foreign policy, and was condemned in absence to death. In this the Spartans led the agitation in the hope of ridding themselves of a powerful enemy. They sent agents to arrest Themistocles in Argos, but with characteristic audacity and skill he evaded them and went by a long tour first to Corcyra and then to north-west Greece. At the house of Admetus, king of Molossia, when the king was out of the house, the queen told Themistocles to take their child in his arms and sit down by the hearth as a suppliant. When the king came back, he listened to his plea, and, when soon afterwards the pursuers arrived, refused to give him up. Then Themistocles slowly found his way to Persia, where the Great King, who knew his worth, sent for him and gave him an important post as governor of Magnesia. So daemonic a figure could not expect to live without trouble in Athens, where powerful forces were massing against him. The result was that his extraordinary talents were wasted when he wished to exert them in new directions, and it is likely that if he had not been exiled he might have helped his country in the years after Salamis. The historian Thucydides thought him admirable for his natural genius and particularly 'remarkable at looking into the future and seeing there the hidden possibilities of good and evil'.[6] Themistocles saw that Persia would not be a real danger for some years, but that Sparta might well wish to hinder the growing power of Athens. This was what he wished to prevent, and he was prepared to switch all the energies of Athens to such a policy. He was ahead of his time, and his work was cut short, but he left followers who in due course revived his policies.

The struggle between Themistocles and other Athenian leaders began soon after the Persian War, and we can see traces of it in some powerful propaganda made for him. In 476 he himself paid for the staging of a play by the tragedian Phryni-chus, probably the *Phoenician Women*, which dramatized the defeat of the Persians from their own point of view and was clearly intended to remind the audience of the part taken by Themistocles in winning the victory. In 472 Aeschylus produced his *Persians* on the same theme and gave attention to Themistocles. He mentions both the silver mines of Laurion and the trick by which Themistocles deceived the Persians into attacking the Greek fleet in the waters of Salamis. The visit of Themistocles' agent to the Persians is exalted to a vengeful intervention of the gods:

> Princess, the first beginner of all the woes
> That afterwards ensued, though whence he came
> None knoweth, was some genius of wrath,
> Some wicked spirit such as lures men on
> To their destruction.[7]

By such means Themistocles was kept in the public eye when his fortunes were about to take a very bad turn, and the man who paid for the production of the *Persians* was Pericles, a young man just in his twenties.

These efforts to keep Themistocles in power were unavailing, and when he himself was rejected, his policies were rejected with him. The extreme democrats were without a leader, and for at least ten years the chief figure in Athens was Cimon, the son of Miltiades, who was not actually hostile to the existing democracy but did not wish it to be extended and tried to keep its supporters happy by lavish gifts from his large fortune and by ample appeals to their patriotic fervour against the Persians. The onward drive of Athenian democracy was checked, and Athens was governed by an aristocratic group who respected the existing situation. At the same time it made full use of the naval force which Themistocles had created and which had recently won a new prominence in Hellenic affairs. Seapower for a period absorbed Athenian attention and kept army and navy happily at work.

When the Persians retreated, the Greek allies, many of whose cities were within range of new attacks if the Persians tried to launch them, were determined not to throw away their victories but to press them home on Persian territory. In this their obvious leader was the Spartan regent Pausanias, who had led the united Greek forces to victory at Plataea in 479. But he betrayed their hopes and earned their total distrust. After liberating a part of Cyprus, he sailed to Byzantium, where he caused consternation by his favourable attention to leading Persians and his insolence and arrogance to Greeks. This did grave damage to Sparta's authority. The Greeks no longer trusted her to lead them, and in the winter 478–477 the allies turned to Athens and asked her to assume the command in place of Sparta. The request was made with remarkable unanimity, and Athens accepted at once. The transfer of command was effected in 477, when an allied league was created. Themistocles was out of it, perhaps because he had associated too closely with Pausanias, more probably because his assertive temperament was too much for the Ionian Greeks. Instead the league was organized by Aristides, a member of a good family and an experienced soldier, who was an equally unrelenting enemy of Persia, but whose greatest asset was his personal character, which was ideally suited to the complex task of forming a league on equitable principles. The aim was to maintain the offensive against Persia by preventing the reconquest of cities recently liberated, by devastating territories still under Persian rule and by being ready to meet any possible countermove. The administrative centre of the league was the holy island of Delos, the ancient meeting place of the Ionian Greeks and the traditional birthplace of Apollo. It was chosen not merely for its position in the middle of the Aegean but because, being extremely small, it could not become dangerous with its own policy and private interests. Among Greeks it had a neutral, almost international position. It was exposed to attack by sea, but at the time attack was improbable, and it was easy to defend.

The league was primarily a naval alliance. The allies who formed it wished to control Greek foreign policy through their command of the sea and were in a strong position to do so. Instead of moving armies by land, which was always a slow business in Greece because of the mountainous terrain and the lack of roads, they could move with ease and speed by ship to any part of the Aegean or other neighbouring waters. They had the advantage that many of the Aegean harbours belonged to members of the league, which included the cities on the western coast of Asia Minor, the coastal islands from Rhodes to Lemnos, a large number of towns on the strategically important Propontis (Marmora), the greater part of the Cyclades, and Euboea with the single exception of the city of Carystus. The league dominated the Aegean and held the entry to the southern coast of Asia Minor and to the large island of Cyprus. Athens was the only land power among its members, and among Aegean islands only the small Dorian islands of Thera and Melos and the big but strangely ineffective island of Crete did not belong to it.

The aim of the league was to maintain an allied fleet and it was founded on the principle that each member should furnish ships or money to the united navy. Many of the states were small and poor and unable to furnish more than one or two ships. Such a system was liable to lead to a lack of central control, to conflicting purposes and policies, and waste of manpower and resources. There would be differences of equipment and armament: it would be hard to find a place for such a force to assemble at a single time; there would inevitably be disputes about command and discipline, since national honour, always powerful in Greece, made it hard for one city to take orders from another. Aristides solved these problems by allowing a number of contributions to be made in money instead of ships. The payments were to be made yearly to a common treasury on Delos. Aristides decided that the total should be 460 talents, of which half was to be in money and half in ships. A careful estimate was made of the capacity of each city to pay and the total sum was then divided proportionally among the contributors. This complex and difficult work was done in a very short time and seems to have evoked no serious complaints. Aristides won such a name for fairness that when Aeschylus' play, *Seven against Thebes*, was produced in 467 and the hero Amphiaraus was described in it, the words about him struck home with irresistible force:

> He wishes not to seem just but to be it,
> Reaping from a deep furrow with his mind,
> From which his noble counsels come to fruit.[8]

Everyone looked at Aristides, thinking how well the words fitted him. The league was born with promising auspices. It was not imposed on the allies, but asked for by them, and the man who settled its constitution was honoured with an almost unprecedented trust.

By power and pre-eminence Athens was the obvious, the

only choice to lead the league, and events enforced her authority. Of the two kinds of league member, those who contributed ships and those who merely contributed money, the second class was very much the larger. Even some of the bigger states preferred to join this class because it relieved their citizens from doing military service away from home. The tribute was received by ten officers called Hellenotamiae, 'treasurers of the Greeks', but despite the promising title all were Athenians. The council of the league met at Delos, where Athens could control the votes, partly because she was by far the most powerful member, partly because the smaller states, each of whom had a vote, joined with her against other large states who might wish to bully them. Athens kept the executive power in her own hands, and the treasurers were men of standing who included at one time the poet Sophocles. There was no doubt that Athens was mistress of the organization. This system had solid advantages. It meant that policy, dictated by Athens, avoided the adjustments and compromises which are inevitable when allies work on uneasily equal terms. The allies had to submit to her decisions, and this might lead to complaints, but so long as the common aim was agreed, the league was more closely knit and better controlled than most alliances. It was much in the interest of Athens to have the willing co-operation of the allies.

The league soon got to work. Its first action was, surprisingly, against the Spartan Pausanias, who was playing a double game with Persia and at loggerheads with his own people. The allies, led by Cimon, helped to drive him out of the strategic point of Byzantium, which covered food supplies from the Black Sea. This was preliminary to clearing the Persians out of Europe. At the important stronghold of Eion in Thrace the Persian commander resisted to the last. When food ran out, he lit a large funeral pyre, slew his wives and concubines, children and slaves, and threw their bodies on it. He then flung his gold and silver into the river Strymon and himself leaped into the flames, which were for him the visible form of the fire god whom he worshipped. The capture of Eion indicated the lines on which the league was likely to develop. The Athenians annexed Eion and secured a well-fortified port with a hinterland of cornfields and forests. They sent colonists to it and intended to make it an external district of Attica rather than an ally. They were not really ready to undertake imperial projects on any scale, and inland their efforts came to very little because the wild Thracians were too strong for them; but Eion itself held out and later became the port for the new colony of Amphipolis.

An incidental advantage of the league was that it was in a strong position to suppress piracy. The Aegean provided many promising opportunities and many convenient hiding places for pirates to attack merchant ships on the main routes, while states not on good terms with one another could employ privateers to harass their opponents. Hitherto no power had been strong enough to stop this. But the league took active steps. Since its members were on peaceful terms with one another they did not need pirates to help them; and in these years the Aegean was clearer of piracy than either before or afterwards. A typical enterprise took place in 476–475 when Cimon led a naval force to reduce the island of Scyros, which was a nest of Dolopian pirates from mountainous fastnesses in northern Greece. Cimon scoured the island and rounded up the pirates. His exploit was the more praised because he found a skeleton of enormous size which, on the strength of oracles and legends, he decided was that of the ancient Athenian hero Theseus. The bones were brought to Athens with a devotion like that with which the Crusaders brought back relics of saints from the Holy Land. The pirates were sold into slavery, and Scyros was colonized by Athenians and provided a valuable port of call for ships sailing from Athens to Thrace and the Dardanelles. It may have been a lucky coincidence that what was good for Athens was good for the league, but so far there was no serious conflict of interests. If each new action tended to strengthen Athens in the Aegean, it also guaranteed the freedom of the seas for many Greek cities.

The elimination of pirates and the protection of food routes were incidental to the possession of sea power and did not interfere with the main task of harrying the Persians. Some ten years after the retreat from Europe the Persian king, Xerxes, recovered his confidence sufficiently to build a new army and a new navy. Cimon's strategy was to strike at him on the southern coast of Asia Minor, which the Phoenician ships of the

Persians tended to hug as they sailed west. Cimon delivered Caria from Persian rule and persuaded or compelled the communities of Lycia to join the league. Neither Carians nor Lycians were Greeks or Greek-speaking, and for a moment the league seemed likely to become an international body; but the experiment was not pursued. The Persians countered in 468 by sending a fleet to Pamphylia, the rich plain in the part of the southern coast of Asia Minor between the Taurus mountains and the sea. The fleet sheltered in the river Eurymedon, which, unlike Greek rivers, brims with water even in high summer. Cimon pursued the Persians, struck, and destroyed two hundred Phoenician ships. When soon afterwards he defeated reinforcements sailing from Cyprus, his victory put the southern coast of Asia Minor in the Athenian sphere of influence and added many new members to the league.

Cimon's successes against the Persians thrilled the Athenian populace. He brought it glory and loot and kept it happy. Athenians did not care that the fall of Themistocles had robbed them of a possible leader or that as yet no successor to him had appeared. The young Pericles had not emerged again to any effect after his support of Aeschylus' *Persians*. Though Cimon was the leading representative of the rich families, he held Athens by his military and naval successes. The struggle for power and rights was secondary to the lure of glory. The spirit which inspired the Athenians and their allies in these campaigns was very much that of the earlier Persian Wars, of which they were a natural sequel. No soldier or sailor doubted that by losing his life in such a cause he fulfilled his true nature and realized the *aretê*, or all-round excellence, which was the goal of a man's endeavours. Stone memorials, with Hermes' bust atop them, were erected in Athens, and on them were inscribed epitaphs in verse for those who fell at Byzantium or Eion. The language is cool and restrained. After the resounding victory of the Eurymedon, the common grave of some of the fallen, in the potters' quarter just outside the walls of Athens, carried its simple statement of what had happened:

> By the Eurymedon these lost youth's glory,
>   Fighting the best bowmen of the Medes;
> They died, on land and on swift-sailing galleys,
>   Leaving valour's loveliest monument.[9]

This has not the austere magnificence of the verses which Simonides wrote for the dead of the Persian Wars, but it shows a like spirit and assumes that nothing is finer than to die in battle. We may also notice that sailors and hoplites, once divided by social and political barriers, are now classed together as fellow fighters in a single cause. What counts is that both fought against the Persians. These had again become a danger, and Athens led the resistance to them. For the moment other possible enemies were forgotten or neglected.

For the most part the allies seen to have been happy with this vigorous policy. It might aggrandize Athens, but it did not humble the allies, who shone in their own glory as well as in the reflected light of Athenian achievement. Yet the policy which found so splendid a culmination on the Eurymedon hardened the assumptions on which the league was built. To be truly representative of Greece and to have the utmost striking power the league had to include all possible members. Thera and Melos stood outside on the excuse that they had old links with Sparta, but elsewhere in the Aegean unattached cities were expecting to join. Carystus, in the south of Euboea and very close to Attica, had not done so; in 472–471 she was subjugated and forced into membership. The excuse was political necessity; all possible forces were needed to keep the Persians off. Nor was the price exacted on a brutal scale. Carystus had to pay a contribution of five talents a year, but remained in control of her own affairs.

A more serious situation arose in 471 when the island of Naxos in the Cyclades seceded from the league. We do not know what case the Naxians made for this, but they may have felt that, since Persia was defeated, the league had lost its purpose and did not justify the money which they contributed to it. Naxos was besieged by Athens and compelled to rejoin, but probably suffered nothing more savage than having to accept an Athenian settlement. Her attempt to secede justified force because she was thought to be guilty of treachery and breaking her oath of allegiance, and any desire to leave the league was treated as seriously by Athens as secession from the Union was treated by Abraham Lincoln. Athens could argue that a series of such secessions would mortally imperil the league and lay Greece open to Persian attack. Athens had also her own motives for severity. The league was the source of her strength in the Aegean, and so long as she was in control of it, she was safe from trouble by sea. Desire for power impelled her to strengthen her hold on the allies and to act with severity in dealing with late or incomplete payments of tribute or with other derelictions of duty. In this the Athenians lost some of their first popularity. But the allies were in no position to resist them. By agreeing to contribute money instead of ships they left themselves defenceless. If the Athenians sent a force to reduce them, they had no alternative to surrender. So Athens moved inexorably to stronger control and with each step became more rigorous.

The danger of secession, even of dissolution, was real. After the Persian defeat on the Eurymedon it was natural for the allies to assume that Greece was reasonably safe and that there was no need to continue payments which, though not crippling, were not light and brought no visible return. In 465 the island of Thasos in the Northern Aegean came into conflict with Athens. Thasos was rich and seems at this time to have contributed not money but ships, a sign of wealth and independence. This wealth came from gold mines on the island itself and on the opposite mainland in Thrace. Athens cast covetous eyes on them. A dispute arose, and the Thasians revolted. Help expected from Sparta did not come. The Thasian fleet was defeated by Cimon and, after a long siege, they surrendered. Their walls were pulled down. They handed over their ships to Athens, gave up all claims to mine on the mainland, and agreed to pay tribute. In this case Athens forced a quite powerful ally to yield much of her wealth and to be reduced to a tributary position. Nor is it certain that Thasos had been moved to revolt by disloyalty or treachery; it seems rather that she resisted the unscrupulous attempts of Athens to grab what did not belong to her.

The league had now three classes of members. First were the true allies, who provided ships, but were few in number (Chios, Lesbos and Samos); second the allies who paid tribute instead of ships but remained politically autonomous and whose status was probably determined by a single general covenant; third the tributary allies, who had revolted and been subdued and were governed by separate treaties, which often imposed special obligations such as democratic governments. Though Cimon seems to have treated the allies with a certain generosity and lack of enforcement, the preliminary steps had been taken to transform the league into an empire. Any disloyalty could still be construed as treachery to Greece and justify disciplinary measures.

Athens did not at first impose democratic systems on all allies, and a few of them waited for many years before they accepted such. In smaller cities there would be little difficulty in insisting on a change of government but in large and wealthy states opposition could have been formidable. Indeed, when Cimon was in command, Athens probably allowed most states to keep their existing forms of government. He himself was not so wild a democrat as to try to transform other cities. No doubt many Athenians did not approve of his restraint, and some of the allies even may have welcomed help from Athens in establishing democracies. There are perhaps faint echoes of some such struggle in Pindar's *Olympian VII*, which he composed in 464 for a member of a rich athletic family in Rhodes. Something has clearly happened, and Pindar does not trouble to explain, but since all seems to be well again, we may surmise that the local nobles, who were Pindar's friends, have survived a crisis. In Samos Athens tolerated oligarchic rule until 440–439, when it was dissolved after a difficult war. In Mytilene the old oligarchy lasted, perhaps intermittently, until 428, and in Chios until 412. These were rich islands, and the governing class probably consisted of prosperous landowners who were prepared to accept Athens as an ally or helper provided that she did not interfere with their internal arrangements. So long as Cimon was in power, oligarchies were almost welcomed, and indeed it was some time before the introduction of a democratic government became an indispensable element in Athenian imperialism.

The Delian League represented only one-half of the Greek world, and indeed split what had hitherto vaguely recognized Sparta as its leader. Sparta kept her own allies and remained separate and intractable. The Delian League had come into existence because Sparta shirked her duties to a united Greece, and once Athens had taken this new responsibility, there was no chance that Sparta would serve under her or in any loyal spirit with her. The two states were divided by great differences of training and outlook. Sparta was by some ancient and not very explicit tradition the leader of the Greek states in time of trouble and she claimed the right to interfere in their affairs if, in her opinion, they went wrong. She feared the emergence of Athens and had tried unsuccessfully to manage her in the first years of the democracy. Despite her claims, she was slow to assert her powers. She did indeed lead the Greeks to victory at Plataea in 479, but she had given no help to the Ionians across the Aegean when they revolted against the Persian king Darius in 499–498, and she had been slow to help the Athenians in 490, when her troops arrived after the battle of Marathon was over. Yet despite her hesitations and refusals Sparta claimed to be the leading power in Greece. She had during nearly a century extended her rule in the Peloponnese, and in the years after 479 she was well established in it. Among her allies was the rich city of Corinth which held the isthmus called after her and provided reckonable naval power. The doubtful factor was Argos in the north-east of the Peloponnese. She suffered from delusions of grandeur and held aloof, as did also Achaia on the northern coast, which despite its fertile plain played little part in Greek history. Sparta was well established long before Athens emerged as a possible rival.

The Spartan empire was held together by Spartan arms. Her allies were bound to her by the knowledge that if they seceded, she would send an army to force them back, probably on worse terms. In all of them the government was in the hands of a privileged minority. On this point Sparta was obdurate. Her own government was not so simple. It was an inheritance from the past, though not perhaps from so remote a past as she claimed. At its head were two hereditary kings, who boasted descent from Heracles. In war they led the army, but in peace power was concentrated in the land-owning families, and that was why Sparta favoured oligarchies elsewhere. Below them was a large population of Helots, who were the local serfs, and of Messenians, descended from a pre-Spartan people but treated as Helots. Both were kept in strict subjection. This stern system explained Spartan policy. She was afraid of outbreaks at home and therefore of outbreaks elsewhere which might disaffect her subject populations. This archaic system had some special points. Free citizens were not numerous, but treated each other as equals and resisted special privileges for anyone. Some neighbours, not of pure Spartan blood, enjoyed a degree of local autonomy but had no part in the Spartan state.

Free Spartans were bred and trained for war and lived in austere simplicity. Long after other states had regular coinage, Sparta still used her old iron spits, as if silver could only corrupt. In their distrust of change her citizens were slow to risk adventures abroad, since they feared that foreign wealth might deprave their innocent and ignorant young men. In this they were right. Their kings, despite their strict upbringing, found that outside Sparta money was easily gained, and did not scruple to gain it. Though Sparta regarded herself as the leader of Hellas, she was nervous of venturing too far. She did not insist on quite the same severity for her allies, but supported the rich in Corinth for their impeccable orthodoxy in politics.

Sparta was not an armed camp, but her free citizens followed outdoor pursuits which were helpful in war, rather as in England the fox-hunting set used to claim that its activities were necessary to the training of cavalry. Nor were the arts neglected. In the seventh century Sparta was the chief home of lyric song, and the fragments of Alcman's verse show how good it was. In the sixth century she produced remarkable painted vases which in their own quite different way compete with Athenian and Corinthian wares of the same time. But in the fifth century the arts were in decline. There was little poetry, and the pottery had lost its happy charm. Sparta seems to have become self-conscious and have spent too much time in thinking about the evils which threatened her. Her success in the Persian War was a triumphant justification, but after it she felt an urge to revert to her old ways and confine her activities to the Peloponnese. She had failed to stifle democracy at its birth in Athens; she was now uneasy and suspicious about it. A democratic Athens was bad enough, but if she was also going to be powerful by land and sea, Sparta had reason for alarm. If traditional caution impelled her to abandon the leadership of the Greek allies, she created a new danger for herself by allowing a huge access of strength to the distrusted Athenians. She might put the blame on her unbalanced regent Pausanias, but she was not eager to pursue further operations against Persia, and this unwillingness did not enhance her prestige in Greece. When Athens took command of the alliance, it was agreed that its object was to harry Persia. She was not irremediably defeated, and with her unlimited resources in men and money there was no reason to think that Persia could not soon produce another army and navy and return to the attack. The Great King was not likely to acquiesce in defeat by the Greeks, a people whom he regarded as contemptibly insignificant.

The league found an able leader in Cimon. No doubt in bringing him to power the Athenians felt that they were making amends for past injustices to his father, Miltiades. But Cimon was not only a good soldier; he was well liked by the chief aristocratic families. He inherited his father's wealth and position and some of his gifts. He had a large circle of friends. He was freehanded, easy-going, and affable. It was largely his easy habits that made him popular. The comic poet Eupolis summed him up:

> Not a bad man but fond of drink and careless,[10]

while Cratinus, not usually a kind critic, was more generous:

> Cimon the godlike, most generous to strangers,
> In every way the noblest of the Greeks.[11]

Such a man was well fitted to lead the league so long as Persia was a real menace. He would at the start feel no qualms about attacking the Spartan Pausanias, whose own country was against him, and in Cimon's simple system of loyalties this settled the matter. Pausanias was brought back to Sparta, where he fled for sanctuary to the Brazen House of Athena but was kept a prisoner there until he died a hideous death from starvation. If in this Cimon acted mainly on Sparta's behalf, he would not in any way offend the Athenians; for they disliked and feared Pausanias, believing he wished to make himself tyrant of all Greece under Persian suzerainty. While Sparta was already developing suspicions of Athens, Cimon had no suspicions of Sparta, but was glad to do whatever she wanted.

Cimon liked Sparta and did his best to maintain friendly relations with her. This was partly an aristocratic propensity, the taste of a country gentleman for others who shared his pastimes and his prejudices. But there was more to it. Cimon

43

thought that democracy had gone far enough in Athens and saw in Sparta a possible source of support if things went too far for his liking. Moreover, he must have been grateful to Sparta for what she had done at Plataea and seen in her a safeguard for the balance of power in which he believed. Sparta had accepted the creation of the Delian league with no Sparta had accepted the creation of the Delian League with not it might be turned against her.

Cimon led the league with skill and success, first against odd pockets of Persian resistance, then against the main enemy which he defeated on the Eurymedon in 468. The new maritime class was happy enough to serve under a man who won victories even though he had no liking for its political ambitions. On the surface things looked not too bad. There were awkward moments, like the antics of Pausanias, but after some anxious doubts the Spartan system broke him and survived. Nor can Cimon have been happy when he realized that Themistocles was trying to turn Athenian hostility from Persia to Sparta. But this was easily dealt with. The Spartans were determined to get rid of Themistocles and poisoned the Athenians' minds against him. In this process no doubt Cimon took the Spartan part and felt that he was saving his own country from disaster.

The loyal support of Cimon and his party was of special value to Sparta because in these years she had her own troubles in the Peloponnese. Argos, shaken by earlier blows from Sparta, began to recover, first captured Tiryns, to which she had legitimate claims, and then formed an alliance with the Arcadian city of Tegea. About 470 her forces were defeated by the Spartans, but the city of Tegea was not taken. Other Arcadian cities joined Tegea, but Argos now retired from the field. A little later Sparta, under her young king Archidamus, defeated them at Dipaea, and Tegea had to submit. But Sparta's troubles were not over. New dangers arose when the villages of Elis formed a single city with a democratic constitution, and Argos continued to assert her independence. The one thing that need not trouble Sparta was that Athens would come in as an ally of one of her enemies. This Cimon would see to, and the Spartans ought to have been glad.

Meanwhile at Athens the memory of Themistocles was in

disgrace. But it was not forgotten, and persisted under the surface. After his death, about 459, his body was refused burial on Attic soil because he was judged to be a traitor. The *Persians* had been produced in 472 before his fall, and afterwards it kept his memory fresh. It embodied his greatest achievements and was regarded as the quintessence of patriotism, so that some seventy years later, in the last days of imperial greatness Aristophanes makes Aeschylus say in the *Frogs*:

> Then next the 'Persians' I wrote, in praise of the
>   noblest deed that the world can show,
> And each man longed for the victor's wreath, to fight
>   and vanquish his country's foe.[12]

The *Persians* proclaimed the worth of Themistocles when he was on the brink of total discredit, and reflected the feeling which some Athenians still had for him. The men who manned the ships might for the moment be content with the rewards and the renown which Cimon made available to them, but they must have seen that in other respects they got little of the special attention which Themistocles had given to them when he formed them into a radical section of the political public. They might not fully realize what the present situation was or have an embracing programme of reform, but subterranean forces were at work and a crash of some kind was in the offing. It came, unexpectedly, from Sparta.

In 464 an earthquake laid Sparta in ruins, and the Helots revolted. They joined with the Messenians and fortified themselves in the mountainous refuge of Ithome. The Spartans were thoroughly frightened. The rebels were numerous, and their stronghold was almost impossible to reduce. The Spartans subdued their pride and appealed to their friends, including Athens, for help. A new Athenian political leader, Ephialtes, later to be more prominent, was opposed to giving it, but Cimon was in favour, saying: 'We must not leave Hellas lame; we must not allow Athens to lose her yoke-fellow.'[13] Athens sent him with four thousand hoplites to Messenia, where they failed to take Ithome. Then Sparta abruptly announced that she had no more need of them and asked them to leave. Even for Spartans this was gratuitously offensive. Perhaps they were afraid that with their democratic talk the Athenians might affect the

Peloponnesian peoples who had not yet revolted but might with sufficient stimulus do so. But the Spartans may have had another reason. They may have seen that if they were to allow the Athenians to rescue them now, they would have to admit them again in later times of need. This was not a pleasant prospect for Spartan pride. Cimon came home humiliated. The public turned against him and in 461 ostracized him for ten years. A new era in external politics began, in which Sparta was no longer treated as a friend. The change brought submerged forces to the surface and changed the whole pattern of Hellenic affairs.

3

THE GREAT REVERSAL

WHEN the Spartans dismissed Cimon and his army in 462, they
ended the period in which Sparta and Athens still claimed to be
on friendly terms and ready between them to guide Greece. It
was now abundantly clear that Sparta disliked and feared
Athens and was glad to humiliate her before the world. Such
an affront would enrage the whole people of Athens and particularly those who did not agree with Cimon or his policies. It
discredited the Athenian oligarchic parties' trust in Sparta and
any foreign policy which was built on it, and provoked a sharp
reappraisal of first principles. If the pro-Spartan policy was rejected, so also was the aristocratic outlook which supported it;
if foreign policy underwent a change, so too did domestic
policy. The leading character in this change was Ephialtes, son
of Sophonides. Early in his career he distinguished himself in
command of a fleet on the south coast of Asia Minor. He was,
like other political leaders, of a good family, but he was not
rich. He assumed the policies of Themistocles, and while
Cimon was in the ascendant, could not be very prominent. But
he opposed giving help to Sparta when she asked for it in 463,
and the only words of his which have survived are that 'the
Athenians should not attempt to rescue or restore a city which
was their rival but rather let Sparta's pride be trampled under-
foot'.[1] This was the direct inheritance from Themistocles, who
had decided that after the defeat of Persia Sparta was the most
formidable enemy of Athens. Ephialtes was more than justified
by the result when his advice went unheeded. The behaviour of
Sparta provoked a sharp reaction and greatly increased the influence of Ephialtes and his friends. It was they who secured
the disgrace of Cimon on his return and his ostracism in 461.
But before this, perhaps even while Cimon was in Messenia,
Ephialtes led a powerful movement for internal reform and
appeared as the first truly democratic reformer since Themistocles.

Ephialtes and his fellows thought that the Athenian state was still too much in the hands of the rich families and that there was no way for the poor to increase their share in the control of affairs. They saw that the last bulwark against full democracy was the court of the Areopagus, which had survived the reforms of Clisthenes, presumably because at the time it looked harmless enough. But now it had gained in power and become almost a House of Lords, able to stop popular measures and to concentrate authority in the hands of the rich. Ephialtes began his attack by trying to discredit individual members of the Areopagus by accusing them of corruption, probably in various minor offices to which they appointed each other. Then he set out to deprive the Areopagus of its legislative and judicial functions and to reduce it to a high court which dealt mainly with cases of homicide. He carried his motion, and the Areopagus could no longer punish public officials if they broke the law, or exert a general supervision to see that the laws were kept, or inquire into the lives of private citizens. Now in addition to cases of homicide it looked after the sacred olive trees of Athene, and supervised the property of the gods worshipped at Eleusis. Its other powers passed to the Council, the Assembly, and the law courts. These changes do not look very extreme, but they cleared the way to more reforms by abolishing an obstructive authority. In this they confirmed the democrats in their confidence of power and removed the distinction by which only the wealthiest citizens had places in the supreme seats of government. Unfortunately we know too little about Ephialtes. What we know suggests that he was a highly intelligent man, abreast of the intellectual movements of his time, and also that, unlike Themistocles, he was scrupulously honest and therefore in a strong position to attack those members of the Areopagus who had used their position to make money.

Reforms on this scale could easily be circumvented and power confined to the wealthy if steps were not taken to prevent it. This problem arose in the matter of juries. Once the Areopagus lost its special place in the Athenian legal system, more responsibility fell to juries, and the great growth of legal work meant that there was more for these to do than could be done by a few enthusiastic amateurs. If juries were to come from all classes, they must not be too out of pocket from doing their duty, and the solution was to pay them for attendance. In 462–461 a measure was carried to this effect. Athenians took happily to sitting on juries, once the pay made it possible, and indeed they seem to have enjoyed the work for its own sake. Aristophanes often pokes fun at them for their juridical propensities and pretends that sitting on juries is their favourite pastime. In the *Wasps* (422) he shows how litigation and jury work create addicts and how simple Athenians derive immense enjoyment from them. This comes some forty years after the reforms but it catches a characteristic foible of Athenian democracy and shows how a public duty had a popular appeal.

In these reforms Ephialtes challenged the governing class, and though he had the populace behind him, he aroused violent hostility. In 461 he was murdered by an assassin who was never identified, presumably because other conspirators covered his traces. In Athens murder was not a common weapon of political warfare, for ostracism was available and much more merciful. But the conservatives may have seen that Ephialtes had too strong a backing to be ostracized, and resorted to murder instead. He left a successor. In the prosecution of Cimon for taking bribes in the siege of Thasos, in the reform of the Areopagus, and in the institution of pay for juries, Pericles played an important, if secondary, part. These were his first appearances on the political stage, and we may suspect that he shared a good deal with Ephialtes – his cultural interests, his incorruptibility, his strong democratic leanings, his opposition to the pro-Spartan policy of Cimon. Through Ephialtes he could trace his political descent from Themistocles, who had anticipated the major changes in foreign and domestic politics. Pericles did not step immediately into the high power which he was to hold later. He worked with Ephialtes; he was associated with other leaders after the murder. But he was not yet even *primus inter pares*. His decisive rise began in 454 when he was elected general. Yet in the interval changes characteristic of his later policy were inaugurated, and provided a training for what he was to do later.

Once the pretence of friendship between Sparta and Athens had been exposed, war was inevitable, and broke out in 459, ending unsatisfactorily with a truce in 451 and peace in 446–445. It started soon after the extension of democracy in Athens, which stressed the deep divergences between the two states. Persia did not at the moment seem to be a danger. The league had grown greatly in power, wealth, and experience, and could now be turned against Sparta as it could not have been at its start. The new rulers of Athens, Pericles among them, saw in Sparta the real enemy. She had shown intermittent hostility since the end of the Persian Wars; she had humiliated Athens by rejecting her after Ithome; she stood for a system of government which Athenian democrats rejected. The Athenian leadership may also have felt that the division of Greece into Athenian and Spartan spheres of influence could not last but was fated to lead to violent conflict. In that case it was wise to be prepared. It was true that the two powers had existed side by side, but the relation had never been easy, and now it had broken down. How far the Athenian leaders, Tolmides, Myronides, and others, who swayed policy in the Assembly and held command in the army, thought it possible to humiliate Sparta by arms we do not know; but they clearly thought that Athens could hold her own. Even if Sparta could not be annihilated, Athens might succeed her as the chief power in Greece, and the defeat of Sparta would bring incalculable glory. To combine security with honour was not an ignoble aim, and this is what the Athenians had in mind when they turned from the example of Cimon to that of Themistocles. War came, not as a head-on clash between the two main powers but in attacks made by Athens on places which Sparta considered to be in her special orbit.

Athenian policy was to strengthen herself near home. Naupactus on the north coast of the Corinthian Gulf was seized in 460 or 459 and settled with Messenians who had escaped the clutches of Sparta and were now able to harass her from a powerful base. In the same year the Megarians, after a frontier dispute with Corinth, left the Peloponnesian League and put themselves under Athenian protection. This gave Athens a much stronger frontier to the west. She set to work to build a line of double walls from the city of Megara to the port of Nisaea on the Saronic Gulf. The Corinthians protested, and there were some desultory skirmishes. An Athenian squadron was unsuccessful at Halieis in the Gulf of Argos, but nothing much else happened here. Soon afterwards came a real clash, when the Athenian fleet met the Peloponnesian off the small island of Cecryphalea to the west of Aegina. Aegina was an old friend of Sparta and an old enemy of Athens. Seeing how critical the situation was, the Aeginetans joined the war and brought it into the home waters of Athens.

Aegina was near enough to Athens to be a permanent menace. She maintained a powerful fleet, which had distinguished itself at Salamis and had long protected a vigorous overseas trade. The coins of Aegina with their image of a sea turtle and the coins of Corinth with their image of the winged horse Pegasus are the only Greek coins whose circulation comes near to that of the Athenian owls. Athens had long disliked the unfriendly presence of Aegina in full view from the Acropolis. So early as the seventh century Athens had landed forces in Aegina and been heavily defeated. In the first years of Athenian democracy the struggle had been intensified and reached its climax in 487 when the Athenians tried to gain a foothold through local collaborators but failed. Aeginetans continued to plunder Attic shores, until both cities found themselves on the same side at Salamis and shared the honours of victory.

Some Athenian circles had friends in Aegina as they had also in Sparta. Among these was Melesias, a kinsman of Cimon and father of that other Thucydides (not the historian) who was to be the most formidable opponent of Pericles. Melesias was a renowned trainer of athletes and much admired by Pindar for the successes of his pupils, but we can see prejudice growing against him because of his Athenian origin, when in 460 the Boeotian, Pindar, writing for an Aeginetan, says abruptly:

> If for Melesias I have run back in my song
> To the fame he wins from young athletes,
> Let no sharp stone of hatred strike me.[2]

The games-loving aristocracy of Greece was largely international in its attachments, but when war was in the offing, such ties were dropped. Pindar knew this, but courageously stood out against it. Several of his poems at this time are written for Aeginetans but, though he implicitly foretells that all will be well, he hardly comes out into the open. Yet in his mythical allusions, which hint at an atmosphere of crisis, he suggests that Aegina is being wickedly slandered and draws a parallel with Ajax who killed himself because he was dishonoured by lying stories:

> Of old too was hateful trickery;
> She walked with wheedling words and plotted death,
> Slander who works evil;
> She does violence to glory
> And sets up a flimsy fame for the unknown.[3]

No doubt there was a campaign of propaganda against Aegina, which Pindar resented. In fact she provoked the conflict, but Athens welcomed it and did not shrink from the full consequences.

A naval battle was fought off Aegina, in which each side had allies. The Athenians captured seventy ships, made a successful landing, and blockaded the city of Aegina, which held out manfully. The war spread, as if other Peloponnesians wished to combine in giving a death stroke to Athens. The Corinthians advanced over the mountainous slopes of Geranea and came down into the Megarid, hoping that Athens was too busy to stop them. But the Athenians rose superbly to the occasion. Under Myronides men above and below military age marched into the Megarid and fought the Corinthians. At first they were victorious more in name than in fact; then by a sudden outbreak from the city of Megara, they won a handsome victory. The year 459 was crowded with incidents for the Athenians, who acquitted themselves splendidly in all, but in addition to these tasks they had assumed another which was much more hazardous and offered dazzling rewards. Before they reduced Aegina in 457–456, after two years of siege, and forced her to pay tribute at the same level as Thasos, they were looking for a richer prize further afield.

In 459 when the Athenians and allies were conducting minor enterprises round Cyprus, they received an invitation to sail to Egypt. This came from Inaros, a prince of Libya but probably of Egyptian stock, who had taken advantage of the confusion after the murder of Xerxes in 464 to revolt against Persia. We do not know to whom his invitation was delivered, and indeed on the whole enthralling episode we are very bleakly informed, but whoever received the message decided that it was too alluring to be refused. If the Athenians established a stronghold in the Nile Delta, they could not only strike Persia in a sensitive part of her huge empire but open rich new realms for commercial exploitation. This could make her the wealthiest city in Greece and enable her to outstrip and reduce all her rivals. Nor was this a mere dream. Greek mercenaries had in the middle of the seventh century given valuable help to Psammetichus when he revolted from Assyria and established a new dynasty over an independent Egypt. If the Greeks had done it before, why should they not do it again, especially as Inaros was a leader with some of the same assets and prospects as Psammetichus?

The expedition to Egypt occupies an ambiguous position in the change of foreign policy after the ostracism of Cimon. At first it looks as if a compromise had been reached by which Cimon's old followers continued, in new circumstances, the offensive against Persia, while the strictly anti-Spartan group continued their offensive against Sparta. But Egypt may even have attracted this latter group. With a strong base there Athens could control the eastern Mediterranean, and it might be argued that overseas expansion was part of Themistoclean policy. For him the narrow lands of Greece were inadequate for his ambitions, and he looked beyond them with the eyes of a man accustomed to think in naval terms. Themistocles cherished ideas of expansion to the west in Italy and Sicily and is said to have called one of his daughters Italia and the other Sybaris. We do not know what Pericles thought about the Egyptian venture, but if it was a new application of Themistoclean strategy, he may have approved of it. Certainly he did not in later years condemn these distant ventures in retrospect, though he did not himself much encourage them. It is surely of this kind of thing that he is thinking when in his Funeral Speech he says:

Our adventurous spirit has forced an entry into every sea and into every land; and everywhere we have left behind us everlasting memorials of good done to our friends or suffering inflicted on our enemies.[4]

The friends of Pericles may in the high hopes of 459 have

persuaded themselves that they could combine the expedition to Egypt with a continued war with Sparta.

All began well. Inaros had routed the Persians in the Delta, and there the Athenians found him well established. They sailed triumphantly up the Nile and took the city of Memphis, but not its citadel, the 'White Castle'. Darkness then falls on the record, but the Athenians seem to have blockaded the White Castle without success. Their plan no doubt was to control Egypt from Memphis with the support of Inaros. This was perfectly feasible with enough troops, but Athens was so busy elsewhere that troops could not be sent, and the time lost enabled the Persians to dispatch a large army under Megabyzus and support it from the sea with a Phoenician fleet. The Athenians were driven out of Memphis and shut up in Prosopitis, an island between the Canopic and the Sebennytic mouths of the Nile. It was now their turn to be blockaded. Megabyzus drained the water away, and not only left the Greek ships high and dry, but was able to march his own troops to the island. The Greeks burned their ships, which were now useless, and surrendered to Megabyzus, who allowed them to retire to Cyrene and thence to find their way home. Inaros, whose life the Persians had promised to spare, was crucified. Soon afterwards a squadron of fifty triremes arrived from Athens, not knowing what had happened. It was attacked by the Phoenician fleet in the Mendesian mouth of the Nile, and only a few ships escaped. Persian rule was restored over the whole of Egypt. Thus after five years the Athenian expedition ended in total failure, foreshadowing the even greater failure in Syracuse forty years later.

The cost in ships and men was ruinous, and yet Athens remained intact and undiscouraged. Her enemies had tried to take advantage of her troubles but she had outfought them. These five years were a time of tense and strained exertion. The degree of her commitments and sacrifices may be judged from a memorial stone of the Erechtheid tribe to the fallen of the year 459. The words preceding the list of the dead tell the story:

Of the Erechtheid tribe these are they who died in the war, in Cyprus, in Egypt, in Phoenicia, at Halieis, in Aegina, at Megara, in the same year.[5]

So too we hear an echo of these events when in 458 Aeschylus produced his *Eumenides* and in it made Orestes summon Athene, the divine protectress of Athens and himself:

> So whether on far shores of Libya,
> By Trito's waters, where she came to birth,
> Her foot be planted, covered or erect,
> Defending those that love her for her eyes,
> Like some brave captain's watch on Phlegra's heights,
> O may she come – far off she still can hear –
> And from these miseries deliver me![6]

Phlegra is where the Gods fought the Giants, and its mention connects Athene with the most momentous of battlefields. Aeschylus regards the present struggle in Africa as comparable with the fabled struggles of the gods.

In these campaigns the hand of Sparta is not very obvious. From a twinge of old-fashioned honour or simply from suspicious caution, she refused to aid the Persian king Artaxerxes by invading Attica. Her own needs were met by her allies, who engaged Athens on her frontiers, while the Spartan army sat at home. But in 457 she embarked on a new plan which meant serious war. Her objective was to create north of Athens a power in Boeotia sufficiently strong to hold Athens in check. A Spartan army eluded the Athenian ships and crossed the Corinthian Gulf. Thebes was made head of a Boeotian confederacy which Sparta forced the other Boeotian cities to join. The Spartans could not return by the way they came, for their transports would be sunk by the Athenian galleys, now fully alerted, so they decided to march on Athens and fight their way through. They reached Tanagra near the Boeotian frontier, but before they could cross it, an Athenian force, assisted by some Argives and Thessalian cavalry, went to meet them. The conflict was violent and deadly. The Thessalians deserted in mid-battle, and the Spartans won. But the battle nonetheless saved Athens, for though she was dangerously vulnerable because she was at the time busy building long walls to the Piraeus, the Spartans were sufficiently discouraged by their losses to avoid Athens and go home through the Megarid. Athens, who seemed to be at the mercy of a powerful enemy, escaped disaster by her formidable spirit even in defeat.

The Spartan army had at least won an indisputable victory and sustained its reputation as the best land force in Greece. No doubt the leaders were content with having, as they thought, set up Boeotia as a united state under the oligarchic leadership of Thebes. But two months after the Spartan departure an Athenian army under Myronides invaded Boeotia and won a decisive battle at Oenophyta, which made Athens mistress of the whole country except Thebes itself. The Boeotians, who were inveterate landlubbers, were not enrolled in the league of Delos but made to supply contingents to the Athenian armies. An echo of what the battle of Oenophyta meant to the Boeotians may be heard in a poem which Pindar wrote soon after the battle for a young athlete whose family had suffered heavily in it. Though a Theban, Pindar himself may not have suffered as much as other Boeotians, but he feels that those who have died for their country are like the legendary heroes of the past:

> Honour is laid up for the brave.
> Let him know this clearly, whosoever
> In this cloud keeps off the hail of blood
> From the country which he loves,
>
> And pays back havoc to a host of enemies,
> And swells huge glory for the race of his townsmen,
> In life and in death.
> You, son of Diodotus, matched
> The warrior Meleager, and matched
> Hector and Amphiaraus,
> When you breathed out your youth in all its flower-time,
>
> In the foremost press of the fighters,
> Where the bravest kept up the struggle of battle
> In desperate hopes.[7]

The provocation from Sparta had resulted in Athens annexing a large part of the mainland area of Boeotia. This was a new feature in her policy and went well beyond what a mainly naval confederacy, such as she led, could sustain. Naval power was almost useless for it, and Athens had not enough land troops for a full occupation. She had to rely mainly on co-operation from local people who preferred her to their own rulers. These might be disgruntled members of the old oligarchy, but such would be rare and command little respect. Or they might be local democrats who welcomed power for themselves and were not averse to Athenian support in holding it. Athens seems to have tried both groups. Of the first a sour pamphleteer known as the Old Oligarch comments: 'Whenever they tried to choose the best men, it was not a success, but within a short time the people in Boeotia were enslaved.'[8] Of the second group Aristotle says that after Oenophyta, owing to bad government, the newly established democracy was destroyed.[9] The democrats in Boeotia had not held power before, and their inexperience made them easy victims to aristocrats eager to regain lost authority. Athens was slow to grasp the enormous difficulties of running a land empire and never succeeded at it.

The conquest of Boeotia was the climax of the war for Athens, and if she could have made peace and kept her gains, she would have had much the better of it. She held the neighbouring states of Megara and Boeotia and the adjacent island of Aegina. She was strongly settled in the Corinthian Gulf. But she had suffered heavy losses, notably in Egypt, and the Peloponnesians, especially Corinth, were unwilling to make any concessions to her.

In the war's first years Pericles had played no major part but in 454 he was elected general and in the next year commanded a fleet in the Corinthian Gulf, where Tolmides had prepared the way two years earlier and captured the Corinthian town of Chalcis opposite Patrai. Pericles failed to take either Sicyon or Oeniadae, but his fleet presented so brave a show that the Achaean cities on the southern shore prudently adhered to Athens. In 451 Athens secured a respite with a five years' truce, negotiated by Cimon, who was summoned back from exile and behaved with loyalty and understanding. Meanwhile the revived Persian fleet, encouraged by its successes in Egypt, sailed to Cyprus, where Cimon was sent to deal with it, but where he died in 449. Peace was soon made with Persia, and Cyprus was sacrificed to her, perhaps to make it easier to concentrate on the Peloponnesians.

The policy failed. Athens encountered a series of disasters. In 447 exiled Boeotian aristocrats seized some towns in Boeotia, and the Athenian general Tolmides advanced with a small force against them. Pericles gave a warning against the expedition, which was clearly set for failure, but Tolmides nevertheless went forward. He took and garrisoned Coronea, but on the way home was set upon by the exiles and defeated. He himself was killed, and many of his small force were taken prisoner. Athens could do nothing but accept defeat and make what terms she could. In return for the restitution of the prisoners she gave up all claims to Boeotia. The blow to her prestige was disastrous. Her enemies saw that, however powerful she might be at sea, she was not nearly so powerful on land. Other losses followed. The Athenian garrison in Megara was massacred; Achaea was lost; a Peloponnesian army threatened Attica. Meanwhile Euboea revolted, and Pericles moved there at once with an army. It must have looked as if Athens were likely to be crushed, but she rose magnificently to the occasion. Pericles returned and added his troops to those in the Megarid. The Spartan king, Pleistoanax, even if he was not, as rumour said, bribed by Pericles, lost his nerve and went home. Pericles then returned to settle Euboea. Histiaea, which had been most obstinate in resistance, was treated most harshly; her people were driven out, and her territory annexed to Athens. In each case a separate arrangement was made to suit individual conditions, and that made with Chalcis survives carved on stone. At the same time Athens got more military support from her allies, who had fought with her at Tanagra and borne a heavy share of the losses in Egypt.

The series of dangers and defeats made Athens ready for peace, and in 446–445 she and her allies signed a thirty years' peace with the members of the Peloponnesian League. On the whole this was a confession of Athenian failure. On the credit side Aegina remained tributary, but her autonomy was guaranteed. Athens gave up her posts in Achaea, the Megarid and all Boeotia. She had, for other reasons, already abandoned Cyprus. So ended the first war between Athens and the Peloponnesians. It had lessons for both sides. To Athens it demonstrated what was important both politically and militarily, that she was not equipped to hold a land empire. The actual conquest of Boeotia was possible, but its retention was a failure because Athens had not sufficient troops to garrison it nor adequate Boeotian agents and collaborators to manage it. With her large navy and the demands which it made on manpower and money it would have been next to impossible for her to maintain a large army as well, especially if it were to be used outside her frontiers. Her army was composed of citizens who had work to do at home. Though in moments of intense crisis, as in 458, all the male population was away from home, this could not happen often. It is also likely that even when she was in possession of a land empire, Athens lacked skill and tact in its management. It would be difficult to find men to keep an eye on recalcitrant Boeotians without exacerbating them. Nor did Athens succeed in holding Boeotia by dividing and ruling. She learned by her failure. Not for many years did she repeat the experiment of trying to win a land empire, and then she failed even to win it, let alone to hold it.

Athens indeed survived, largely through the fighting spirit of her troops, who when it came to defending their own land displayed an incomparable prowess. But their heroic morale and self-confidence had a dangerous side. The Athenians were liable to think that they could not fail and did not always make adequate preparations or provide enough troops. This was the trouble with Tolmides in the disaster of Coronea in 447. Some nine years earlier he had won notable successes in the Corinthian Gulf and may have formed too high an opinion of his own and his troops' abilities. With only a thousand Athenians and a few allies he hoped to stop the revolt in Boeotia, but was hopelessly defeated. Something similar may account for other failures, notably when in 453 Pericles failed to take either Sicyon or Oeniadae in his efforts to secure the maritime route to the west. The abounding ardour of the Athenians may have been worth many battalions, but at times it was not enough, and more care and more troops would have done better. This too was noted, and influenced Athenian strategy when she next found herself at war with Sparta.

Sparta also had lessons to learn. The first was that without her help her allies were not strong enough to resist Athens. In the end Sparta herself had to come in, but typically she delayed too long, and too much was lost. She might have attacked Athens when Pericles was occupied in Euboea, but she left it to her allies, and when she herself took the field, Pericles was back in Attica and able to get rid of the invaders. The reasons for this hesitation are to be found in the strange convolutions of the Spartan character. They were in part no more than the habitual prudence of an unusually conservative people. This was strengthened by fear that Spartan leaders, freed from the bonds that held them at home, might cherish dangerous ambitions, as Pausanias had done, or take bribes, like Leutychidas, one of their kings, had done, or by other fears that with the army away from home the subject classes of Helots and Messenians might revolt. It is even possible that Sparta did not fully realize how dangerous Athens was but clung to the illusion that most Athenians really resembled Cimon. Among their allies the Spartans had a reputation for being dilatory. The historian Thucydides understood this when in relating events of a later date, he makes the Corinthians say to the Spartans:

You alone do nothing in the early stages to prevent an enemy's expansion; you wait until your enemy has doubled his strength,[10]

and a little later in the same context:

Your nature is always to do less than you could have done, to mistrust your own judgement, however sound it may be, and to assume that dangers will last for ever.[11]

This was the normal view of Sparta. She was in the first place slow to start. But in the second place, after she had taken successful action, she did not stay to gather the full benefits of success. This was the case after Tanagra in 457. The Spartans had won a decisive victory against a gallant enemy. They seem to have thought that in view of their heavy losses this was enough, and decided to go home without taking any steps to bolster up the shaky government of Boeotia. The result, in the succeeding autumn, was the Athenian victory at Oenophyta and their possession of Boeotia. The Spartans remained cautious in their general policy, but learned that it was profitable to act with more speed and to follow a policy to its end.

Though Athens and Sparta were the main antagonists in this war, they very seldom met in the field, and the only serious occasion when they did was at Tanagra, where Sparta won. Even then the Spartans failed or refused to attack Athens. Yet the war was essentially between Athens and Sparta, and ultimately it was fought for the control of Greece. It was becoming clear that Greece could not hold both of them, or rather that if Athens intended to extend her dominions. Sparta must stop her from doing so. Neither side can have had a clear idea of how a decisive victory was to be won or how, if won, it was to be exploited. Neither side had enough troops to keep the other's possessions if it got hold of them, and neither had any experience, comparable to that of Persian satraps, in running large districts populated by alien subjects. At this stage both the desire for a final decision and ideas about the right use of it may have been vague. The Athenians may have thought that they had made a notable advance when they conquered Aegina; the Spartans much the same after Tanagra. Yet Athens did not get the full advantages from Aegina, nor Sparta from Tanagra. In the next few years the desire for an ultimate solution became more insistent, but it was already present in many minds, even if it had no firm outline.

The differences between the two states, from a military point of view, were enormous. Sparta prided herself on training her citizens for war. They were professional soldiers strictly drilled and disciplined and ready to make any sacrifice. With this the Athenians, who were volunteers and amateurs, could never fully compete. When Themistocles said that the Athenian army was no match even against the Boeotians, he may have strained the truth in order to get a fleet, but there may be something in the Old Oligarch's view that 'the Athenian infantry has the reputation of being very weak'.[12] The Athenian army had its ups and downs. The Spartans were led to battle by their kings; the Athenians by generals elected by the Assembly. The Spartan kings had the advantage that they had been trained to war from childhood. The price for this was that they sometimes reacted against their training, causing fear and anxiety at home. Athenian generals were chosen by free vote, and on the whole well chosen. The voters were often soldiers or ex-soldiers who would be hardheaded on what was wanted in a general. Themistocles at Salamis and Cimon after it were popular choices abundantly justified. But even experienced Athenian generals might be amateurs in comparison with their Spartan counterparts. In general the Spartans hoped to do by discipline and training what the Athenians did by improvisation and high morale. Each military style had its defects. The Spartans might be too cautious and too wooden in their methods, the Athenians too slapdash and too liable to make insufficient plans. The Spartans had the better of it by land, but the Athenians now ruled the sea as Aegina once had, and their command of it gave access to anywhere they wished. Only by some stroke of luck could any other fleet, such as that of Corinth, do anything against them, and this was seldom attempted. But a navy could only secure the empire by sea; it could do very little for it by land. The Athenians might be the foremost sailors of the age, but they could not also be the best soldiers. When in 446–445 Athens made peace with Sparta, nothing was really settled. Each side was given a respite to restore its resources and train its manhood for another war.

In the process of imperial expansion Athens evolved a new means of strengthening herself away from home. After coming to power Pericles decided that if some places, of vital relevance to Athens, were to be held firmly, they must be occupied by Athenian citizens. So he promoted such settlements abroad. They might help to solve the question of superfluous population at Athens, but that was of minor importance. What counted was that men were sent to different places where they served as garrisons among subject allies. One of these cleruchies, as they were called, was established in 447 in the Thracian Chersonnese – the western shore of the Dardanelles – under the personal supervision of Pericles. Land was acquired from the existing inhabitants, and a thousand Athenian citizens, for the most part impoverished and unemployed, were allotted farms and assigned to the various towns. The land was paid for by a reduction of tribute from the places affected. It was dangerous country, and a wall was built across the isthmus to keep out the barbarous Thracians.

This move was followed by others of a similar kind, though not always with the same purpose. When cleruchies were established in the northern islands of Lemnos and Imbros, it could be reasonably argued that they too helped to protect the trade routes through the Dardanelles. But this could not be said of the cleruchies settled a little later in Euboea, at Histiaea, and in the Cycladic islands of Naxos and Andros. In these much the same procedure was followed as in the Chersonnese, but the number of settlers in a single place was not more than five hundred. There was a case for such posts in the Cyclades since they would help ships in their direct passage across the Aegean, but this could hardly be said for a cleruchy in Euboea. It had revolted from Athens, and the task of the new settlement was to keep watch against another outbreak. The methods of settlement were not humane. The dispossessed landowners were faced with starvation or emigration, while the new settlers were presented with three or four times as much land as the previous owners, which suggests that it was not always the rich who suffered. The formation of cleruchies was one of the most disliked activities of the Athenian empire and indicates that Athens was not only conscious of the need for military outposts but not too scrupulous in establishing them. The cleruchs were Athenians settled outside Athens. Sometimes they forced the local inhabitants to work for them. In general the cleruchs retained their Athenian citizenship and were bound to their new homes by military duties in them. Each community had a degree of self-government, with council, assembly, and magistrates on the Athenian pattern. The total number of cleruchs can never have been more than ten thousand; and thus the cleruchies were less like colonies than garrisons. It was this that made them odious in the eyes of the allies.

Life in a cleruchy cannot have been easy. The cleruchs had to keep constant watch, and their improvised life must have been much less comfortable and less secure than at home. But this separation from their own land made them more attached and more proud to belong to it. In one case we can see how their loyalty took a practical, even visible form. Among the foremost works of Phidias was the so-called Lemnian Athene. Made of bronze, it was placed on the Acropolis at Athens by the Athenian colonists of Lemnos. The critic Lucian regarded it as the most beautiful of the works of Phidias, and though we have only late copies of it, a head now at Bologna catches the magic of Phidias as no other copy does. Athenians settled overseas felt no inclination to disown their birthright.

The war with the Peloponnesians had at its start seemed to promise Athens enormous rewards; it ended with very few solid gains. In itself it was remarkable for the prodigious efforts to which it inspired the Athenians. Almost any other Greek state would have given in before the impact of such attacks, but Athens held out with incomparable determination. At no other period in her history did she display such resource and such ardour, and though she did not gain much that she wanted, she was at the end no worse off than at the beginning. Her citizens could not fail to think that next time they might be a little more successful and therefore victorious. The extremity of effort which she displayed made her form a more realistic assessment of her powers and limitations without weakening her self-confidence or her stamina. Among the harsh lessons which she had learned and was to bear in mind was that Greece was hard to conquer and even harder to control from a single centre. Yet at the same time the Athenians, enjoying the heyday of their achievement, lost nothing irrecoverable from their expenditure of life and treasure. The first years of Pericles' leadership were the zenith of a splendid age in which were laid the foundations of much that was to last for the next forty years. By holding off her enemies Athens became more acutely conscious of her own capacities and more eager to set them fully to work.

4

PERICLEAN DEMOCRACY

In the last years of the war Pericles played an influential part, and from it we may deduce certain principles of action which were to be constant throughout his life. First, he was opposed to unlimited, scattered objectives. The Egyptian expedition had pointed a moral, and he applied it when peace was made with Persia. Secondly, he saw that a land empire was difficult to secure, and that was why he opposed Tolmides' advance into Boeotia. Thirdly, he saw that sea power was Athens' most powerful resource, and he tried to use it making the Corinthian Gulf her monopoly. In the following years we see him at work, but we must first ask what kind of man he was.

Pericles was an aristocrat, the son of that Xanthippus who had finished off the Persian fleet at Mycale and captured Sestos on the Dardanelles. In politics Xanthippus led a democratic group in opposition to Miltiades, whom he may have regarded as a potential tyrant; he then threw in his lot with the other Athenian leaders in the struggle with Persia. His wife, Agariste, mother of Pericles, belonged to the powerful clan of the Alcmaeonids and was the niece of the reformer Clisthenes. Story told that when she was pregnant with Pericles, she dreamed that she gave birth to a lion. Some at least of the Alcmaeonids had been in favour of extending democracy at Athens, if only because it would strengthen them against rival cliques. Heredity and family tradition suggested that Pericles would follow an independent policy. We do not know when his father died, but there is no reference to him later than 478. Pericles succeeded and surpassed him in every task and though he took time to establish himself, he figured in politics first as the supporter of Themistocles, then as the ally of Ephialtes, and one of the leading opponents of Sparta, until finally he so endeared himself to the Athenian people that he was elected general annually from 443 to his death in 429. Since he was born about 490, he would have been too young to fight in the Persian

Wars, but would know all about them from his elders. He belonged to the next generation, which inherited the spirit of the fighting men of 480 and 479 but went further and gave a new impetus and a new direction to Athens.

The ancestry of Pericles revealed itself in his appearance and manner. He was, if we may judge by the several copies of a bust of him by Cresilas, of a notably intellectual cast of features with an air of calm command. No doubt the sculptor improved upon reality and stressed what struck him as Pericles' most significant traits, but the portrait is of a living man who could hardly have failed to impress anyone who saw him. Pericles had some oddity in the shape of his head, which was thought to be too long, and for this reason he preferred to be depicted wearing a helmet, rather as Julius Caesar wore a laurel wreath to hide his baldness. Pericles' look is in no sense of one anxious to please or able to be all things to all men; it is strong and controlled but friendly and paternal. Such no doubt he was, and it is to the credit of the Athenians, who liked everyone to be approachable, that they did not hold his remoteness against him. In his aristocratic independence he pursued policies which he had decided were right, and, instead of anticipating the desires of the people, tried first to instil into them his own principles. This reflected his moral integrity, of which his famous incorruptibility in money matters was but another sign. In a democratic age he kept a high detachment which smacked of a more select society. This marks almost everything that we know about him and separates him decisively from his successors in directing the destinies of Athens.

Pericles was brought up in the new intellectual movements of the fifth century and was much attracted and affected by them. His chief teacher was Damon, a distinguished musician who was said also to have taught Socrates. Music, as he taught it, was much more than a technical accomplishment and provided the Greek equivalent of a humanistic training. It was hoped that by mastering harmony and rhythm and responding to all kinds of music a young man would develop his human qualities to the full, including his taste for the beautiful and the good. Damon was a teacher with unusual gifts, compared in his own speciality with the trainers of athletes who were honoured all over the Greek world. He was also a creative artist who extended the scope of music with new effects and worked on the principle that certain rhythms created certain kinds of character. He was a man with a mission, a counsellor who encouraged Pericles in his reforms. The enemies of Pericles thought that Damon's influence was too great, and in due course ostracized the teacher for it.

It may also be relevant that when Pericles was young he heard Zeno of Elea lecture. Zeno refused to live in Athens, and his visit was an exceptional event. He was a philosopher of mathematics, who examined the nature of motion and provoked thought by advancing paradoxes which seemed to be insoluble, but which were easily solved when it was recognized that motion was not divisible into discrete units. His importance was enormous in his own field, but in a more practical sphere he could have given little help except in stimulating clever young men to a taste for ingenious argument. This Pericles enjoyed and practised, though in his later years he saw it as a youthful folly; for when the young Alcibiades trapped him in an argument, Pericles said 'We were clever at that kind of argument when we were young!'[1]

Pericles' taste for action and for problems connected with it drew him to other thinkers of a more practical turn, but his interests were not limited to politics. In Protagoras of Abdera he had a friend who loved science and philosophy for their own sake and combined a searching and sceptical approach to religion with a deeply considered respect for law as a means for holding society together. That the two men were on friendly terms appears from an anecdote which tells how they spent a whole day arguing whether, when a boy was killed accidentally in a competition for javelin throwing, the thrower and the javelin were more to blame or those who arranged the competition. It sounds like a trivial case of casuistry, but it is from such simple issues that ethical systems are born, and at least it illustrates how Pericles' conscience worked and forced him to thrash the matter out with an expert on behaviour.

Protagoras was not a member of the inner circle round Pericles, but Anaxagoras, who came from the Ionian city of Clazomenae, was. He was primarily a scientist in the grand Ionian tradition of the sixth century, who wished to discover the nature of physical reality, and made acute and imaginative suggestions concerning it. His lofty view of his own calling appears in his answer to the recurring Greek doubt, expressed in the notion that it was better for a man not to be born, when he said that a man would choose to be born 'in order to study the heavens and the whole universe'.[2] Such was his confident faith. He sought for a single principle in things and found it in Mind, but he was also an observant scientist. An anecdote illustrates his difference from his more hidebound contemporaries. A countryman brought to Pericles the head of a ram which had a single horn in the middle of its forehead. The soothsayer Lampon interpreted this as an omen of victory for Pericles in his rivalry with his chief opponent, Thucydides, son of Melesias. Power would fall to Pericles since he had received the head. Anaxagoras however had the skull split open and gave instead an anatomical explanation of the single-horned ram. The gap between two generations and two systems of thought is clear, nor are we surprised to hear that people soon afterwards praised Lampon for being right when Thucydides was ostracized and Pericles became sole leader of Athens. Anaxagoras advanced scientific explanations of natural phenomena, and though they were elementary, they might run against established beliefs. How much Pericles owed to him may be seen from some words of Plato. In maintaining that all arts, including rhetoric, demand a study of nature, his Socrates says:

This is what Pericles acquired to supplement his natural gifts. In Anaxagoras he found, I think, that kind of man, stored his mind with astronomical lore, and learned the nature of mind and thought – matters on which Anaxagoras was continually discoursing – and drew from it what was useful for the art of speaking.[3]

Socrates might have a grudge against Anaxagoras for not posing the right questions about Being, but he recognized that he exerted a powerful influence.

If Pericles sharpened his mind on science and philosophy, he also enriched it with the arts. The poet Sophocles was his colleague as a general in the Samian War of 441–439, when Pericles warned him not to indulge his sexual tastes too obviously in time of war and added: 'A general should keep clean not only his hands but also his eyes.'[4] Pericles treated his office with so austere a seriousness that he could chide even the poet who had recently won a national success with his *Antigone*. A more productive and more intimate friendship was with the sculptor Phidias. Pericles put him in charge of the sculptures of the Parthenon, both inside and outside, and must have given him control over a large band of assistants and a free hand in the composition. Pericles was said to have inspired Phidias, and though we cannot define this at all precisely, a close connection may be seen between the national spirit as Pericles put it into oratory and as Phidias put it into stone.

Pericles was both a soldier and a man of affairs. Since generals were elected annually, political talents might help, and it paid to be able to speak before the Assembly. Thucydides the historian ascribes three complete speeches to Pericles, and though these cannot be word for word what he said, they must surely reproduce his substance, his manner, and even some of his phrases. From them we can see how he treated his audience. He did nothing to flatter it; his main aim was rather to make it rise to his own level of thought, understand the complexities of his policy, and not be carried away by transitory emotions. That Pericles had a gift for the apt and telling phrase is clear from stray scraps from his speeches which have survived outside Thucydides. He called the island of Aegina, which lies in full view from Athens, 'the eye-sore of the Piraeus',[5] because to an imperial vision this independent city spoiled the prospect. He spoke of Boeotia, divided by civil war, 'like an oak split with oaken wedges'.[6] Of the dead in battle he said: 'The city has lost its youth; it is as though the year had lost its spring.'[7] He caught the imagination of his audience, appealed to its proper pride, and associated himself with it in large undertakings. The comic poet Aristophanes, writing in 425, six years after the outbreak of the Peloponnesian war, has a vivid recollection of Pericles' eloquence when he spoke on it:

> For then in wrath, the Olympian Pericles
> Thundered and lightened and confounded Hellas.[8]

Aristophanes is by no means entirely in his favour, but happy to ridicule his part in starting the war; yet he cannot conceal how formidably impressive Pericles could be, and admires him for it. A similar, perhaps unwilling tribute comes from another comic writer, Eupolis, who records the unique powers of Pericles as an orator:

> In eloquence no man could equal him –
> When Pericles arose and took the floor,
> By ten good feet our common orators
> As by an expert runner were outstripped.
> Not only voluble, but with persuasion
> Sitting upon his lips. He bound a spell,
> And had this power alone of orators,
> To prick men's hearts and leave behind the sting.[9]

The sting is the sting of shame which Pericles sharpened and set to work when he wished to remind the Athenians of their political ambitions and the responsibilities which these entailed.

Pericles was a master of words in other spheres than strict oratory. He was a debater of unusual agility and resource. His chief rival, Thucydides, son of Melesias, complained of him to king Archelaus of Sparta: 'When I have thrown him in a wrestling match, he says that he has not fallen, wins his case, and persuades the spectators.'[10] His notable talent for political manoeuvre is illustrated by the way in which he eliminated his political adversaries and was elected general every year from 443 to his death in 429. From different angles we form a picture of this remarkable man, at once detached and passionately committed, idealistic and practical, so trained in art and philosophy that he enjoyed them for their own sake but also made them serve his political ends. It is not surprising that he early caught the imagination of the historian, Thucydides, who when young must often have seen and heard him. Thucydides is an expert on political ability and judges men by their possession of it. It is this that he finds to a consummate degree in Pericles:

During the whole period of peace-time when Pericles was at the head of affairs the state was wisely led and firmly guarded, and it was under him that Athens was at her greatest ... Pericles, because of his position, his intelligence, and his known integrity, could respect the liberty of the people and at the same time hold them in check. It was he who led them, rather than they who led him, and, since he never sought power from any wrong motive, he was under no necessity of flattering them: in fact he was so highly respected that he was able to speak angrily to them and to contradict them. Certainly when he saw that they were going too far in a mood of over-confidence, he would bring them back to a sense of their dangers; and when they were discouraged for no good reason, he would restore their confidence. So, in what was nominally a democracy, power was really in the hands of the first citizen.[11]

This is a strictly political estimate. It says nothing of what Pericles did for the arts or of what principles guided him in private affairs. It analyses his success in controlling Athens and gives him the highest praise for it. He had many other qualities but was primarily a wise and resourceful statesman, with a consummate gift for the management of men. How he did this we can see in the three speeches in Thucydides, which show a wider range of genius than his summary suggests. In the first we see the hardheaded leader who calculates his chances with care and knows what he intends to do; in the second, the devoted spirit in which he serves Athens; in the third, his courageous temper when things seem to be going wrong and must be faced with candour. The impassive head presented in the famous bust had more to it than Olympian grandeur and detachment.

Though most Athenians must have regarded Pericles as a remote and almost superhuman figure, they had safeguards against him. They were free to listen to his arguments in the Assembly and judge them on their merits. If they disagreed with him, they need not re-elect him to be general, and in that case much of his power would be lost. Indeed in 430, at the end of his life, Pericles was deposed from his office as general, fined, and then reappointed. This may have been due to war nerves, but it showed what could happen.

The citizens of Athens might respond to his resonant eloquence and his soaring vision of Athens, but the comedians made endless fun of him, and had their own disreputable explanations of his public policies. They won innumerable laughs at his expense, but his position remained undamaged. If he was confident in answering his critics, it was because he was sure that they must listen when right was so obviously on his side.

Yet his hold on the Athenian people was secured by more than his capacity for persuasion; he had the unanswerable asset of authority. He forced audiences to pay attention to him, and this would explain why his opponents, lacking his special gifts, felt so strongly against him. Though he was rich and well-born, he did not mingle with his own class but kept himself to a small group of highly gifted friends. The circle of Pericles deserved the rare and paradoxical title of an aristocracy of intellect, and was all the more remote from other Athenian circles in that its chief members did not come from Athens. Social distinctions in Athens were less rigid and less exacting than in most modern societies and could easily be neglected. Pericles solved the problem by creating his own small circle for his private life, and in his public life by raising democratic issues to so lofty a level that they almost lost their social colour. Living in a time of transition, he was able to shape a position of some detachment and to maintain his personal idiosyncrasies, notably in quiet and modest habits, without making them conform to political and social demands.

No other Greek in this age wielded the same kind of power as Pericles on a like scale. His Athenian adversaries gradually yielded to him, and none of his successors had so lasting an influence. In other parts of Greece parallels can hardly be expected, largely because in most of them power was in the hands of oligarchies which maintained their solidarity by not yielding too much to any single man and had no need to convince a sovereign assembly of the need for this or that course of action. So special a position seems to have been possible only in Athens, and there largely because the change to democracy had been so rapid and so thorough that the people, used to more authoritarian systems, still looked for a leader. Their belief in Pericles owed something to memories of Pisistratus, who had helped the underprivileged and had a similar taste for national display in noble buildings, while even the anti-democratic nobles understood that they must not alienate the mass of the population. With a sound sense of political realities the Athenian democrats saw that they could maintain their influence and get what they wanted if they followed a single highly competent leader. This was simple enough. What was less easy to foresee was that this leader would, in return for doing what the populace wished, impose his own ideas on it and give it a course in political education. This education need not have sunk very deep or been at all subtle or complex, but it was a great deal better than nothing at all, and meant that Athens set about its purposes with a fairly clear notion of what they were. Once this became familiar, it would explain why Pericles kept his position for so long. As the aristocratic leader of a democratic state, he was not free from troubles. At the beginning of the war in 431 the Spartan king Archidamus was a friend of Pericles, and Pericles was afraid that for this reason the Spartans, in invading Attica, might spare his own estate. If this happened, prejudice would certainly be aroused against him, since other men's estates were being ravaged and invidious comparisons would be made. Pericles grasped this at once and dealt firmly with it by announcing in the Assembly that, although Archidamus was his friend, this friendship should not extend to the harm of the state, and in case the enemy were to make an exception of his house and lands and not pillage them, he gave them to be public property. It was a wise precaution, by which Pericles skilfully overcame the handicap of his background.

The historical importance of Pericles owes as much to his personality as to the political conditions at Athens which enabled him to exert his talents to the full. In a democracy where decisions were taken openly in the Assembly a man's presence and manner counted for a great deal. This impact, in the last resort, we cannot recapture. Pericles in his actual person eludes us, and we can only speculate about what impression he made on those who saw and heard him. It seems that the mask, if there was one, was very close to the man and that the captain of democracy never lost his confidence and gift of command. His family background trained him to regard politics as a normal activity which any man might practise, and he would certainly see nothing wrong in wishing to gain power for himself, since this would enable him to do what he thought necessary, and reveal his true *aretê*, his worth, in the spectacular way which the Greeks regarded as worthy of glory. His successors may not have been quite so brutal as Thucydides later suggests, but they lacked Pericles' breeding and background and tried to make up for it by violence. This was at least a change of manners, and not only Thucydides but Aristophanes regarded it as very much a change for the worse. Pericles, by his Olympian detachment and his magnificent gift of the word, gave to public affairs a special dignity, comparable with that of tragedy in a very different sphere. He not only practised the fine art of speech but used it to evoke principles which were not debased by over-employment, and which by their moral grandeur threw a glow over common, daily things.

When he was firmly established in power, Pericles' actions were consistent with his first political activities when he was working with Ephialtes. Just as then he had established the payment of jurymen as indispensable to democracy, so now he extended payment to other public duties. First, there were those who were appointed to administrative posts by lot, notably the archons or presiding magistrates, and the five hundred members of the Council. These were paid not in respect of their attendance but in respect of holding office. More strictly administrative posts also called for pay, and this applied to other officers of state, notably generals, cavalry commanders, and other soldiers and sailors. Choice by lot for certain posts and payment for services for all enabled the poorer classes of Athens to take a larger part in public affairs than in the democracy of Clisthenes. The conservatives viewed the practice with horror and advanced the usual argument that it corrupted the people and, as Plato thought, encouraged the rabble to interfere in matters which should be left to their betters.[12] We do not know what proportion of the Council consisted of poorer members, and it is possible that the very poor never belonged to it. But with these changes Pericles completed the process of democratization and made Athens draw its servants from a wide field and recompense them for their services.

Periclean democracy was founded on slavery and could not have existed without it. Though most free citizens had to work for a living, they could create leisure by employing slaves to do the heavier part of their labours for them. Slaves were used in workshops and mines, on the land and in domestic service. All Greeks regarded slavery as an unalterable condition of society, and accepted it as such. It may not have troubled them very deeply or raised ugly questions of natural justice. But they were aware of it, at times uneasily, and at least sought excuses

there was a horrifying tendency to enslave the women and children of the defeated.

In the long run slavery did irreparable harm to the ancient world. Because it provided a large pool of cheap and usually unskilled labour, it gave no incentive to the invention of machines as substitutes for human hands. The failure of the Greeks to apply mathematics to practical needs such as engineering, and their increasing reliance on slave labour, accounts for their failure to improve their material circumstances and for the static monotony of their culture in the centuries after Alexander's conquests. Applied knowledge was rejected by creative minds as below their proper dignity, and even war, which sometimes stirs the inventive faculty, continued to use its age-old weapons and armour. Yet in the fifth century slavery had not revealed all its weakening influence and was in some degree still beneficial. It was not extensive enough to create a huge, unskilled class living at a very low level and performing only menial tasks. Some slaves must have been skilled artisans and even artists. Mass production hardly existed, and though of course cheap knick-knacks abounded, they were not always shoddy and were fully counterbalanced by the high level of domestic articles and ordinary ornaments. A slave who did work at this level was not only close to free men in his interests but able to speak to them on their own terms. Many Athenian households were small enough for slaves to be almost members of the family and mix easily with them, thus avoiding the segregation which ruins self-respect. Slaves could be given their liberty and often were, perhaps because their owners felt that they were human beings like themselves. Yet it is a sad paradox that democratic Athens, which built so much on its belief in the individual worth of every man, endured a system which completely contradicted it. Athenian slaves were probably treated better than Spartan Helots, but they cannot have enjoyed the high sense of personal honour which Athens proclaimed to the world as the right end of man.

Allowing for this grave limitation, the Periclean system gave power not to a favoured few but to a large part of the population. In particular it brought to the fore that section which had hitherto been socially submerged and excluded from office.

This section provided crews for ships and workers for the dockyards. Each man-of-war had one hundred and seventy oarsmen, many of them foreigners and slaves but some of them free men of poor financial standing. Each ship was manned by a crew of ten free men and a guard of twenty soldiers, who provided their own accoutrement and came from a relatively prosperous background. As Athens increased her power at sea these sailors and marines became increasingly conscious of their political chances and responsibilities. They saw that they were indispensable, and they demanded something in return. Their presence in politics kept Pericles to his democratic course but also eventually strengthened the opposition to him.

The dependence of Athenian democracy on the naval section of the population is stressed in a remarkable little pamphlet ascribed to Xenophon and called *The Constitution of Athens*. It is certainly not the work of Xenophon, and though by convention we call its author the Old Oligarch, he seems rather to be an arrogant young mugwump who shows off by advancing what he thinks to be tough, hard-headed ideas. He may have written after the death of Pericles, but his ideas are close to what was said against Pericles when he was still alive. For this author there are two classes of men. The first, to which he himself belongs, is variously called the rich, the good, the noble, while the second, which is roughly identified with the populace, is called the base, the low, the poor. On the latter he has much to say, but he begins with the paradox that, allowing that they exist, it is reasonable that they should have power:

because it is the people that mans the ships and gives strength to the city; and as for the helmsmen, the coxswains, the ship-captains, the forward steersmen, and the shipwrights, it is these who give strength to the city far more than the hoplites and the noble and the good.[14]

He goes on to say that this democratic element is more powerful than its opponents and makes more speeches in the Assembly. Allowing for exaggerations, the Old Oligarch grasps an important truth about Athenian politics—the growth of the navy brought a large submerged section of the population to power. The process began with Themistocles, and was enhanced by Ephialtes and Pericles.

If this sour little pamphlet speaks for one aspect of the hostility to Pericles, we get another from an unexpected source. In his account of the way in which Darius made himself king of Persia, Herodotus presents a short discussion between him and two other conspirators on the comparative merits and demerits of tyranny, oligarchy, and democracy. He insists that this discussion was actually held, but that is too good to be true. Nonetheless it is an example of the simple political thinking that was popular in Athens about 440 in the heyday of Pericles' power. The critic of democracy has much in common with the Old Oligarch when he says of it:

There is nothing more lacking in understanding, nothing more uncontrolled than the useless rabble. It would surely be insufferable to reject the insolent domination of a tyrant only to fall under the equally insolent domination of the reckless mob. At least the tyrant knows what he is about; the mob knows nothing. How can it when it is untaught and has no natural sense of what is right and rushes thoughtlessly into affairs like a river in winter flood? Let our enemies have democracies; but let us pick out a group of outstanding men and put the government in their hands.[15]

Herodotus himself admired the Athenian democracy, but knew what was said against it. All through the fifth century it was opposed by a class of relatively rich men, who were able to provide their own armour and therefore formed the land army, regarding themselves as superior to everyone else in manners and morals and vastly superior in intelligence and practical judgement. The cleavage between the two parties was not absolute. Pericles himself was a landowner, and there must have been others who abandoned family traditions for a new ideal. Equally the rich must have had their toadies who valued the prestige of mixing in good company. But the gap was real enough. One of the main problems for Athens was to prevent the two groups from breaking into hostilities which would rend her to pieces. On the whole she was remarkably successful in doing so, and even when she failed in 411 and endured the establishment of an oligarchic government, she soon got rid of it.

This security was largely the result of Pericles' policy of uniting Athens through his vision of what she ought to be. By persuading the Assembly to share his own convictions he achieved a consistency which could not be expected from a disorganized mass of voters, and it was this that Thucydides admired when he said 'Pericles led, rather then was led by, the people.'[16] When after his death this unity endured it signalled the firm foundation of Athenian democracy. Of course Athens was for a large part of the time at war, and war often unites a divided people by appealing to patriotism and to fear of defeat and its consequences. The Athenian leaders may have disagreed with each other and therefore varied in their policies, but the main body of citizens remained orderly and loyal. Pericles did not create a polity whose different elements were united on most points, but he gave a passion and conviction to Athenian patriotism, and this carried the Athenians through some dark times in which a less devoted people would have given up the struggle. Something of the kind could be found in most Greek states, but in few did sheer love of country have so strong an advantage over loyalty to class or faction or private interest.

There were still individuals and families who favoured the Spartans and would have liked to work with them, while others were prepared to treat them as possible allies. But Athens was not during the fifth century divided by such violence as ruined Corcyra and reduced her from a potentially powerful state to impotence and unimportance. The well-to-do in Athens must have gained from the great expansion of foreign trade and the large advances in skilled industries, while the poor found themselves tolerably cared for and could not only look themselves in the face but feel assured that they were in many reputable respects the equals of the hoplite class. Moreover, though the business of the one was war at sea, and of the other, war on land, most expeditions were amphibious and all ships carried a certain number of hoplites. The shared thrills and horrors of war must have broken down class distinctions, which consist mostly of differences of manners and speech and matter not at all when urgent issues are at stake. When men of different origins are united in some common risk for the state, and inspired by a like idea of it, petty barriers vanish until failure or discontent revives them, and in Periclean Athens it was a long time before this happened.

In any case class distinctions can hardly have been very

marked. Some families were, by the standards of the time, rich from the possession of land, like Pericles; or of mines, like Thucydides the historian; or of factories, like Sophocles, whose father made armaments. But such wealth was by our standards modest and not at all showy. Houses were small, and if money was spent, it was on entertainment and horses and not much else. Nor can we doubt that all Athenians spoke freely to each other, no matter to what class they belonged. There was none of the flunkeyism which marked Victorian England or the Kaiser's Germany. Similarity of interests, many of them out-of-doors, made this almost impossible. If we may judge by tragedy and comedy, servants talked without inhibition to their masters, and in the *Electra* of the realistic Euripides a humble farmer treats openly with the royal house. This equality was strengthened by the public duties which all Athenians shared. Men could hardly serve together on juries without forming neighbourly relations. Easy association of this kind exists in some societies where there are enormous differences of income as in Russia before 1917 and in China at all ages; it is attempted, with some success, in the United States. But in Athens it worked differently. Liberty enjoined fraternity, not unrestrained or facile, but still workable and invaluable in welding the state together. There was a strong opposition against many men for their policies and personalities, but the opposition would not dare to demand that Athens should not be a democracy. Of course there was always a group of moderates led by worthy if uninspiring leaders, but Athens was fortunate in that her economy did not allow the emergence of millionaires who might wish to bribe themselves into power and promote Spartan conservatism over Periclean liberty.

The democracy which Pericles reshaped and inspired reveals at least its main characteristics to us, but his own motives remain mysterious. Why did this Athenian aristocrat devote himself to shaping so complete a democracy? His enemies were ready with a simple answer – he wished to make himself a tyrant and to use the populace, as Pisistratus had, to do so. Yet Pericles did not seek any of the fine trappings favoured by tyrants and much preferred a simple life. He liked power, not necessarily for its own sake, but because it enabled him to do what he wished for his country, and his sincerity in this is clear from the courage with which he accepted harsh criticism, but still kept to his decisions. Democratic propensities were not universal in his family. The Alcmaeonids went their own way, and helped to destroy Themistocles. The paradox of Pericles' career is that he took up the work of Themistocles where it had been left incomplete and remained faithful to its principles for the rest of his life. In this, patriotism played a part, but with very special meaning, unlike its meaning to other leaders, equally patriotic but not so deeply committed.

The ideal of Athens which Thucydides puts so eloquently on the lips of Pericles rings true in its fervour. It is unlikely that Themistocles held views so complex or so deeply meditated as these, and it is in them that we can see the inspiring centre of Pericles' own life and the explanation of his policies. He believed that the Athenian people, freed from old hindrances and charged with new responsibilities, was unique and uniquely valuable in the world. In him the old love of country, consecrated by a noble poetry of glory and sacrifice, had been enriched by new developments in political thought which tried to probe and analyse what an earlier generation had simply taken for granted. Pericles infused the old imaginative devotion with new intellectual conviction. Because he believed in Athens, he believed in everything that she had and was, and above all in the worth of her private citizens, no matter of what class or origin. His extraordinary achievement was to see beyond the limits set by his upbringing and to recognize that if Athens was to be a great city, it was because all her citizens played their part for her and must be allowed to do so to the full scope of their abilities.

5

THE NEW IMPERIALISM

In the league of allies Pericles found a powerful weapon to enforce Athenian policies. The concentration of strength in Athenian hands was welcome so long as the league was directed against Persia. But Athenian power expanded beyond strictly naval and military requirements. The stronger the central organization, the better equipped the league was to meet fresh menaces from Persia. Signs of these were quickly marked, and action followed. The culmination came in 454 when the treasury of the confederacy was transferred from Delos to Athens. For this there was an excellent reason. Delos was exposed to attack by sea at a time when Persia had begun to reestablish her hold on Egypt and to become again a menace to the Athenian navy. There was a real possibility that the treasury might be raided and looted before Athens could come to the rescue. But good though this reason was, it could not conceal the unpleasant truth that Athens now had the money completely in control and could spend it as she pleased. It was now kept in the custody of the national goddess, and, to refute any possible charges of corruption, all payments made to her were handsomely inscribed on stone for everyone to see. The Athenians were determined that Athene should be the protectress of the allies as well as of themselves, and under her patronage the league became an empire. Athens collected the money and spent it as she liked; she enforced discipline by keeping garrisons in allied cities; she became progressively more ruthless against any assertion of independence from the allies; she used the alliance against other enemies than Persia. If Athens decided on some military expedition, the allies had no effective voice against it. In years of peace the tribute piled up in the treasury and gave the Athenians an assurance that they were prepared, as no other state was, for any emergency.

At the same time Athens insisted more forcibly on control of the allies. Specific evidence comes from Erythrae, which lies east of Chios on the coast of Asia Minor, and was brought to heel about 453–452. Careful rules are made for the appointment of the local Council, which is the keystone of democratic government. It is to be formed with the help of Athenian officers, and Athenian soldiers are to remain as a garrison. Precautions are taken against any support being given to Persia, and thus the first aim of the league is still observed. On the other hand Erythrae is compelled to bring offerings to the national Athenian festival of the Panathenaea, and this indicates a more exacting control than mere headship of a league would require. The tributary states had to furnish troops in war and accept Athenian garrisons at all times. What began as a naval league extended its functions to wars on land, which could seldom have been of vital concern to maritime cities.

The transformation of the league into an empire showed the guiding hand of Pericles, but in this too he followed in the steps of Themistocles, who, while the Persian war was still unfinished, used the fleet to extract money by threats from Aegean islands, especially from those which were thought to have collaborated with the Persians. Pericles, by concentrating control in Athenian hands, made her truly imperial. He saw that in the allies he had a splendid instrument for making Athens powerful, but he was not content to keep it loose and flexible. Athens must have the first and the last word, and the end must be her greater glory. So Pericles took steps to make the league more homogeneous and more manageable. Not all his changes were liked, and some of them disclosed the harshness of Athenian ambition. Behind each appears the same desire to strengthen Athens as the head of a new kind of empire. Since she collected the tribute, held it, and spent it, it was a logical and not necessarily offensive step to abolish local currencies and to insist that only that of Athens was legal tender. The local coins, with their multifarious, charming designs, were called in and melted down, and from the silver so obtained more coins on the Athenian model with the Athenian emblems were minted. All such coins were of silver. Gold was coined in Persia but not yet in Greece, and this meant that there was a single basis for metal currency. But before the standardization local coins might be cast on systems of weight different from the Athenian, and this can only have caused delay and irritation in changing from one currency to another. Every payment calls for bargaining, in which one or the other party loses money, and the waste of time is not justified by any result. The establishment of a single standard coinage was a solid advantage for all commercial undertakings. Nor is there any evidence that the allies really disliked the change. No doubt for reasons of local pride they deplored the disappearance of their own crests and symbols and the ubiquitous appearance of the Athenian owl on one side of a coin and Athene's head on the other. This left no doubt that Athens was in charge, but though the allies may have felt some resentment, their finances were made more workable.

More likely to provoke discontent was the jurisdiction which Athens asserted in criminal and other cases. At the start it was logical that, if there was a case between Athens and an ally, it should be decided at Athens; if anyone were accused of treason to the alliance, it was no less logical. But Athens enforced her powers beyond this point. In the settlement with Chalcis after her revolt in 446 it was laid down that in all cases which involved the death penalty or loss of civic rights the trial should be held at Athens. For this too there was something to be said. Such offences might be intended to damage the league or individual democracies in it; local bias might interfere with justice. Yet any dispute on breach of contract between an Athenian and an ally was decided in the defendant's own city, for Athens claimed that she did not use her power to further her own interests. The claim was only partially true, but the result was fair enough. In general we may suspect that while allied democrats were well treated, perhaps even beyond their deserts, allied oligarchs were not so sure of justice, and this would strengthen their antagonism to Athens.

While Athens extended her power, she also stressed her exclusiveness. Though all Greeks regarded foreigners as barbarians, they did not regard other Greeks as foreigners. For them Hellas, despite its political, geographical, and cultural disparities, was a unity for which in an extreme emergency they were prepared to take joint action and which revealed its character in the conduct at regular intervals of Panhellenic festivals like the games at Olympia and Delphi. The members of the league were bound to Athens by common interests and in many cases by common use and wont, since they shared the language and the for it or pointed out the good points of slaves. The Athenians were as aware as Homer that slavery robs a man of half his life and remarked more than once that some slaves had the minds and the self-respect of free men, that for a free man to become a slave was the most terrible thing that could happen to him. The tragedians portray slaves who speak on equal terms to their masters and are sometimes more admirable. Slaves were protected to some degree by law and owned a certain amount of property. No doubt many were well enough treated. Since the higher class of artisans in the workshops of sculptors were often slaves, it was much to their owners' interest to look properly after them. We do not know how far slaves did really skilled and difficult work as, for instance, in carving the sculptures of the Parthenon, but we may assume that at least some such labour was done by them.

Slaves seem to have assumed a greater freedom of manners in Athens than elsewhere, and one sharp critic of the democracy says:

At Athens there is the greatest licence among slaves and aliens, and neither is it permissible to strike them then and there, nor will a slave make way for you.[13]

This at least indicates that slaves were treated quite well, if only because they were indispensable. Free Athenians valued leisure because it enabled them to exercise their minds and bodies in agreeable ways, and to secure this they needed slaves to perform the duller, and not only the duller, chores of common life. They themselves were thus free to meet and discuss politics, enjoy the arts and athletic sports, take their seats on juries, listen to debates in the Assembly, and vote on its motions. When war meant that they were not able to supervise their farms and workshops, workmen might take their place. If they had qualms of conscience, they could perhaps argue that most slaves were not Greeks but barbarians, aliens who did not share the Greek outlook or Greek habits. The Greeks assumed without question that they were superior to all foreigners and, though they might admire Persians and Egyptians and at times form friendships with them, they saw nothing wrong in making slaves of them. Greek slaves were rather a different matter. They certainly existed and, as war brutalized its participants, habits of the Ionian section of the Greek people. We might therefore have expected Athens to strengthen this sense of commonalty and to make members of the league feel that they shared the privileges and the rights of the Athenians. But the opposite happened, when in 451–450 Pericles carried a law by which only those who had Athenian parents on both sides could become full Athenian citizens. For this policy, which strikes us unfavourably, there may have been sensible reasons. The rapid growth of prosperity drew a large number of non-Athenian Greeks to live in Athens, and Pericles may have thought that, since they could not be guaranteed to put Athenian interests first, they should not enjoy the true Athenian's privilege of governing his country. He may even have believed that the Athenians were congenitally superior to other Greeks and that this should be recognized by practical measures. Yet at the same time Pericles was anxious to counteract xenophobia and took pride in the sanity of the Athenian attitude towards foreigners:

> Our city is open to the world, and we have no periodical deportations in order to prevent people observing or finding out secrets which might be of military advantage to the enemy.[1]

Though this may seem to be contradicted by Athenian practice, what Pericles has in mind here is the suspicious and intolerant attitude of Sparta to strangers, and this he does not find in Athens. Athens is open and friendly to visitors but politically keeps herself to herself, if only to be free to pursue her own destiny. Moreover, members of the allied cities enjoy everywhere the protection of Athens and can invoke her help in need. No doubt many of the allies felt that they were treated as second-class citizens, but even this might bring advantages, since it meant that they were relieved of some of the burdens and responsibilities which the Athenians took upon themselves.

Despite this limitation on citizenship Athens kept open house for visitors from all parts of Greece. The historian Herodotus not only spent some years there but made Athens the heroine of his History. He came from Halicarnassus, a Dorian city on the south-west coast of Asia Minor, which paid tribute to Athens. His association with Athens gave him the inspiration for his life work, and even among Athenians few show so lively an appreciation of what the city stands for. Though Athens did not yet produce philosophers and scientists of any special distinction, she welcomed them from outside and became a second home for many men who had ideas, good or bad, about matters so various as the structure of the universe or how to gain success in the law courts. She attracted them less by material rewards than by the interest excited by their work and the opportunity to meet other men of like tastes and calibre. Such men came, as often as not, from allied cities and were not hostile to Athens. Ion of Chios came from an island which claimed the dignity of a full ally; but he became a friend of Sophocles and avoided involvement in local Athenian squabbles. Ion wrote tragedies, which were performed in Athens, and compiled reminiscences, of which a few tidbits survive, about men whom he had met and known.

The union of the allies with Athens was not taken for granted as a mere convenience; it was given a special dignity under the supervision of the gods. Sometimes an allied state entered into an agreement with Athens and bound itself on oath to keep its promises. Examples of such oaths survive on inscriptions, and though details differ, all make solemn pledges of friendship. At Eretria, Chalcis, and Samos the Athenians swear that they will do all they can to benefit the ally concerned. Nor were such oaths an empty form. The Greeks believed that to break an oath invoked the vengeance of infernal powers. Oaths imposed a solemn obligation on both parties in a contract and gave it a religious authority. In the same spirit attempts were made to associate the Athenian gods with the working of the league. A portion of each contribution was paid to Athene, in whose temple on the Acropolis the money was kept. The payments were made at the spring festival of Dionysus, when tragedies and comedies were performed, and Athenian comedians were expected to behave with decorum in the presence of allies. If they did not, they might be prosecuted, as Aristophanes was in 426 for having derided the democratic leader Cleon in his *Babylonians*. The allies had obligations to provide animals and weapons for the Panathenaic procession in honour of the national goddess. Conversely the Athenians kept their own special temples in allied territory as at Chalcis, Mytilene, Aegina, Cos, and Samos. Allies sometimes built these precincts, but they were nonetheless visible emblems of Athenian domination and of the divine power which supported it.

Something of the same spirit, but more exalted and more exclusively Athenian, underlay the policy of Pericles in paying for the resplendent buildings on the Acropolis with money accumulated from the tribute. For this excuses could be found. In the interval of peace, from 451 to 431, between two wars with Sparta, the balance from the tribute was piling up to more than was needed for armaments on even a generous scale. Pericles seems to have assumed that the allies ought to be delighted that their money should go to buildings such as the Parthenon and that they themselves should be under the protection of the goddess to whom it was dedicated. For this he was harshly criticized, and much of the criticism must have started with the allies. But he carried his people with him. They were proud of this glorious embodiment of the national spirit and their national goddess. Behind it was an idea, that Athens might inspire Greece to a spiritual unity stronger than any league bound merely by agreements and treaties.

Yet though this display was meant to impress the allies and make them feel that they shared some, if not all, of the glories of Athens, the allies did not always respond with enthusiasm. It has been claimed that, in imposing her will on them, Athens went against a sentiment which insisted that all Greeks were equal if only in the face of barbarians. Even if this sentiment was not so deep or so conscious as is supposed, it was useful as propaganda against Pericles and his supporters, who defied it. But it was probably exploited by those who had most reason to complain. These were the richer classes in the allied cities. It fell to them to pay the larger part of the tribute, and they did not get much in return. For Athens preferred democracies to oligarchies, and after the rise of Pericles was more determined in supporting them. To the aristocratically minded this was an odious policy, since it meant that their privileges and properties were reduced, and the poorer citizens, who thus got a share in local government, were regarded as unworthy members of the community. These aristocrats Athens regarded as potential enemies, with good reason. They preferred the Spartans to the Athenians, since the Spartans favoured local oligarchies, did not interfere with them, and even supported them in times of danger. If they saw a chance of gaining power, they took it. It was they who led the revolt in Euboea in 447, in Samos in 440–439, and in Mytilene in 428. In no case were these uprisings on a national scale, and in each the leaders seem to have been a small class which had its own reasons for hating Athens and hoped to undermine her authority. They did not necessarily wish their countries to be independent, but they certainly wished to exert more power at home than existing democratic systems allowed. In Mytilene the rebels issued a programme which claimed to be in the general national interest, but it failed to win support. When much later, after the fall of Athens, her critics pointed to the hostility which she had aroused and gave this as a reason for her failure, they had in mind the oligarchic parties which preferred Sparta to her, and independence to both. So long as Athens was strong, these revolts were crushed, and this suggests that they were not wholehearted. But the critics of Athens both at home and abroad pointed to them as evidence for a festering discontent. The hatred which oligarchs felt for Athens and her democratic friends can be seen from Corcyra, which was a non-tributary ally. There the oligarchs began a campaign of brutal savagery, and the democrats retaliated in full measure. In general, oligarchs felt that it was bad enough to lose their old privileges; it was worse to have them destroyed by Athenians, and worse still to have to pay for it. There was a substantial opposition to Athens among the allies, but in so far as it had a shape or a direction, it came from disgruntled aristocrats, who were more numerous in the large than in the small states and at times asserted themselves ruthlessly.

The proof that the Athenian domination of the allies was not entirely abhorrent to them comes not from words but from actions. Despite every opportunity to turn on her when she was in danger, the democratic allies hardly ever did so until long after the death of Pericles, and then always under oligarchical inspiration. The serious revolts were plotted by oligarchs, and when they failed, their place was taken by democrats who remained faithful to Athens. In this there was a large element of prudence. If the local democrats joined in turning against Athens, their own countrymen would in all probability show their ingratitude by trying to reduce them to their old humble position and take back any lands or liberties which they had gained in the interval. If at home a democracy was in power because it controlled the majority of votes in the local assembly, in foreign affairs it was essential to combine under Athenian command if it was to deserve Athenian support in times of crisis. No doubt such considerations, and not purely love and admiration for Athens, kept the allies loyal to her, but loyal on the whole they remained. In the fourth century, when the great days of Athens were past, men who just remembered them regarded the empire as an admirable and beneficent system which guaranteed to many Greeks liberty in more than one sense. While it existed it evoked conflicting feelings, but its survival for so long shows that it cannot have been universally loathed. Class war in Greece could breed bloodthirsty brutality, and the atrocities in Corcyra were by no means unique. It was in the interest of democrats to avoid anything of this kind, and the violence shown to them by their opponents indicates how much they were feared and how strongly they were thought to be entrenched in power. Athens gave to the masses a sense of their rights and their dignity, and for these they were prepared to fight, not only against immediate enemies at home but against Sparta and other enemies who embodied the sentiments which they rejected.

The facts speak for themselves and make it all the more remarkable that the judicious Thucydides should have gone out of his way to claim that the empire was hated and always a potential danger to Athens. He states this as his personal view when, speaking of the outbreak of war between Athens and Sparta in 431, he says that all Greece was in favour of Sparta :

So bitter was the general feeling against Athens, whether from those who wished to escape from her rule or from those who feared that they would come under it.[2]

The same view is repeated in different forms by the enemies of Athens, notably by the Spartan king Archidamus, who speaks of 'the general hatred against Athens',[3] by disgruntled Samians who tell the Spartan admiral Alcidas that they are allies of Athens against their will, and by other enemies of Athens in Sicily and elsewhere. This is natural enough, and there is no difficulty in believing that the Spartans and their allies comforted themselves with the thought that Athens, despite her air of enormous power, had a fatal weakness in the disloyalty of her allies. What is more surprising is that the same view is put forward by Athenians – in 427 by the demagogue Cleon when he denounces what he calls the Athenians' 'weakness,[4] to their allies, and in the winter of 416–415 by the Athenian envoys at Melos who say that they are concerned about 'subjects who have already become embittered by the constraint which our empire imposes on them'.[5] Finally, Pericles himself seems to share this view when he speaks of the empire and 'the dangers arising from the hatred which we have incurred in administering it'.[6] It is true that this hatred may include that of Sparta and her friends, but it cannot be confined to them.

That the oligarchical parties among the allies were hostile to Athens is confirmed by the Old Oligarch, who says that 'it is necessary for the ruler to be hated by the ruled'[7] and accepts this as a law of life which is exemplified by the Athenian empire. Anyone who mixed in his circle would take for granted that the Athenians were loathed. Nor is it really surprising that Thucydides agrees. He recorded his views after the collapse of Athens in 404, when the desertion of her allies in the last years was fresh in his mind. He read this into a more distant past than was warranted. It may even have been what he himself feared before he was exiled. As a rich Athenian he would know men among the allies who were as rich as himself and disliked democracy. This attitude existed, and much propaganda was made with it, but it need not have been universally true.

What Pericles thought about the empire into which he had transformed the league must be deduced from the three speeches which Thucydides gives to him, and which embody the substance of what Pericles said on important occasions towards the end of his life. In the first he delineates with realistic details and cool judgement his policy for winning the war, describes the Athenian advantages over the Spartans in resources and money, and lays down a grand strategy. In the second, which is a speech in honour of the fallen in battle, he commemorates them by praising the city for which they have died and puts forward his ideal of Athens. In the third he counterattacks the critics who have blamed his conduct of the war in its first two years and at the same time passes some just and considered verdicts on the burdens of empire. In each speech phrases occur which have an authentically Periclean ring, and it is difficult not to believe that he said : 'What I fear is not the enemy's strategy but our own mistakes' or 'the whole earth is the sepulchre of famous men' or 'you cannot continue to enjoy the privileges unless you also shoulder the burdens of empire'.[8] The three speeches are consistent with one another and drive their points home with a fierce intellectual passion, as if they presented a single personal attitude which is that of Pericles. They imply rather than state a view of what the empire is and what it ought to be; Pericles takes it so much for granted that it needs no explanation. It has become part of his political thinking and enters alike into his financial and his strategic calculations.

First, Pericles regards the empire as an indispensable instrument of war. It provides ships and money, which are, in his opinion, Athens' greatest assets and most promising instruments of victory. The first enables her to take the war anywhere that she wishes; the second means that she has large reserves which the Peloponnesians, living in an archaic agricultural economy, can never hope to acquire. He assumes that if Athens were to be defeated by land, she would lose her allies 'on whom our strength depends', but he plans to avoid any such eventuality. Against this he sets the complete command of the sea which Athens enjoys :

With your navy as it is today there is no power on earth – not the King of Persia nor any people under the sun – which can stop you from sailing where you wish.[9]

Pericles saw that the empire was indispensable for the growth and maintenance of Athenian power, and this was his first defence of it.

Secondly, Pericles regarded the formation of the empire as a noble achievement for which his countrymen deserved the highest praise, especially those of the preceding and the present generations :

For to the inheritance they had received they added all the empire which we have now, and it was not without blood and toil that they handed it down to us of the present generation. And then we ourselves, assembled here today, who are mostly in the prime of life, have, in most directions, added to the power of our empire and have organized our state in such a way that it is perfectly well able to look after itself both in peace and in war.[10]

Any Greek would think it his duty to make his city safe and prosperous, but he would not necessarily think that he must extend its dominions. All Greek cities had intermittent quarrels with their neighbours, but the conception of a large empire was not in their purview. Even with Sparta the dominion over the Peloponnese, partly through subject peoples, who had for centuries been almost serfs, partly through alliances with self-governing states, was in theory a development of Sparta's ancient, historical role as the leader of Greece. In this matter Pericles went his own way and imposed his own conception of Athenian imperialism on his people. Yet he may have had Sparta at the back of his mind; for he makes a special point that 'of all Hellenic powers we held the widest sway over the Hellenes.'[11] For Pericles it was a matter of pride for Athens to rule over other Greeks as if barbarians were hardly worth the effort.

Thirdly, the Thucydidean Pericles says nothing solid to the credit of the allies but suggests that they dislike Athens and will turn against her if they get the chance. This is a reason why Athens must not suffer reverses on a large scale. He sees Athens not as their benefactress, which after all she was in many ways, but as a stern mistress. He compares her power with an actual tyranny in that, though she may have been wrong to seize power, it is deadly for her to give it up. This is a nice refinement on an idea of the time. It was easy to compare Athenian rule with a tyranny in that it was run by Athens in her own interests and guaranteed by force. This was familiar later to Aristophanes, when, making his Chorus address a personification of the Athenian people as Demos, he says:

> Proud, O Demos, thy sway.
> Thee, as Tyrant and King,
> All men fear and obey.[12]

This is friendly and genial, as suited some tyrants, but the attribution of tyranny to Athens, though skilfully skirted by Pericles, was accepted by his less agreeable successors and became a commonplace to her enemies. Greek oligarchs who suffered from Athenian policy regarded her as a tyrant in the worst sense – upstart, unscrupulous, and bloodthirsty. The accusation came with more force because in its beginnings and even afterwards the league claimed to oppose tyranny, at least as Persia embodied and encouraged it, and some of the oaths which bound its members disclaimed any propensity for it. Of course 'tyranny' was still an ambiguous word and could be used in high literature as an equivalent for 'kingship', but that is not what Pericles' opponents or he himself meant. His opponents, who were usually aristocrats, regarded tyranny as an attempt to organize the proletariat under a single leader in some deleterious cause. Pericles knew that this was said about Athens, and was not ashamed to repeat it and admit that there was something in it. It is for the Athenians to recognize the facts and act accordingly. Though he knew how indispensable allies are, he had no liking or trust or gratitude for them, and could not rid himself of the fear that, if they got a chance, they would leave Athens in the lurch. Though he talks of Athens being the school of Hellas and thinks that her mission is to further democracy, he is not convinced that this is always possible, and he makes too many allowances for its failure. Though his doubts may have stiffened the Athenians, they can not have warmed the hearts of the allies.

Pericles was aware of the fears which haunted some of his countrymen about the allies, and himself shared them to an unexpected degree. In this he probably miscalculated. Things were not so dangerous as he thought. His misgivings show the measure of his anxious care for Athens and were justified by the probability that, if Athens were defeated, her allies, willingly or unwillingly, would desert her, if only because they would have no option of doing otherwise. He felt this fear, and it may have hardened him in his treatment of the allies and made him insufficiently appreciative of their efforts. His whole attitude shows that so far from being a reckless exploiter of imperial power he was cautious to the point of doubt and ready to keep a watch for any possibilities.

It is possible, even probable, that in working up these

speeches of Pericles Thucydides has, without realizing it, given them a bias against the allies which they did not originally contain on this scale. Yet Pericles had some such bias, and it was dictated by uneasiness about the allies' loyalty. That is natural enough, but what is strange is that Pericles seems never to have seen how much Athens would gain if she treated her allies better. If instead of imposing her power on them she had treated them as real equals in a common task, she could surely have feared less from them. In practice she must often have done so, but Pericles says nothing about it, and it does not seem to be part of his thought about empire. Perhaps such an idea was alien to Greek thinking at this time, for even in later times union on the basis of equality was never very popular. Perhaps such ideas as existed about empire emphasized the importance of holding it by force, as the Persians held theirs. But if Athens really had a civilizing mission, it would have worked better on more generous terms. The obstacle seems rather to have been that Pericles accepted power not merely as natural and indispensable but as something worth exercising almost for its own sake. As we shall see, it was this concept – nourished by what Athens was and by what he wished her to be – which gave so unusual a turn to his notions of empire.

6

THE PHILOSOPHY OF EMPIRE

CONQUEST is a dominant feature of the second and first millennia B.C. The god-kings of the Near East spent their arrogant energies in fighting one another, and empires rose and fell with sensational expenditure of blood and effort. These conquests did not bring any real profit to the conquerors. Loot and slaves were the most substantial gains. Otherwise the destruction of captured cities and defeated populations was the common rule, and though this gave ample opportunities for ingenious refinements of savagery, it brought no lasting advantages. Nor was it meant to. Wars were fought for the glory of the god-kings, who boasted of their successes in grandiloquent phrases carved in public places. If economic gains meant almost nothing to them, ideologies meant less, and there was no pretence that the victims were being led into a nobler way of life. But in the seventh and sixth centuries the powers who reigned on the edge of the Asiatic Greeks and ruled Asia Minor saw that conquest could have more practical uses than mere glory. Conquered peoples could be made to pay tribute and to provide soldiers for the army. This was what Persia, under Cyrus and Darius, demanded as it reduced the Greek cities of Asia Minor in a series of highly efficient campaigns. The Persian empire might be ruled by a half divine King of Kings, but he allowed his subjects a certain measure of autonomy. He employed local tyrants in his Greek cities, but kept them in control through his powerful satraps. The pyramidal structure of this empire was well suited to its vast extent but called for a strong grip at the centre. This was provided, and though it might at times show faults, these were usually remedied. Persia under Cyrus made sure of the Asiatic Greeks, then with Darius and Xerxes moved to the Greek mainland and forced its inhabitants to face her in battle and to think about her in relation to their own traditions.

In the long run the Greeks were to respond violently to the

confrontation with Asia, when in the third quarter of the fourth century B.C. Alexander of Macedon conquered the whole of the Persian Empire and would probably have ruled it on Persian lines if his premature death had not left his vast dominions to be parcelled among his generals. But he was not the first Greek to think of creating a monarchy on the Persian pattern. The Spartan regent Pausanias, after defeating the Persians at Plataea and moving to Byzantium, plotted to make himself a king of all Greece with Persian help. In sending some prisoners as a gift of Xerxes he sent also a letter which contained the words:

> I propose also with your approval to marry your daughter, and to make Sparta and the rest of Hellas subject to you. I may say that I think I am able to do this, with your co-operation.[1]

Pausanias at least proposed to act under the Great King, but his plan of ruling over a united Hellas had no parallel since heroic times when Agamemnon led a confederacy of kings to Troy. Pausanias suffered from megalomania and grossly underestimated the difficulties of his plan on the Greek side, but his words, which are preserved on excellent authority, suggest that such ideas were possible in Greece even if they were not popular. After him no Greek of the fifth century seems to have cherished ambitions on this Panhellenic scale. Imperial aims existed but were shaped rather differently.

In their colonial enterprises overseas the Greeks grabbed land from indigenous owners whom they killed or enslaved. Such colonies maintained relations with their mother cities but were not subservient to them, and however many colonies a city might found, they did not form anything resembling an empire. The founding city might assert religious and other prerogatives, appoint some officials, or in times of danger call for help, but that was about all that she dared to do. A colony like Corcyra could be on the worst of terms with her mother city of Corinth, and if the Greeks had been content to confine expansion to founding colonies, no imperial system would have emerged. When it did, it was the brain child of democratic Athens and highly anomalous. When Pericles turned the anti-Persian league into an Athenian empire, his motives were not at all like those of the Persian king or his imitator Pausanias.

The Athenian empire was a new phenomenon with hardly any precedents or parallels. It was built on assumptions that would have been unintelligible to omnipotent autocrats, who had no aim beyond their own glorification and took even that so for granted that it called for no justifying theory.

The Athenians had an idea of empire, and it was new and disturbing. When Pericles claimed that Athens was an education to Greece, he was thinking of her active advocacy of democratic government and of the presuppositions behind it. In general he believed that a state should not be content to remain unchanged but should justify its existence by developments in various directions. The conservative states of Greece, under their oligarchies of landlords or merchants, believed that political change was unnecessary and probably evil. Their ideal was of a harmonious order in which everyone had his own place and kept it, and public tranquillity reflected an inner tranquillity of mind. Such ideas were suited to a world which still believed that gods must be held in honour and men must not seek divine prerogatives for themselves. But in the fifth century other ideas were at work, and though the gods were still held in honour, religious belief was supplemented, even countered by naturalistic theories, and the progress of mankind was ascribed largely to its own efforts. In Athens this meant that action was sought for its own sake and regarded as an honourable pursuit for the city. So in the *Suppliant Women* of Euripides, the Theban herald, who speaks for an old-fashioned polity, exchange ideas with Theseus, who represents all that is best in Athens:

HERALD: Your way is action, and your city's too.
THESEUS: True. Great her toils, and great her happiness.[2]

Such a doctrine appealed to the Athenian sense of honour and desire for glory, but it was resented by less purposeful and less energetic cities.

This spirit inevitably created opposition and trouble, for one of its chief outlets was the extension of Athenian power over other states. Athens might fail in Egypt and Boeotia, but if her allies revolted they were soon brought to heel, and even if they did not revolt they might have additional burdens laid on them and be forced to pursue Athenian ambitions rather than their own. The Athenians were notorious for their unquenchable activity. The Corinthians, who hated them, are reported to have said of them:

Their view of a holiday is to do what needs doing; they prefer hardship and activity to peace and quiet. In a word they are by nature incapable of either living a quiet life or of allowing anyone else to do so.[3]

In the Athenian view the active life was in itself so good that it counterbalanced any objections that might be raised against its hardness and harshness. This was the price paid for glory, and justified by its acquisition.

Such a view was not inconsistent with the Olympian religion, and Pericles harmonized the two in his own way. The cardinal point of his creed was a belief in the divine character of Athens. For Pericles she was more than the 'citadel of the gods', as Pindar called her.[4] He saw her in a special light and felt that in their moments of glory her sons resembled the gods. So he declared that those who fell in the Samian War had become immortal like the gods:

... the gods themselves we cannot see, but from the honours which they receive and the blessings which they bestow we conclude that they are immortal.[5]

Even if there is a touch of sophistication in this, there is no doubt about Pericles' reverence for the fallen.

We have abundant visible testimony to what part Pericles thought that religion should play in public life. About 449 he summoned the states of the Greek mainland to discuss what could be done to the temples ruined by the Persians, but Sparta frustrated any cooperative response. So Pericles set out to rebuild those of Athens on a magnificent scale. The new shrine of the virgin goddess Athene, the Parthenon, was to surpass all other temples in size and splendour, proclaim the glory of Athens to ships sailing across the Saronic Gulf and strike awe and admiration into their crews. But though Pericles was well aware of the political considerations involved in such building, he was moved by more than mere patriotism. In his supreme attention to Athene he showed what he wished men to think about her as the presiding goddess of Athens. Her head had long figured on Athenian coins; on the pediment of the temple built by Pisistratus and destroyed by the Persians she was shown in triumphant battle against the Giants; in 458 she appeared on the stage in Aeschylus' *Eumenides*. The Athenians honoured her as their own goddess, and though she had important cults in other places, Athens was her special home. It is not easy to analyse what she meant to the ordinary or even to the extraordinary Athenian, but her main characteristics are clear. First, she was a warrior goddess – the Champion – and as such a statue of her by Phidias was set up in the open air on the Acropolis facing all who came up through the great gateway of the Propylaea. Secondly, she was a virgin goddess, and this gave her a distinction and a dignity which were a little lacking in, for instance, the Corinthian Aphrodite, and fitted her to be the supporter of manly pursuits, the loyal companion in action and adventure. Thirdly, she was the patron of craftsmen and artists, and as such happily suited to the Athenians, of whom Pericles said: 'We love the beautiful without extravagance.'[6] She was well fitted to her post, and Pericles saw the inner implications of the prominence which he gave to her. She embodied that active, creative intelligence which finds satisfaction in making and doing, alike in political action and in the fine arts. As such she deserved all the honour that she could get.

Among Greek temples the Parthenon is unusual in that it is almost entirely concentrated on the goddess whom it serves. The noble temple of Zeus at Olympia was by no means concentrated on Zeus. He had his gold and ivory statue inside, but on the exterior the metopes displayed the labours of Heracles; one pediment displayed the intervention of Apollo in a fight between Lapiths and centaurs, the other the moment before the chariot race between Pelops and Oenomaus, in which Zeus had the central place but very little to do with the story. It was not compulsory or even customary for the sculptures of a Greek temple to celebrate only the god to whom it was dedicated. Yet the Parthenon is almost entirely concerned with Athene and her special task of civilizing mankind. Its name means 'the shrine of the Virgin' and emphasizes the main point. That Phidias supervised the sculptures we cannot doubt. He cannot have carved them with his own hands, for that would have taken some hundreds of years, but we can see his guiding spirit and personal style in those that survive, and since he was a close friend of Pericles we may assume that the two discussed the themes and the temper of the decorations to some purpose. The sculptures were on a larger scale than on any other temple known to us, and all the latest devices were used to make them majestic and lively. They presented the power of Athene from more than one angle and made her people vividly conscious of her presence among them.

At first sight the metopes might seem to have little connection with Athene. They show men fighting against Amazons, Centaurs, barbarians, and Giants. In these fierce struggles, in which men often get the worst of it, normal, rational beings are set against other beings who are variously superhuman, inhuman, subhuman, or non-human. The men illustrate Athene's special gift of inspiring effort and struggle through intelligence and self-respect. They provide a general background of conflict for the human state. In contrast with them, the dominating role of Athene was emphasized by placing her statue in the centre of the building. The interior was never lit by the full glare of day, and the statue would be partly concealed in a half-light, but its subdued glitter would be visible through the open doors on the east. The work of Phidias, it was about thirty-eight feet high, and the crest of the goddess's helmet nearly touched the roof. The whole was made of ivory and gold; that is, on a wooden core the flesh was made of ivory, and the clothing and armour of gold. Any undue glitter would be countered by the dim light in which it stood. The goddess was armed in her character as champion of Athens; in her right hand was an image of Victory. On the outer surface of her shield were depicted Amazons at war, heroic counterparts to the fighting goddess, and among their opponents two figures were said to have the faces of Phidias and Pericles, who were thus associated closely with the goddess. On the inner surface of the shield was depicted the war between the Gods and the Giants, a cosmic theme which accorded well with Athene in full armour. In contrast with the shield the base of the statue showed on its front Athene and other gods adorning Pandora, the woman created by them in the beginning of things. Though she must have been quiet and graceful enough in contrast with the fighters on the shield, she too was a symbol of struggle, for Pandora was the original source of human sorrows and troubles, which have to be overcome quite as much as more visible enemies. The totality of these emblems meant that Athens is from the beginning the friend of effort and achievement and the adversary of darkness and disorder. The statue was known as 'Athene the Virgin' and as such distinguished from 'Athene the Champion', who stood in the open air outside. Her virginity signified independence and self-reliance and superiority to the common calls of the flesh. To the Athenians it meant a similar detachment and self-control in the service of their city.

The famous statue has perished, and we know it only from cheap small-scale copies and literary descriptions. But the further development of the theme of Athene on the eastern and western pediments is easier to follow, since substantial remains survive, largely in the British Museum, which acquired them from Lord Elgin in 1816, and partly on the Acropolis at Athens. Though the western pediment was very severely damaged in an explosion in 1687, when the Venetians were besieging the Turks in Athens, a good drawing gives some idea of it a few years earlier. The eastern pediment portrayed the birth of Athene fully armed from the head of Zeus. The sculptor sets the scene on Olympus at the moment when day succeeds night, as the horses of the dawn come up on the left while those of the night go down on the right. The sleeping gods and goddesses are woken by a tremendous event, the emergence of a new goddess from the head of Zeus. They stir in their sleep and gaze with amazement at the new divinity. This scene conveys in a mythological form what the emergence of Athens into the world means at the most exalted level. She has a mission, and this is embodied in the divine figure of Athene. Phidias translates a political event, with many implications and ramifications, into a single mythological scene. This is an apt parallel for the rise of Athens. Through it Phidias makes his human situations reveal their divine associations and their place in the scheme of things. For all Greeks human events were inextricably mingled with divine, but in this case an ancient myth gives a full meaning to a human state of affairs. Phidias felt the omnipresent power of the gods and had his own dazzling vision of it. It is this which enables him to see the divine spirit at work in Athens as it stirs awe and amazement among suddenly awakened powers.

The western pediment is more severely damaged than the eastern, but we know its original outlines. Its subject is the struggle between Athene and Poseidon for the possession of Attica. The two contending gods occupy the centre of the design, Athene armed with a spear, Poseidon with a trident. Between them stands an olive tree, the symbol for Attica, which lives largely by the olive. The goddess claims Attica because the land is hers, the god because the sea is his, and Attica is almost encompassed by it. Each has supporting divinities; indigenous heroes and heroines are divided between them. It is natural that the gods of land and sea should compete for Athens, but to such a struggle there can be no solution. Athens continues to be mistress of both elements, and that is the point of the myth. Her land empire might not be so large as she wished, but she was nonetheless a formidable power; at sea she was supreme, and Poseidon's desire for her is a tribute to her mastery of it. The lesson is that Athens is great alike by land and sea because in both a god is eager to own her. If the eastern pediment shows what the birth of Athene means, the western turns to the birth of Attica when two great divinities contend for her.

The pediments presented the destiny of Athens from a supramundane, Olympian angle. In conscious and illuminating contrast to them the frieze went all round the temple and depicted the national festival of the Panathenaea, which took place every fourth year and was marked by a grand procession, which assembled outside the city, came up the Acropolis, and ended by presenting a robe to the goddess. The frieze gives both the human and the divine sides of the occasion and thereby exalts the people of Athens to the company of the gods. They sit calmly and decorously in their elegant chairs and converse with one another. When we recall how passionate and terrifying Greek gods can be and how much of their divinity is displayed through explosions of destructive wrath, it is comforting to see them tranquil and controlled as they watch the ceremonial on earth. Their mood is unlike their awed amazement on the east pediment or their excited commitments on the west. They are at their most intimate and most friendly, and reflect that union between gods and men which the grand procession embodies.

Most of the frieze depicts the human beings who bring offerings to their goddess – animals for sacrifice or fine vessels for libations. A single spirit permeates the vast accomplishment of the design. Here are the inhabitants of Athens, men and women, old and young, presented at their best, as they would like to be seen, as they might even look in a moment of unclouded happiness in the presence of the gods. Phidias does not falsify his subjects; he transfigures them. He does this because the Panathenaic procession sheds a divine spirit on its participants and brings them nearer to the felicity of the gods. The young men on horses, the women carrying large pitchers, have an effortless distinction. They keep this high style when they might have lost it through too great dissemination, and they all share it. In their restrained gaiety, their quiet converse with one another, their affectionate attentions to the animals that they lead or ride or drive, the graceful simplicity of their clothes, the figures of the frieze recall what Pericles says of his people :

Each single one of our citizens, in all the manifold aspects of life, is able to show himself the rightful lord and owner of his own person, and to do this, moreover, with exceptional grace and exceptional versatility.[7]

This personal dignity is at its best in the procession, and is an important part of the Athenian spirit as Pericles saw it. The artists have caught the transfiguring influence which comes when men and women take part in a ceremonial which emphasizes both their individual parts and their common association as members of a great city, while at the same time both personal and common qualities are lit by the approval of the gods. This vision of Athens is coherent and logical and exalted. It has not risen by accident from some whim of history. It is the work of a shaping mind, of a great artist interpreting a great ideal.

The artists of the Parthenon, guided by Phidias, translated into stone what Pericles and his intimate circle believed about Athens and its significance. Their work influenced the Athenian public at more than one level. The ordinary man, seeing himself more or less represented in the frieze, could not fail to be exalted. What was dim enough in his daily round became suddenly radiant, and his trust in the gods, however mechanical, might take on a new importance. The frieze creates an atmosphere, suggests what it is to live under the protection of benign gods, how fine a ceremony Athens devotes to them. The incarnate divinity of Athens and her people could not fail to touch, however vaguely, many people. At quite a different level the display of power on the pediments did not so much shed light on the present scene as suggest mysteries lurking in the world and specially relevant to Athens. The gods were the masters of power, and when this was made visible it was an inspiring revelation and gave a fresh angle to public life and policy. Phidias deepened and enriched the average Athenian's view of his country and its destiny. In this Pericles was wholly with him. By concentrating on Athens Pericles found a new outlet for national devotion. It might not mean so much to all men as it did to him, but many of them would be touched by it to finer issues. The Parthenon enforced the wish which he reveals to the Athenian people:

What I should prefer is that you should fix your eyes every day on the greatness of Athens as she really is, and should fall in love with her.[8]

The task of the Parthenon was to speak to Athenian devotion and love of grandeur.

Athene is first and foremost a goddess of war, who inspires her people to it because she desires them to win honour. The Maiden goddess, as Phidias saw and created her, embodies what Aeschylus put on her lips in his *Eumenides* in 458:

> In the glorious
> Arrays of battle I shall strive until
> This city, over all victorious,
> Enjoy an honoured name throughout the world.[9]

This is a traditional view. Athene will help Athens to win honour, and the honour will come from a vast extension of power. This was what Pericles also wished and believed, but he tempered it with other considerations. Though the renown of his city was the central article of his creed, he did not confine it to victory in war. The range of his vision matches the Parthenon frieze, which is concerned with peace and lacks those scenes of battle and bloodshed which were commonly represented on temples. The happy mood of the frieze might be explained as the result of victories in war, or at least of power sufficient to frighten or repel enemies, and this was certainly inherent in Pericles' theory of government.

The safety of Athens lay in the hands of the gods; their presence was an assurance of their readiness to help. The importance which Pericles attached to their cults can be seen from the construction of four other temples at about the same time as the Parthenon. In Athens were built the temple of Ares, the god of war, and the temple of Hephaestus, the god of fire, who presided over the factories which made Athens rich and equipped her for war. Of these the second survives almost complete, and though it is by Athenian standards of no special distinction, its position above the agora, or market-square, set it at the centre of Athenian life. The other two temples were outside Athens. On the high promontory of Sunium was the temple of the sea god Poseidon, visible to all ships coming back to Athens from the east, the first assurance of home. So Sophocles makes a chorus of sailors from Salamis sing in their homesickness at Troy:

> May I be where the wooded cape
> Lashed by the waves stands over the sea
> As I pass below Sunium's lofty peak
> To greet holy Athens.[10]

At Rhamnus on the north coast of Attica, at the top of a cliff that slopes steeply to the sea, a temple was built to Nemesis, who was not a member of the Olympian hierarchy but as the embodiment of fate or destiny could not be neglected by a people so bent on challenging fortune as the Athenians. These four temples – and no doubt others were built at the same time – show how seriously Pericles took the religious organization of Athens. The choice of the sites and of the gods to be honoured was no doubt determined by existing cults at these places, nor can we discern any precise policy in the actual choices made. But the main intention is clear. The gods of Attica must be honoured in full measure, and their ceremonies must not be confined to Athens itself. The scientific spirit from

Ionia had not seriously discredited respect for the gods. Pericles knew that Athens needed them and took steps to see that they were properly treated. For him Athene was the most important, but the others supported her and helped to enlarge the fields in which Athens excelled.

In so far as the arts were needed to honour the gods, they were taken for granted, and the finer their performance, the more the gods gained from it. Yet though the arts aimed to serve the gods, this did not mean that their interest for their own sake was neglected. It was possible both to share their religious temper and to enjoy the special delight which they gave. The pleasures of the mind were honoured in Athens as an important element in what she gave to her sons. The arts flourished in her free atmosphere and in the seriousness of her civilizing mission. In the spring of 431, just before the outbreak of the long and disastrous Peloponnesian War, Euripides produced his *Medea*, though he had poor success with it, since the judges put it at the bottom of the list. He was a patriotic Athenian, whose patriotism had little to do with the Olympian gods, even if they had been modernized and made more intelligible. Yet even for him, despite his searching scepticism, Athens was something holy, which lifted its people into a rarer and more exalted air. Rather in contempt of his plot, he makes his chorus sing of the Athenians:

> From old the sons of Erechtheus know felicity;
> The children of blessed gods,
> Born from a land holy and undespoiled,
> They pasture on glorious wisdom,
> Ever walking gracefully through the brightest of skies,
> Where once, men tell, the Holy Nine,
> The Pierian Muses,
> Created golden-haired Harmony.
>
> On the fair-flowing waters of Cephisus
> They say that Aphrodite fills her pitcher
> And breathes over the land
> The sweet gentle air of breezes,
> And ever she crowns her hair
> With a fragrant wreath of roses;
> She sends her Loves to be throned at Wisdom's side,
> And with her to work all manner of excellence.[11]

Euripides may not see the Muses and Aphrodite as living, div-ine personalities, but they are real enough, born from the soil and water and air of Athens and shedding their enchantment over her. The Greek gods could be interpreted in many ways and given many functions, nor did it much matter if they became abstractions and ideals. The important thing was that they gave a meaning to human actions. Of this Pericles was certainly conscious. So too at this period was Euripides, who still saw his country as favoured beyond all others with the finest gifts of the spirit. Religion was moving from the close limits of cult and ritual to a wider but vaguer sphere. For the moment it gained in majesty and generosity.

Just as religious worship inspired works of art which en-hanced its appeal and were at the same time admired for their own sake, so the needs of social existence inspired a conception of law as the foundation of order and liberty. The Greeks had for long regarded law as indispensable to just government be-cause it set explicit rules, known and recognizable, in the place of subjective, personal whims. Whatever form of government might exist, law was indispensable, and public actions were expected to conform to legality. Athenian democracy was the product of laws proposed by Clisthenes and later by Pericles and confirmed by the Assembly. Part of the strength of the Athenians was that, though they enjoyed a large measure of liberty, they remained law-abiding, knowing that anarchy or disorder would play into the hands of those who hated de-mocracy and wished to destroy it. Pericles makes a special claim for the Athenian attitude towards the laws :

We obey the laws themselves, especially those which are for the protection of the oppressed, and those unwritten laws which it is an acknowledged shame to break.[12]

Here are two separate propositions, each of which calls for attention. The first is that Athens looks after the oppressed. Her democratic system brings the underprivileged into the tasks of government and looks after them in return. This claim went back to Solon, but Pericles extended its meaning in regarding the oppressed not as a special class, but as all who suffered from some social disadvantage. We may also suspect that, per-haps with some lack of precision, Pericles refers to the help which Athens gives to the oppressed of other cities. She saw herself in this role when she imposed democracies on her allies and when she went to the help of states like Corcyra which were in trouble with their superiors. In the next century both the soldierly Xenophon and the political pamphleteer Isocrates held it to the credit of Athens that she helped the injured. As Athens consolidated her empire, the chances of aiding the oppressed must actually have diminished, and she herself was now seen as the oppressor; but she clung to her claim, and her poets helped her. The principle remained that one duty of the law was to protect the oppressed whether at Athens or elsewhere.

Pericles follows this with a reference to the 'unwritten laws'. The idea was common and had more than one meaning. In Athens, for instance, it had a special reference to the rules that governed the conduct of the Mysteries at Eleusis. These were controlled by special officials, but though they placed strong obligations on the initiated, the state was not the authority that enforced correct behaviour. In any case it is doubtful that Pericles had these in mind, for it would surely be an anticlimax after what he had just said. The conduct of the Mysteries was not in the same class as the laws of Athens. Conversely, the unwritten laws were claimed in some circles to be laws given by the gods on which all other laws were based. This at least gave divine sanction to human laws and enhanced their authority. But we may doubt whether Pericles meant this. He once told Alcibiades that a law is 'whatever seems good to the people',[13] but, though he had a high opinion of the people, he can hardly have believed that *vox populi vox dei*. It was enough that the people should make laws which expressed their will. There is in fact no need to seek for clear precision in the concept of unwritten laws. Athenians, like other Greeks, observed certain rules which were not enforced by law but were none the less respected. These rules came from ancient use and wont and were largely concerned with domestic sanctities and relations between members of a family, including the duties of burial and of vengeance and the avoidance of adultery and incest. They dated from a time when the family, not the state, was the seat of order, and their authority was canonized by age. They dealt with matters beyond the scope of official regulation but were important for the dignity and honour of Athenian life. In mentioning them Pericles indicates that a democratic public has just as high standards of behaviour as any aristocratic clique with its claims to be 'noble' and 'good'.

In his ideal of Athens Pericles does not limit himself to political aims. He recognizes that the full life contains more than these and that leisure too has its uses, especially for enhancing the grace of living. He makes the point briefly but firmly :

When our work is over, we are in a position to enjoy all kinds of recreation for our spirits. There are various kinds of contests and sacrifices regularly throughout the year; in our own homes we find a beauty and a good taste which delight us every day and which drive away our cares.[14]

The festivals were held in the honour of the gods, but were none the less occasions for display and rejoicing. The Old Oligarch disapproved of them as symptoms of democratic decadence. But they were not holidays without religious significance; they were the Periclean way of showing what the gods really meant in the lives of men. In these quiet words he refers to such magnificent and holy occasions as the Panathenaic procession, depicted on the Parthenon frieze, which embodied the divine nature of Athens and yet was entirely human in the most delightful sense. Though naturally such occasions provide recreation, they are not mere recreation, but the expenditure of energy on something exalted and exhilarating.

Pericles' second point is about the ordinary conditions of life in Athens. He is plainly content with the elegance and beauty which he finds in them. By modern standards they would seem very simple, though what we know of Athenian furniture and pottery shows a high level of craftsmanship and taste as befitted an age when manufactures had not become mechanized. In the fourth century it was customary to look back to the glorious past and be proud of the simple conditions in which great men like Miltiades and Aristides lived, but sharper critics complained that most houses in Athens were cheap and very few convenient. Pericles was clearly quite happy that houses were cheap if they had a certain style, and this he claims for them. In so far as Athens was expected to maintain the old aristocratic luxury, it must be in her public buildings, and on these no expense was spared. If men were to live together in harmony, it was prudent to encourage them to enjoy similar habits of elegance. But the vital point was that beauty is possible without extravagance, and it is this which restores the Athenians after their labours.

At an important point of his Funeral Speech, Pericles says:

Taking everything together, then, I declare that our city is an education to Greece.[15]

It is wrong to take this as referring to Athens as the intellectual centre of Greece. This she certainly was, and was recognized as such by the many sophists and scientists who enjoyed her hospitality. But it is clear from the context that Pericles has much more in mind. His words are a short summary of what he has said so far, and this includes his most detailed and considered estimate of what Athens does for her own citizens. The inevitable conclusion is that the education which Athens gives to Greece is her own manner of life, her special kind of democracy, and the self-development and the self-respect which it encourages. This may be adopted voluntarily or it may be imposed by force, but in either case it is the most valuable thing that Athens has to give. Nor does the distinction much matter. What matters is that the Athenian example should be followed and all kinds of Greeks inspired to realize her ideal of the full life. Athens of course could not begin to set such an example unless she was unusually powerful, and Pericles even claims that she has won her great successes without others complaining, because they accept it as natural to be defeated by her:

In her case, and in her case alone, no invading army is ashamed of being defeated and no subject can complain of being governed by people unfit for their responsibilities.[16]

Pericles asserts that because Athens is good at war, she is fit to govern other cities. The claim has often been made for other countries, and is usually untrue. But for Pericles it has a real meaning since it underlines his belief that what Athens does for other cities is what no other power can do. In return for some diminution of independence they are offered a wider and more glorious life. The empire awoke dormant powers and made cities conscious of their potentialities. Not all the allies welcomed either the claim or its implementation, but those who did showed by their vigorous actions and their intellectual vivacity what Athens had done to educate them.

The Periclean ideal for Athens was of creative activity inspired by liberty and secured by law. This activity reflected ideals which other cities could only profit by adopting, and Athens was ready to help them. Yet despite all the benefits which she claimed to bring to other cities, her capacity was based on power and on her ability to get them to share her burdens and to accept her leadership. If they did this willingly, well and good, but Pericles was too realistic to think that they always did, and was almost unnecessarily sceptical about their loyalty. Even by the most brutal calculations the democratic parties in the allied states would rather remain under Athenian rule than be the victims of vengeance from their own despoiled rich. But there was always a chance that some allies might set independence above security, and Athens had to bear in mind the need to enforce control. If the cult of Athene, and through her of Athens, was largely religious in intention, that did not give a moral sanction to all that Athens did. Religion and morality were not very closely allied in the Greek consciousness, and even in matters dealing with gods what mattered was not goodness but power. Their difference from men lay in their vast superiority in mind and physique, and this enabled them to act as they wished. In enforcing power Athens behaved in a divine way, in which most Greeks would see nothing wrong. Where it was exceptional was that Athens recognized no limits to the use of power. Others might argue that there must be a mean in power as in other things and that the Athenians went too far and were much too active in extending their dominion over other Greeks. Old-fashioned aristocrats, who were as common in Athens as elsewhere, thought that this unceasing activity was a sign of low breeding, but perceptive Athenians gave it quite a different interpretation. In his *Suppliant Women* Euripides, giving voice to the society of Pericles, regards this energy as a form of happiness beyond the comprehension of most Greeks and one of the many advantages brought by Athenian freedom. Such energy could find satisfaction only in power, and this raised one of the most difficult questions of the age. How far were men entitled to exert power freely as the gods did? To an old-fashioned Greek aristocrat, who was not an Athenian, the answer was clear. Gods and heroes have one way of life with its own rules, and men another with different rules. Men may at times enjoy moments of divine felicity but it is not for them to seek to resemble gods. The fault of Athens, in the view of many Greeks, was that she not only strove to pass beyond what is allowed to men but gloried in it and thought it a matter for pride and congratulation. That it caused suffering to others did not much matter if in the end it enhanced the power and reputation of Athens. In the last analysis this was the Periclean philosophy of empire.

Pericles knew quite well the dangers of power, but thought that they could be surmounted by courage and intelligence. If Athens really believed in herself and her mission, there was no reason why she should not succeed. Though glory was his aim, he did not confine it to war. Nor did he pursue war for war's sake. In his early years perhaps he may have been carried away by dreams of imperial splendour, but he learned from experience. When he found himself again at war with Sparta, he said:

If one has a free choice and can live undisturbed, it is sheer folly to go to war. But suppose the choice was forced upon one – submission and immediate slavery or danger with the hope of survival: then I prefer the man who stands up to danger rather than the one who runs away from it.[17]

He was certainly not eager to throw away the lives of his countrymen or to see this as an unmixed good. On his death-bed he is reported to have said that his most glorious title to fame is that 'No Athenian ever put on mourning because of me.'[18] He reveals a sense of reality which is not commonly found in the heroic temper. Pericles need not have been entirely consistent in this attitude or content with it. When things looked better, the desire for the onward march of events was vivid in him, and he felt that just as the previous generation had increased the dominion of Athens, so the present generation must follow its example. This belief in success and glory exacted a heavy toll from the Athenians, especially as it was an article of belief that every citizen must care for the city and be ready to do his best for it. So Pericles affirms:

We do not say that the man who takes no interest in politics is a man who minds his own business; we say that he has no business here at all.[19]

It was right to mind one's own business so long as it was also the business of Athens, but wrong to detach oneself from public affairs and obligations.

The sense of belonging to a city and having deep obligations to it was natural to almost all Greeks. To live outside such a frame a man must, as Aristotle said, be 'either a god or a beast'.[20] Pericles examined the matter with care and came to hold special views on it. First, he insists that in a democratic state the citizens must be well informed on political matters and be ready to discuss them properly without rushing into headlong decisions. They must be 'capable at the same time of taking risks and of estimating them beforehand'.[21] He saw in the Athenian people the possibility of qualities which he himself possessed and liked to foster in others. With an insight extraordinary for his time he knew that a people can be educated in politics and that the best means of education is through full consideration of what steps it has to take. Secondly, he knew how prone all Greeks were to internal strife, how savagely partisans of the class war attacked each other. He hoped that Athens might avoid its more violent manifestations and exercise a positive, almost instinctive goodwill on the principle that 'we make friends by doing good to others, not by receiving good from them'.[22] He saw the Athenians as a single body, highly diversified in detail and all the better for it, but also at one with each other in all matters which concerned the good of the city. This was an ideal more than a reality, as Pericles knew well enough from the opposition which he encountered with more than one policy, but when it was tested by war, its strength was revealed. His ideal was not far from that which Aeschylus in 458, soon after the murder of Ephialtes, had set forth in the *Eumenides*:

> N'er, I pray, n'er may that
> Root of evil, civil strife,

Rage within her boundaries;
N'er may the earth's dust drink of the blood of her children,
And wroth thereat thirst greedily after revenge,
Blood in requital of blood;
Rather in friendly communion
Gladness be rendered for gladness,
All at one in love and hate,
Therein lies a cure for human ills.[23]

If Athens was true to herself and abjured the feuds of inferior cities, there was no reason why she should not dominate Greece.

Any Greek would feel that he was so intimately tied to his city that he owed great obligations to it. Pericles picked up this belief and made it more explicit by defining what the responsibilities were. He insists that every citizen must play his part in making public decisions, and he assumes that once the decisions are taken, all must unite in putting them into effect. Such loyalty is demanded by honour but also by expediency, and Pericles characteristically explains what this means:

However well off a man may be in his private life, he will still be involved in the general ruin if his country is destroyed; whereas, so long as the state itself is secure, individuals have a much greater chance of recovering from their private misfortunes.[24]

This was almost a commonplace, used by poets to enforce lessons. For Pericles it is not a pious sentiment, but a realistic policy. Because he believes it, he is able to carry the people with him in taking risks and knows that his own patriotism is beyond cavil. In his statement of his ideals there may be an element of wishful thinking, but in the last resort he bases his case on experience and a rational assessment of human character and its vagaries. In his speeches there is a conscious persuasiveness, a desire to make things look more attractive than they are or even than he believes them to be. But on the fundamental issues he speaks from a coherent point of view. He knew what he wished Athens to be and worked out the means by which she could become it.

The aggressive policy which Pericles inspired made enemies for Athens, among her allies as well as her recognized rivals and enemies. He was himself acutely aware of it, and in the speech which he made shortly before his death he gives his own answer to what must have been quite a common complaint:

All who have taken it upon themselves to rule over others have incurred hatred and unpopularity for a time; but if one has a great aim to pursue, this burden of envy must be accepted, and it is wise to accept it. Hatred does not last for long; but the brilliance of the present is the glory of the future stored up for ever in the memory of man.[25]

To a traditional Greek theme Pericles gives a new variation. So much of Greek behaviour at all times was shaped by the desire for glory and the honour which comes from success that there is nothing new in Pericles' notion that the Athenian empire will have a renown comparable to that of the great heroes of the past. But to this he joins another traditional notion, that envy and hatred are actually tributes to success and must be accepted as part of it. Pindar, in addressing Hieron, king of Syracuse, about his high position, says: 'It is better to be envied than pitied.'[26] Glory is so worth having that it can afford to pay the price of hatred. But behind this Pericles implies something less usual. The Athenians of his time were much concerned with finding a modern equivalent to the heroism of the legendary past. They believed that in the Persian Wars they had equalled the achievements of heroes long dead, but they saw that any modern equivalent would have its idiosyncrasies, since a man lived not for his own honour but for his country's, and this called for a different type of behaviour. Athens set out to be superior to the other cities of Greece, and her superiority lay partly in her being above such common human weaknesses as sensitivity to criticism or resentment at abuse. In this respect Pericles sees her not as one city among many but in glorious isolation. This attitude he fostered. If Athens was to be true to the divine spirit which infused her being, she must be remote and formidable. She might claim that she brought many benefits to other cities, but these were possible because she had enough power to guarantee them against hostile or rival causes.

Athens did much good, but it was done largely by force and fear. She had friends who stood loyally by her, but her enemies were numerous and unrelenting, and we know something of what they said. On this matter we get important inside information from the Boeotian poet Pindar. He is an admirable witness for more than one reason. As a professional poet he visited many parts of Greece and consorted as an equal with Sicilian tyrants and the king of Cyrene, but more happily and more often with aristocratic families such as those of Aegina. As a boy he had learned his art in Athens, and for Athens he kept a certain affection until the emergence of Pericles and his treatment of Boeotia and Aegina made tolerance impossible. Pindar even got into trouble at Thebes in 474 for praising Athens in a famous dithyramb which began :

> O glittering, violet-crowned, chanted in song,
> Bulwark of Hellas, renowned Athens,
> Citadel of the gods.[27]

For this he had to pay a heavy fine, but he did not apologize, and insisted that he had the right to praise even an enemy, such as the Thebans regarded Athens, if she did well. In 470 he mentioned Athens with honour for her victory at Salamis. This was the world of Cimon, in which Pindar was at home. But slowly he changed his position. In writing formal odes to be sung in the home towns of successful athletes, he had sometimes to refer to political events. He did so obliquely and presented his feelings and his lessons through myths and legends, which have to be interpreted. This method has its advantages. It reveals the full measure of Pindar's emotion as he interpreted the feelings of his patrons, and though it is seldom precise, it has moral and religious associations which do not emerge so clearly from straightforward statement. Pindar represents an aristocratic point of view which is not very articulate in our other evidence. About 460, when Athens attacked Aegina, Pindar saw what was happening, but hoped for the best. Aegina was his second home, and that was painful enough for him. Soon afterwards Athens attacked his real home in Boeotia.

In *Isthmian* VII, composed in 454 soon after the Athenian victory at Oenophyta and the subsequent Athenian take-over of Boeotia except for Thebes, Pindar's main theme is praise and honour for those who have died fighting for his country, but towards the end he inserts a small moral or lesson in a reference to a famous myth. The hero Bellerophon, who rode the winged horse Pegasus, tried to scale the sky and was thrown to earth. Pindar passes a comment:

> If a man peers at what is afar,
> He is too small to reach the bronze-floored home of the gods.
> Winged Pegasus threw off
>
> His master Bellerophon,
> When he wished to climb to the sky's dwellings
> And the company of Zeus.
> A most bitter end
> Awaits what is sweet in despite of right.[28]

This is not a direct statement about Athens, but its full weight of meaning is applicable to her. Pindar sees in her the ambition which overreaches itself and comes to a bad end. This is his forecast for Athens. More than this, he implies that just as Bellerophon was thrown by his own horse, so Athens will be thrown by her allies. This was a common idea at the time. We may even press the point that Bellerophon sought to partake of the company of the gods; for, after all, this was what Athens was trying to do when she sought to enforce her will to a superhuman degree on other cities. For Pindar the lesson is clear. Athens suffers from the infatuation of pride and will work her own undoing.

Soon afterwards, in the spring of 453, Pindar wrote *Pythian* XI, also for a Theban, to be performed in Thebes. He begins with the theme of justice and then tells with concentrated power the story of the murder of Agamemnon by his wife Clytaemnestra and the vengeance exacted for this by their son Orestes. The myth is introduced in what looks like a very superficial way but that is common with Pindar, and it is meant to be taken very seriously. It ends emphatically with the killing of his mother by Orestes:

> Yet Ares at the last
> Brought him to slay his mother and lay Aegisthus in blood.[29]

This is a myth of deliverance through vengeance, and when Pindar introduces Ares, the god of war, into a family feud, he shows that his intentions go beyond it. Pindar has something heavy on his mind, and this is almost certainly the Athenian hold on Boeotia. This impression is confirmed when a little later Pindar condemns tyrannies, such as Athens is, and closes by putting his trust in protecting heroes, partly Theban but partly also Spartan as if he hoped that Sparta would in due course rescue Boeotia.

In 446, when Pindar was an old man, he wrote *Pythian* VIII for an Aeginetan boy-victor. At the time Athens was in grave danger. She had just lost Boeotia at the battle of Coronea; a Spartan army was inside her border; Euboea was in revolt; Megara had liberated herself. We can imagine the atmosphere in Aegina. Was not this the time to strike a blow and set herself free? Pindar looks at the matter from more than one angle, and recognizes both the hopes and the fears. He sees Athens as the enemy of the gods, comparable with the Giants who fought against them and were hideously defeated. He appeals to 'Quiet, daughter of Right' for help, and this is his way of personifying the moderation and self-control which he and his friends set up as an alternative to Athenian restlessness. This spirit will, he believes, triumph in the end because it keeps its strength when its enemies overplay their parts:

> You too, if any
> Drives home into his heart
> Unsweet anger, will harden your face
> Against the might of your enemies, and clap
> The upstart in the bilge.[30]

Yet though he believes that his cause will ultimately win, Pindar has doubts and misgivings. He knows that unforeseen accidents may upset the best plans. Yet he assumes that the gods are on the side of Aegina, and ends with a prayer for their help:

> Aegina, dear mother,
> Keep this city in her voyage of freedom:
> You with Zeus and lord Aeacus,
> Peleus, and lord Telamon, and Achilles.[31]

His prayer was not answered. Aegina remained in Athenian control for many more years. In 431 her inhabitants were expelled and the island was settled by a cleruchy of Athenians and became part of Attica.

Pindar spoke for the old aristocratic world which Athens opposed both in her empire and outside of it. For him there was little allure in the Athenian lust for action; he preferred the graces and delicacies of a quiet life enriched by the arts and by personal relations. So far from seeing Athens as the darling of inspiring gods whom she wished to resemble, he saw her as their infatuated adversary, who would inevitably be humbled.

In imperialism the Athenians found an outlet for their unquenchable energies and a summons to further efforts. In this Pericles abetted them and created an ideal which caught their imaginations. He was surely also interested in the practical and commercial advantages of an empire, but he speaks rather obliquely of these as if they were not of first-class importance. With command of the sea the Athenians could send their goods to distant markets and pay for food imported from abroad. Athenian commerce flourished, and her fine wares, such as painted pottery, found a market in many distant places. Yet the Athenian empire was not primarily a commercial empire as Carthage had already begun to be or Venice and Portugal were to be in later ages. Athens did not establish colonies or even trading stations outside the Greek world; her attempt to found a base in Egypt ended in disaster. The claim of the empire was that it provided Athenians with something to live for. Many no doubt appreciated its opportunities for making money, but others welcomed its challenge to action, even if this meant war. It appealed to beliefs in the value of action as a test of manhood and helped to make the Athenians feel superior to other Greeks because they took greater risks and won more successes. The empire did much for Athenian prosperity; it did more for Athenian confidence and pride. In this, as in other respects, democratic Athens prolonged and strengthened a spirit that had already existed in the aristocratic age. It gave to its free citizens the sense of authority and freedom which the old order gave to landowners and rich merchants. The humblest Athenian saw himself as equal to the most prominent citizens of other states, and better than most of them. This was what Pericles gave to his countrymen. It explains why they supported him and why they were not frightened when they heard that the rest of Greece hated them. For this ideal they were prepared to fight to the last and to refuse any compromise which offered security instead of honour.

7

POETRY AND POLITICS

IN most histories the fine arts are treated as an appendix to political and social events and relegated to a subsidiary place in any general pattern. They are an interesting side show, with which the main trend of affairs has little to do, and which they themselves do not illustrate to any notable degree. The reason is that, even when they attain a high level, the arts are too much the reflection of a special group and throw a very limited light on the larger prospects of the time. With the Greeks it is different. Their fine arts are an intimate part of their history, closely integrated into politics and public life. Just as the Parthenon was a dazzling advertisement for Athens, and its sculptures symbolized what she stood for, so in the parallel art of poetry current events are seen from exalted, unfamiliar angles and transformed into new shapes. Yet behind it lies the living scene, which makes it worthy of study as a historical record. Poems are both facts in themselves and a commentary on them. In Athens, if they enriched life, they were also a criticism of it, especially in its less immediate and less particular features. For the poets, underlying principles mattered more than individual occasions, but they were drawn, at no matter what distance, from current events. The poet usually transformed them into new shapes in some remote world of heroic conflict, but the first impulse and the abiding intention belonged to the present. Out of it the poetry grew, and it could not have been otherwise. Only very seldom, in the decline of Athenian greatness, was poetry an attempt to escape from reality. Normally it set out in dramatic form some issue which concerned everyone and which it might not solve or explain but saw to be pressing, and presented with all the urgency of the committed imagination.

It has been said with some truth that to the Greeks poetry was a second religion. It was of course closely connected with religion in that it was often concerned with the gods, whether in telling stories of them or in asking them to do something. The epic seems always to have given gods some part in its action, even though its attitude towards them was largely playful and by our standards lacking in solemnity. But poetry was religious in a deeper sense than this. It had its convivial moments of relaxation, but on other occasions it presented in concrete forms paradigms of human behaviour, especially in relation to the gods. These could take more than one shape. When at the beginning of the sixth century Solon codified the laws and regulated the constitution of Athens, he explained his motives and his policy in verse which was recited in public. Outside Athens choral songs had for long been the means by which certain societies became more conscious of their own unity by singing of some mythical event relevant to their experience. In Athens this had become more frequent with the Persian Wars, when hymns for triumphant occasions were composed by Simonides of Ceos, not himself an Athenian but bound by close ties to Athens and fully at home in it. For all this there was more than one reason. Verse was a more effective instrument of communication at a time when reading was rare and most literary works were either sung or recited in some more or less public place. Such recitations were cast in a special language which indicated that their matter was above that of common day. Much of this poetry was delightful in its own right, but it was usually more. It had a serious purpose; it must rise to special occasions and interpret their spirit; it raised large issues and illustrated what they might mean in the scheme of things. The Athenians could not easily do without it, and into it they put their creative taste for words. Though by the Periclean age they had developed some admirable methods for stating abstract ideas in prose, poetry probably meant more to them and offered a more satisfying means of expression for their deeper feelings.

A mythical way of thinking is common with peoples who have not reached a stage at which ideas can be expressed abstractly and with whom scientific thought is still very restricted. The Greeks moved early into abstractions and began to form scientific ideas at the beginning of the sixth century, but their supply of myths to explain almost everything in man and nature was so abundant and so attractive that they were loved for their own sake and provided almost inexhaustible topics for poetry. They were particularly valuable in giving vivid shapes to themes for which abstract words were inadequate because they could not convey all the ethical, religious and imaginative associations needed for a full presentation. The strength of Attic poetry in the fifth century was that it combined a powerful intelligence with an eager imagination. The grand figurative language is not an added attraction but an integral part of a complex whole shaped by more than the analytical intelligence. This manner of thinking is particularly obvious in Pindar, who was not an Athenian, but it is no less present in Aeschylus, who was his near contemporary in Athens. To appreciate the advantages of such mythical thinking we have only to look at the Middle Ages and the Renaissance, when stories from the Bible were treated in the visual arts to produce continually new effects and new impressions, which might lead to new interpretations of familiar subjects and were a more effective means of communication than distilled formulations of old truths. They showed what these truths might mean in a living world of particulars, what riches lay concealed in their depths, what relevance they had to an actual society. The Athenians of the Periclean age had much to think about and were ready to pay full attention to almost any serious problem. For this they found an outlet in poetry, but it was poetry of a new kind.

The poetry most representative of Athens in the fifth century is tragedy. It had grown rapidly from very humble origins, was recognized by the state as a national institution, and dealt with grave questions in the relations of men and gods. It existed before the Persian Wars, but kept its strange original formalities throughout the century, making them perform new tasks for new purposes. Just as in its formal development Attic tragedy grew out of the choral ode by making one of the singers step out of the ranks and deliver an explanatory or introductory speech, so in its social function tragedy grew out of an archaic form and gave it a new grandeur by extending its appeal from a family or a class to the whole people of Athens. A natural indentation, shaped like a horseshoe, in the flank of the Acropolis at Athens, was in due course found to provide a theatre, from which countless theatres were later to be copied.

It held a large audience and was fit for any national occasion. Just as in the visual arts the Athenians added a new dimension of grandeur to aristocratic elegance, so in extending the dramatic and narrative elements in tragedy they created a form able to do much more than merely praise the proud achievements of Athens. This it did often enough, but it went further and by its own methods questioned the larger issues of the time. It is remarkably independent of what we might think to be the more popular causes advocated by Pericles, but this does not imply any hostility to him. Pericles paid for the production of Aeschylus' *Persians*, was acquainted with Sophocles, and found for a time an ardent supporter in Euripides. He might claim for Athens:

We do not need the praises of a Homer, or of anyone else whose words may delight us for the moment but whose estimation of facts will fall short of what is really true.[1]

But this did not exclude a just appreciation of what tragedy might do. What Pericles wanted was not praise, for in his view the actions of Athens spoke for themselves, but a serious treatment of them. This came better in the grave considerations of tragedy than in the lively narrative of epic which was meant primarily to provide enjoyment.

Tragedies were performed at a festival in the spring. The production lasted from dawn to dusk, and the audience must have been well trained to absorb these works of art, especially when much of their content was couched in an elaborate, metaphorical language, which even in speeches and dialogue, let alone in songs, can never have been easy to follow. More than this, the audience had to grasp what the poet was after, what changes he made in an old story, what he meant by his version of it. The Athenian democracy was largely self-educated, but it had a good drilling in music and poetry. The performances were a part of social and civic life and fine instruments of education in that they accustomed men to language of an unusual richness and force. By this means the sensibility cultivated by the old-fashioned well-to-do spread to a much wider public. Tragedy in particular demonstrated a keen and purposeful interest in human worth and depicted the difficulty of the problems which beset mankind in dealing with the gods.

It was set in a majestic mood, and though it sought for surprise and novelty, tragedy never lost its serious care for major issues of conduct and destiny.

In principle, tragic poets did not need to relate their plays to contemporary events, and seldom did so directly. They were deeply interested in their society and its doings, but no single event could satisfy their embracing vision. They must go behind it and beyond it and discern universal forces at work. To this there is what looks like a notable exception. When in 472 Aeschylus produced his *Persians*, he broke the tradition that tragedies should draw their matter from legends of the heroic past. He had the precedent of the *Phoenician Women* of Phrynichus, which is thought to have been produced in 476 and paid for by Themistocles. Why Aeschylus, supported by Pericles, wrote after so short an interval a second play on an almost identical subject prompts a possible answer. Phrynichus, who was subsidized by Themistocles, could not for that very reason give him too great prominence, whereas Aeschylus could, and this may explain the appearance of the two plays in quick succession.

The *Persians* gave to Salamis the legendary honour which already belonged to Marathon, and provided a democratic myth to counter an aristocratic one, finding in Themistocles a hero to rival Miltiades. It was regarded by Aristophanes as primarily a patriotic play, but it was also much more. Aeschylus presented a recent historical event *sub specie aeternitatis*. He stages the Persian War from the Persians' point of view, and shows a fine generosity in handling this enemy dramatically. However much the Athenians, like other Greeks, disliked all that the Persians did to them, they retained a sense of the personal worth of their enemies. In this Aeschylus resembles Herodotus, who admired the good points of his Persian friends. The scene in the *Persians* is set in the capital at Susa, and the characters are leading Persians. There is no doubt of their vast wealth and military strength, nor of their majesty and grand style. The queen mother, Atossa, rules the stage as she was said to have ruled Persia, and the glories of the preceding generation are revived in the appearance of the ghost of Darius, who is presented as a great and wise king. Into this Persian world comes first the Messenger with the news of Salamis, then

Xerxes himself, defeated and humbled but not defiant or ran-
corous. The full extent of the Greek victory would be diminished if Aeschylus presented the Persians in a derogatory light,
whereas to show them in their grandeur gave perspective to his
theme and enabled him to emphasize his lesson: Xerxes suffers
from overweening pride, and for this the gods lead him into
war and punish him with defeat. The idea was old and familiar,
but it had enough truth to allow Aeschylus to make his theme
universally relevant. Such an idea may not have been entirely
to the taste of Pericles, whose own utterances suggest that he
was not afraid of what would happen if Athens herself went
too far. Rather he saw her as destined to greatness and capable
of finding it if she steeled herself to every effort. He was aware
that pride breeds folly, and he condemned anyone who allowed
it to rule him, but he thought that it could be controlled and
turned to proper purposes:

> We all look with distaste on people who arrogantly pretend to
> a reputation to which they are not entitled; but equally to be
> condemned are those who, through lack of moral fibre, fail to
> live up to the reputation which is theirs already.[2]

Pericles may always have believed in something like this, and
perhaps the notion that pride precedes a fall was too simple for
him. He would not think that a power like Persia could be left
to defeat itself. The *Persians* not only breathes a simpler spirit
than Pericles would share but avoids the banal vulgarities
which too often accompany a panegyric of victory. Though its
subject comes from recent history, it succeeds in attaining the
detachment proper to tragedy.

Pericles' affinity to the *Persians* is clearest in its attitude towards Athenian democracy. This is a subsidiary theme, and
just because it is not overplayed, makes a powerful impression.
When Atossa asks the Chorus about Athens, she hears first
about the abundance of silver in the mines of Laurium, and
this is a complimentary aside to Themistocles, who persuaded
the Assembly to use the silver to build a fleet. Atossa then puts
another question, entirely appropriate to her high position:

ATOSSA: Who stands over them as shepherd? Who is master of
the host?

CHORUS: Of no single master are they called the subjects or the slaves.[3]

This is the Periclean conception of Athenian democracy, in accord with his view that at Athens power is in the hands of the whole people. He would equally commend the splendid moment in the battle of Salamis when, as the Messenger tells Atossa, the Greeks go into action:

> We could plainly hear
> The thunder of their shoutings as they came.
> 'Forth, sons of Hellas! Free your land, and free
> Your children and your wives, the native seats
> Of gods your fathers worshipped and their graves,
> This is a bout that hazards all you have.'[4]

This is not far from the spirit which inspired Pericles' imperial aims. The *Persians* is not an advertisement for his ideals, of which some cannot yet have found their full form, but we can see why Pericles supported Aeschylus in reminding the Athenians of their proudest hour, and even in hinting deftly at the formation of the league when a choral song enumerates the chief islands which have been liberated. A recent event is exalted to a heroic level, without losing any of its actual characteristics.

The *Persians* is the only surviving Greek tragedy which deals with a historical event. The other plays of Aeschylus deal with a mythical past and very seldom touch on the present. But in them we can see issues which rise from the present and throw light upon it. So the *Seven against Thebes* was produced in 467 as the last of three plays dealing with the curse on the House of Laius, which comes to an end when the two brothers, Eteocles and Polynices, kill one another in battle. The average Greek would not find such an idea unfamiliar. Solon had at one time made use of it to explain the corrupt behaviour of some Athenian families, and it was still current when Aeschylus wrote, rather as in modern times faults and failures are often ascribed to heredity. But such an idea cannot be pressed very far or provide ample material for drama. In Aeschylus the curse is indeed dramatic when it begins to work, but that is only for a brief moment. The central, persistent theme of the *Seven against Thebes* is war. This was appreciated by Aristophanes, when he made the spirit of Aeschylus say to Dionysus in the underworld:

AESCH: A drama I wrote with the war-god filled.

DION: Its name?

AESCH: 'Tis the 'Seven against Thebes' that I mean, which whoso beheld, with eagerness swelled to rush to the battle there and then.[5]

Aristophanes liked the play for its martial ardour, but Aeschylus is quite as much concerned with the horror as with the glamour of war. He shows what it is to be in a beleaguered city. Any Greek city was hard to take, but if it were taken, a gruesome fate awaited its inhabitants. The chorus of frightened women gives one side of the picture, the terror and the anxiety; Eteocles gives the other. He stops their chattering with a harsh reproof, and, when his time comes, goes out magnificently to battle. This was the approved Greek attitude to war. The Greeks knew its horrors but also its thrills. Pericles understood this and justified it when he said of the fallen:

More to be desired than such things, they chose to check the enemy's pride. This, to them, was a risk most glorious, and they accepted it, willing to strike down the enemy and relinquish everything else.[6]

This trust in courage was indispensable to Pericles' view of Athens and gives strength to his ideal of it. It was quite natural that Aeschylus, who was in some sense his friend, should give imaginative expression to it. He had fought at Marathon and Salamis.

The *Suppliant Women* may have been composed within a few years of the *Seven against Thebes*. It is the first play of three, of which the last two are lost, their main point unknown to us. The action is set in a very remote past when the daughters of the Greek Danaus flee to Argos pursued by Egyptian lovers. They ask for refuge, and this provides the main theme of the play. It is dangerous for the Argives to give it, but they discuss the matter in full assembly and come to a firm conclusion that it is right. This unpromising plot would have little meaning if asylum was not a living and pertinent issue at the time. It happens that in about 470, Themistocles was in

Argos and given asylum when the Spartans and some Athenians wanted his death. We must not assume that Aeschylus has precisely this in mind, for the daughters of Danaus pursued by Egyptians are not at all like Themistocles. But there was an important matter of principle involved, one treated very seriously in Athens and regarded as inherent in the democratic way of life. Help to the oppressed is a duty of democracy and quite alien to Spartan intolerance and suspicion. What draws out the full poetry of Aeschylus is indeed the question of refuge, even though it is refuge for helpless women harried by concupiscent barbarians. The daughters of Danaus present many special points of interest which Aeschylus powerfully exploits. He sees not a specifically political issue but a human issue which concerns states and individuals alike. His attitude is perfectly clear and reflects what many Athenians thought. The provision of a haven for refugees was to become a much prized feature of Athenian democracy, and here by depicting a case in the distant past Aeschylus underlines the nobility and humanity of such behaviour. In this he anticipates what Pericles was later to claim as typical of Athens' attitude to other cities in need of help:

When we do kindnesses to others, we do not do them out of any calculations of profit or loss: we do them without afterthought, relying on our free liberality.[7]

Aeschylus shows what the abstract ideal means when translated into the solid imagery of myth. Exalting the present by relating it to the past, he makes the past more real by showing that it was beset by problems which still beset the present.

In these plays Aeschylus speaks for democratic Athens as Clisthenes shaped it. He shares its values and probes their consequences. But when he composed the three plays of his *Oresteia* in 458 he was fully aware of the reforms imposed by Ephialtes and Pericles on the Court of the Areopagus. He begins by powerfully dramatizing a society in which bloodshed calls for bloodshed, and a feud continues apparently forever. The execution of justice lies with the family and with the primeval Furies who work for it. In place of this system, Apollo and Athene, divinities of light and wisdom, impose a new system, by which trial for murder is confined to the Areopagus. On the surface this means that the reforms meet with Aeschylus' approval and that he welcomes a reduction of the Court's old powers that it may perform new and more important duties. But behind this lies his belief that order depends on law, and that law comes from the gods. In a stately speech Athene proclaims the value of the reformed Court:

> I establish
> This great tribunal to protect my people,
> Brave, quick to anger, incorruptible,
> But ever vigilant over those that sleep.[8]

This is much to attribute to a Court for murder, but Aeschylus has in mind the dangerous situation existing after the reforms, when it looked as if Athens might be rent by civil strife in which bloodshed and murder played a large part. Against this, Athene claims, the new Court is a source of unity and order. She tells the Furies, who are being transformed into pillars of society, that the temper which is wasted in civil war can be used in defence of the country:

> Implant not in my sons the bravery
> Of fighting-cocks, embroiled against their own.
> Abroad let battle rage for every heart
> Possessed by love of glory – that shall be theirs
> In plenty.[9]

This catches the tone of these years in which Pericles, after defying and defeating the Athenian nobles with his reforms, turned the national energies into a new war with the Peloponnesians.

More mysterious is the *Prometheus Bound*. Though the play itself is complete, we lack the two other plays which made up the trilogy and must have developed the theme of power which lies at its centre. Nor do we know when it was written, though it looks like a late work of Aeschylus, who died in 456. It is not concerned with contemporary issues in any direct and obvious way; it contains no recognizable references to passing events. Yet it is largely concerned with power. Zeus, the young god, has recently made himself king of the gods by dethroning his father Cronus. In this, Prometheus, a Titan and therefore not an Olympian god but a divine being of an older generation, has supported Zeus. But Zeus is angry with Prometheus who has helped man in his primitive, helpless wretchedness by bringing the gift of fire from heaven. For this Zeus inflicts on him a savage penalty. He is nailed to a rock in the Caucasus, and every day a vulture eats his liver. Our sympathies are entirely with Prometheus, the friend of man, and not with Zeus, the cruel son and ungrateful friend. Yet, if anything is certain in the matter, it is that the play is not an attack on Zeus, and we must try to find out what it meant for the poet and his audience. The loss of the next two plays makes this extremely hazardous, but in the surviving play there are hints of how the conflict was resolved.

Prometheus is able to endure this punishment because he knows a secret hidden from Zeus: that if Zeus marries the sea maiden Thetis, with whom he is deeply in love, he will beget a son stronger than himself who will overthrow him. In the end Prometheus is able to trade this secret for his own liberation, and this was the theme of the next play *Prometheus Unbound*. It is easy to read into the myth ideas which are not there. There is no reason to think that after thousands of years Zeus has grown wiser and less ruthless in the use of power; that would be against his character, for after all he is as near to omnipotence as any Greek god can be. Nor is he moved by compassion for Prometheus. Greek gods are unforgiving in their hates, and Prometheus has insulted Zeus by helping the despised race of men. The new deal with Zeus is a real deal, on business terms. It is enormously important for Zeus to know the secret; for when he learns it, he averts his doom by getting Thetis to marry a mortal husband and give birth to the paramount hero, Achilles. Aeschylus propounds a practical solution for a dark problem. The myth, as he tells it, need not preach any obscure parable but it makes a point relevant to the age in which he lived. Not only is the pursuit of power the strongest impetus to action and the most ruthless but it can be defeated only by other power. What Prometheus knows is enough to frighten Zeus and force him to an agreement. This is a fair analysis of power, and Aeschylus' method is as vivid as a vivid myth can make it. It has some relevance to Athenian might. Athens won imperial domination by using her power to force cities into a subservient form of alliance, and her former friends the Spartans might complain that by doing so she had betrayed them. But once she had attained power, there was always a danger that she might lose it, especially from some undetected or unforeseen source. The right procedure was to keep watch for this and take the best means to forestall it. We need not assume that Aeschylus thought in so particular a way as this, but the imaginative success of *Prometheus Bound* lies in its demonstration of the price power exacts for its maintenance. As human beings we cannot but sympathize with Prometheus and deplore the tyrannical behaviour of Zeus, but that should not blind us to the true nature of power, which cannot be judged by considerations of right and wrong or like and dislike. Power operates on a level beyond such discriminations and must be accepted for what it is. Aeschylus displays its nature without illusion or consolation.

It is dangerous to generalize about the way in which Aeschylus built his trilogies, for the *Oresteia* is our only complete example of them. In it a story of recurrent bloodshed and vengeance comes to a happy end. Orestes, who seems to be the victim of a merciless doom, is liberated, and the whole sequence of blood for blood ends with the promise of prosperity under the gods under the new rule of law. Here Aeschylus turns tragic misery into positive happiness. It is possible that the third, lost play in the trilogy of which the *Suppliant Women* is the first also came to a happy end, in which extensive carnage somehow led to new honours for the goddess of love. If the trilogy on Prometheus was actually completed, it may have ended in some sort of pact, perhaps with the establishment of a feast for Prometheus in Athens. On the other hand the *Seven against Thebes* ends in the mutual slaughter of Eteocles and Polynices and the fulfilment of a hereditary curse in the third generation. This is by our standards a tragic finale. Eteocles and Polynices both deserve their deaths, but Eteocles goes to his in so heroic a spirit that we cannot but feel admiration and pity, if not fear, for him. Yet to the Greeks death in battle for one's country was a desirable end, and Aeschylus may have meant us to see it in that light. In that case Aeschylus does not, so far as we know, in his endings evoke a sense of irretrievable waste. In his dark events he finds something consoling, and this seems to be characteristic of the years when he was at the height of his powers, from 472 to his death in 456. This was the period when Athens was led, first by Cimon, then by his opponents, and if later Aeschylus approved of the reform of the old Areopagus, in the first part he seems to have thought that even the most brutal actions and the heaviest sacrifices might end in consoling conclusions. This was the spirit in which Athens expended her efforts and her manhood. The sacrifices were made gladly for the benefits which they brought, and though this is clear from epitaphs on the fallen in battle, it is also what Pericles has in mind at a later date when he speaks on a similar topic:

> They gave her their lives, to her and to all of us, and for their own selves they won praises that never grow old, the most splendid of sepulchres—not the sepulchres in which their bodies are laid, but where their glory remains eternal in men's minds, always there on the right occasion to stir others to speech or to action.[10]

Here the theme is that sacrifice and sufferings bring glory and inspire future generations. Something of the kind seems to run through Aeschylus' trilogies when things move from darkness to light, from defeat to victory.

Though most of Aeschylus' plays deal with large, timeless issues, and though even the *Persians* raises what might be a narrowly patriotic theme to a universal grandeur, yet his work is related to his contemporary world and relevant to it. The themes of national pride or failure, of the rule of law, of the nature of power, of the defence of the weak, of death in battle, are natural themes for the second quarter of the fifth century, and it is not surprising that with democracy they took new shapes without losing their essential characteristics. Aeschylus presents them not only through dramatic action but also through choral songs which debate them from several angles and a rich profusion of metaphors that point out what they mean to different points of view. His own is clear enough, though he makes it not analytically but poetically and is more concerned with its general character than its details. Such a method would catch a wider audience than any philosophical disquisition, and Aeschylus had a large influence even on the generation of Aristophanes in the last quarter of the century. Aeschylus is a poet of Athens because he deals at a lofty level with matters that concern it. For him most problems are civic problems, and he is less interested in the personal conflicts of a tragic hero than in his social significance. Even Orestes, pursued by the Furies for killing his mother, is in the end saved by divine intervention in a human law court. Aeschylus' approach to public affairs on this grand scale is a comment on the success with which Athens combined vigorous action with no less vigorous thought. The democracy founded by Clisthenes and now in the process of being remodelled by Ephialtes and Pericles raised many issues. In these Aeschylus found the stuff of his dramas, and thereby enabled his age to think about itself in a way that suited it. By such means Athens cleared her mind and understood what she was doing.

The later plays of Aeschylus belong to the first years of the political emergence of Pericles and share with him an outlook which was both serious and confident. Aeschylus' acknowledged successor, Sophocles, spoke for his country in a different way. His long life (495–406) covered the heyday of Athens. As a boy he took part in the ceremonial dance in honour of the victory over Persia, and he died in extreme old age just before the fall of Athens. Though he began by imitating Aeschylus, he soon found his own manner and bears independent testimony to his time. He works on a much smaller scale, in single plays instead of in trilogies, and does not attempt to solve cosmic problems by generous solutions. But he is aware of them and dramatizes them from different points of view, and though he seldom delivers an explicit judgement on his events, he leads us to make our own. Though Sophocles knew Pericles, he kept his independence of him and looked at common issues with different eyes. While Pericles sees everything from the point of view of Athens and Athenian greatness, Sophocles builds his dramas against a background of divine power, which is vastly more important than human power and acts in dark and menacing ways. In him the poetical vision is separate from any political vision, however exalted, and finds expression in myths which cannot be accepted literally in a modern world but have for that reason all the richer range of suggestion.

We might even think that, in his attitude to the supernatural, Sophocles is less open-minded than Aeschylus. Rather than spoil the unity of his mythical world, he sacrifices realism to it, and sometimes takes a subject fit for scientific inquiry and treats it from a mythical angle. Thus in *King Oedipus* he starts the action with a plague which devastates Thebes, but is no plague known to medicine then or now. It kills the living, destroys the fruits of the earth, and brings miscarriages and premature births. This is all as it should be, for the plague is sent to Thebes by the gods as a punishment for harbouring Oedipus, who has unwittingly killed his father and married his mother. He is defiled and abominable, and while he is tolerated Thebes will suffer. It has been thought that Sophocles got the idea of the plague as a dramatic theme from the actual plague which devastated Athens in 430 and 427. We know all about it from the unsparing, clinical description by Thucydides. He enumerates the symptoms, and though opinions differ on what it really was, that is not his fault, but the fault of nature which changes diseases in the course of centuries. For Thucydides it is a hideous calamity, but there is nothing supernatural in it. It was quite unfamiliar to the physicians of the time, and that is why he describes it so carefully. He suggests that it came from Ethiopia by way of Egypt, and he sketches its destructive and demoralizing effect on Athens. Between Thucydides and Sophocles there is an enormous gulf, all the distance between a world where science is ready with explanations and another where the gods are always at hand to take responsibility. Yet this does not necessarily mean that Sophocles and Pericles were far apart, even if we accept, as we probably should, the assumption that Pericles viewed the plague as scientifically as Thucydides. The plague which attacks Thebes belongs to an ancient story and is the more credible because it is unlike known epidemics. It serves a special purpose for the gods. But the plague of Athens is a historical event, without a known cause and without any beneficent results. No doubt Sophocles felt its horror as Thucydides did, but could hardly put its nauseating reality into a play. This was natural enough, but it shows that with Sophocles a gap had begun to open between myth and fact. They were not perfectly adapted to complement each other as Aeschylus had tried to make them, but now the world of the gods, as known to myth, began to show its idiosyncrasies. Sophocles did not, like Pindar, reject scientific knowledge, and was certainly interested in disease, but his special world was one in which such knowledge could only be incidental and not in the last resort of much importance. For Pericles, the friend of scientists, a balance between natural and divine causes was possible, and each had its place, but for Sophocles what mattered was the part played by the gods.

Unlike Aeschylus, Sophocles makes very few attempts to justify the gods, but they are always at work in his plays, usually behind the scene, and we draw conclusions about them from the dramatic action. In an age when old beliefs were subjected to sharp scrutiny and when science was beginning to find naturalistic explanations for phenomena, Sophocles made man's relation with the gods the central point in his tragedies. To show the interaction of divine and human purposes he used the old religious machinery by which men were supposed to be able to learn the gods' intentions. It is difficult for us to understand how the sharpsighted Athenians of the fifth century still believed that the will of the gods could be revealed in oracles, and that oracles must be treated with the greatest respect and care. That they were however is clear from Herodotus, who likes to tell how oracles are always fulfilled, often in a sense unforeseen by anyone or contrary to what they seem to say. Thucydides, who comes from the next generation and was perhaps not typical even of that, does not share this belief but says drily of an oracle which predicted that the Peloponnesian War would last for twenty-seven years that it is the only one of which people who believe in oracles can say that it was certainly fulfilled. This was not the view of Sophocles, and on this point we cannot excuse him on the ground that he simply responds to the call of his dramatic material. Four of his seven surviving plays are concerned with the fulfilment of oracles, and with each he is at some pains to stress its importance in the scheme of things. In *King Oedipus* the action turns on the discovery by Oedipus that he has in fact done everything that the god foretold by killing his father and marrying his mother. He tries to escape from this, but fails totally and yields to his doom by blinding himself. For a moment he may think that such oracles are lies, and this is what his mother-wife Jocasta says, but very soon she learns that it is wrong, and kills herself.

In the *Women of Trachis* Heracles, having accomplished his last labour, meets with a hideous death from a poisoned shirt which, unwittingly, his wife Deianira gives him in the hope of winning him back from another woman. By this means an oracle is fulfilled which told Heracles that he would at last find rest. So he does, but it is the rest of death after appalling suffering. Oracles of such malignant ambiguity were commonly recorded. Herodotus often likes to show how ingeniously the god has cheated his inquirers. It gives a nasty notion of the god, but such deceptions no doubt took place, and saved the god's professional honour at the expense of his decency. The old notion was that every word of an oracle must be treated with respect. If it were not, the recipient would suffer, but not even the greatest care could save him from the disagreeable tricks which the god was liable to play.

The oracle of the *Women of Trachis* is not dramatically of much importance. Its aim is to stress the doom which awaits Heracles on his return home. It is interesting because it has parallels in contemporary life and reflects a belief which was more commonly held than we might expect. This ironical fulfilment has a curious parallel in an important public event which happened a few years before the play. In 447 a small Athenian force under Tolmides was defeated at Coronea in Boeotia. On the memorial in Athens to those who fell in the battle were inscribed eight lines of verse, which must be translated as literally as possible, since the precise sense is of first importance:

Enduring ones, how you lasted to the end in your struggle in the hopeless fight, and lost your lives by divine power in war—not by the strength of men who opposed you, but one of the half-gods came into the Goddess's Road against you and wrought your undoing. The oracle which he gave with seeming good will, of a prey hard for foeman to hunt, that oracle he himself fulfilled to your ruin by his pursuit. For all men of the future he made the fulfilment of oracles to be trusted and reckoned upon.[11]

This presents three main features of interest. First, it is clear that, whoever the half-god was, he gave an oracle which encouraged the Athenians but was in fact ambiguous and foretold their defeat. It may have been something like: 'For enemy hunters there shall be a prey hard to pursue.' The Athenians assumed that they would pursue the Boeotians; in fact the

Boeotians pursued them. This is an ambiguous oracle of the same kind as that in the *Women of Trachis*. Secondly, the half-god, who may have been Orion, is thought to have taken part on the Boeotian side. In this there is nothing very strange, since tales of the Persian Wars abounded in phantasmal heroes who fought for the Greeks. Thirdly, the poem draws a moral and presses it home with some emphasis: henceforward all oracles must be trusted. It is a large moral to draw from a single instance, nor is there any evidence that Tolmides did not trust his oracle, though he interpreted it wrongly. But Sophocles does much the same thing in *King Oedipus* when the Chorus proclaims that if the oracles about Oedipus are proved false, religion is undermined:

> For now men set at nought
> Apollo's word, and cry 'Behold, it fails!'
> His praise is darkened with a doubt;
> And faith is sapped, and Heaven defied.[12]

That sentiments of this kind should be inscribed on a public memorial is perhaps no stranger than that the events which inspired them should be given a supernatural explanation, but it is evident that in his religious opinions Sophocles had influential persons on his side. Since the memorial was set up in the prime of Pericles, he must at least have acquiesced in it. For Sophocles it was an admission that human actions are at the mercy of the unpredictable purposes of the gods and though a warning may come of them, it may not be understood.

Another point in which Sophocles and Pericles may be compared is in their treatment of the unwritten laws. Pericles leaves his notion of these vague and seems to suggest that they are concerned with various matters outside the reach of ordinary laws. At least he claims that the Athenians respect them. For Sophocles they have a more instant and more definite meaning. The *Antigone* is based on them. Polynices has been killed fighting against his own city of Thebes, and the new ruler of Thebes, Creon, issues an edict that he must not be buried and that anyone who attempts to do so will be put to death. The prohibition is based on Athenian practice, as when Themistocles, a declared traitor, was forbidden burial in his own country. Creon puts his case speciously and advances the familiar arguments about the city being the source and safe-guard of a man's being and worthy of his total devotion. He means what he says, but Antigone, sister of the dead man, defies the edict and conducts burial rites over the body. She is caught and brought to Creon, to whom she defends herself on the ground that she obeys the laws of the gods against the ruler's man-made ephemeral edict:

> Nor did I think your edicts were so strong
> That any mortal man should override
> The god's unwritten and undying laws.
> Their life is not today and yesterday
> But always, and none knows from where they came.
> I would not pay the price before the gods
> Of breaking these for fear of any man.[13]

The issue is raised to the loftiest possible level and has a special point because Antigone accuses Creon of breaking the unwritten laws which Pericles, in his funeral speech, claims that the Athenians respect. So Creon, who makes a good impression at the start by claiming to defend law and order, is shown to be deluded by vanity, while Antigone, who begins by defying authority, has a heroic magnificence. Though Sophocles keeps us guessing as he shifts the emphasis on his characters, he means Antigone to be right and Creon wrong. Though Antigone dies for her action, Creon is shattered by a succession of blows from the gods. We may assume that the unwritten laws did not mean the same to Antigone as to Pericles. Sophocles insists that the claims of the state are not final and suggests that the laws of men do not always follow the laws of the gods. In an age when Athens was almost taking the place of her gods as an object of worship, the poet protested that the priorities were wrong and that if there is a conflict between divine and human law, there is no doubt which claims first obedience. Such a demonstration in a notable masterpiece shows that at the height of the Periclean age a need was felt for some superior authority above the holders of power. Pericles may not have felt this so deeply as Sophocles, and to that degree Sophocles gives range and depth to the Periclean view of the state. It was not after all the last arbiter.

It may be no more than an accident that of the seven surviving plays of Sophocles, four, which seem to be relatively early, are fully and painfully tragic in our sense of the word, while the other three, which were undoubtedly written in the last years of his life, come through much struggle and agony to more or less happy endings. In this the Greeks would see nothing unusual, for a tragedy need not end unhappily provided it deals with serious matters in a serious spirit. In the heyday of Periclean Athens Sophocles seems to have chosen dark issues and drawn their full tragic implications. His actual situations spare no horror and are of a cruelty which calls for the finest endurance and courage in his heroes and heroines. These are greatest in their hour of doom, and though this greatness may not always be to our liking, it is formidable and impressive. When Ajax recovers his sanity and sees that he has lost his honour, he kills himself on his sword – a very unusual action, since most Greeks shrank from self-slaughter. Antigone goes bravely to be buried alive, though her human feelings break through her hitherto unbroken display of courage. Heracles, tortured by the poisoned robe, is still master, still in control of the situation, as he gives his last commands to his son. Oedipus assumes the lead in finding out who pollutes Thebes, and when he finds that it is himself, he takes the initiative in his own punishment by blinding himself. None of these is a case of mere passive suffering; each shows how the heroic temperament fulfils itself in disaster. It may be remote or even inhuman, as it is with Ajax and Heracles, even with Antigone, who rejects with scorn the prudent counsels of her sister, or with Oedipus, who is quick to see treachery and corruption where they do not exist. But this makes these characters grander than ordinary people. This is in full accord with the Periclean ideal. Just as Athens was nobler and more formidable than other cities, so the characters of tragedy, who carry heavier burdens than others, are at a little distance from common humanity. Just as their sufferings are greater than most men's, so their endurance of them reveals a special control and self-reliance.

The grand moment of Sophoclean tragedy in this period is when the hero, faced by a brutal destiny, encounters it with all his courage. He has no escape, no reward, no consolation. The tragic catastrophe is sufficient in itself, part of the scheme of things, never fully explicable. The Athenians were trained to face death without flinching and to redeem disaster by resisting it to the last. On the stage they saw examples of both. There was no need for solace, for it could never be adequate and would even detract from the fierce magnificence of these tragic dooms. Aeschylus seems to have offered explanations in his finales and so saved them from being wholly tragic and given them a place in an orderly plan of the world, but Sophocles so builds up a catastrophe that in death his heroes stand in their own proud dignity against a hostile universe. The gods may have reasons for inflicting such sufferings, and sometimes Sophocles gives a hint of what these might be, but men do not know, and act according to their own human lights. The heroes and heroines of Sophocles are the ideal, imaginary counterparts of the ordinary Athenians who were expected to find their finest hour in fighting and dying for their country. The plays are in their remote splendour a commentary on every day.

The third dramatist in the great Athenian succession, Euripides (480–406), grew to maturity under the supremacy of Pericles and lived on to die in the same year as Sophocles. Yet he seems to belong to a different world, and provides yet another indication of how many varieties of human talent and taste Periclean Athens could sustain. Euripides lacks the consistency of Sophocles, and his uncertainty goes very deep. We are never quite sure that we have found his centre. Yet he too is a child of his age, especially of those years when the Peloponnesian War prompted Athenians to ask sharper questions and to follow unexploited clues. The elements were less happily mixed in him than in Sophocles, and we sometimes feel that he has not fully digested his impressions or finally made up his mind on matters which he handles. He enjoyed new ideas and was sometimes content to play with them rather than to test their truth. His contemporaries thought him an eccentric, but there is no doubt that he spoke for many of them, and that is why they were fascinated by him. In some degree he was quick to grasp and to shape into dramatic form tendencies which were at work before the death of Pericles and continued to grow until the end of the war. Assumptions, hitherto accepted without bother, were doubted; the old belief in the gods turned into nagging questions about them; types of humanity which had been despised or neglected became centres of interest; the scheme of things seemed less important than its multifarious parts, but many of these excited notice and called for scrutiny. An apparently solid structure of sentiments and assumptions was beginning to show fissures, and tragedy, which now sought to grasp the immediate world, became less detached and less imaginative, but more searching and more given to sensation and surprise. Euripides is a less accomplished, less singleminded artist then Sophocles, but in some respects he is more exciting, and though he does not express a single, consistent point of view, he reflects many current speculations and tells more than Sophocles about the shifting lights of the Periclean age and the bleaker years which followed it.

The special light which Euripides throws on his own times is to be found largely in incidental small points, especially in passing remarks made by his characters and not always necessary to the plot. They bring the ancient situations up to date, and this was what fascinated the Athenians. Euripides suggested that these doomed characters of a distant past could be relevant to more modern issues. He makes the heroic age more urgent and more immediate and is not shy of inserting novelties into it. For instance, in various places he echoes some views of Anaxagoras – that the sun is a 'golden clod', that the air is a divinity, that the waters of the Nile come from melted snow, that heaven and earth were once a single unity, that nothing dies that is born, though it may take a different shape, that the study of the ageless order of nature is the highest happiness. He followed the theological modernism of Prodicus in explaining that Demeter and Dionysus are gods because bread and wine give life. He exploited the distinction between 'nature' and 'custom', which was popular in the second half of the fifth century and made havoc of many beliefs. We cannot tell how firmly or how deeply he held these ideas, but he was aware of them and saw enough in them to put them on the lips of his characters. He was moreover deeply influenced by the art of disputation which flourished in his time and was based on the assumption that argument could in the end find the truth and equally that to every argument there is a counter-argument. When his characters in moments of high passion relapse into what seem to us hollow sophistries, it is because these tricks were then new and still kept the glitter of which the years were soon to rob them. For a time some Athenians must have spoken like this. There are traces of it in their early forensic oratory, in which arguments from probability take precedence over the establishment of facts. The respect for argument, which in Socrates amounted to a life-long passion, touched Euripides and accounts for a prominent feature of his dramatic manner. No doubt it echoes something in his nature, but it is also characteristic of his time and is notably absent from Sophocles.

Euripides' lively taste for intellectual novelties makes him a significant figure in the transition from the old way of thinking in myths and symbols to the new way of thinking in abstract concepts. As soon as science and philosophy began to develop, the change was inevitable, and it was fortunate that the Greek language was able easily to form abstract nouns. The change meant that instead of summoning a wide range of imaginative associations by a pictorial image or a mythical tale, the essential facts were stated abstractly in a way that gave greater clarity but also imposed greater limitations. Euripides was still able to set the mind working through mythical imagery and to tell an old story again through its main dramatic points, but he tended to rationalize his stories in the sense that he tried to give a more precise meaning to them. To some extent Aeschylus did the same, but not always successfully, since his myths carried too great a meaning for him to penetrate to some central, abstract theme. Euripides felt the appeal of myths very strongly but it was an artistic and aesthetic appeal, and he tried to get behind it to something plain and rational. This accounts for the harshness and apparent brutality of some of his effects. The exploitation of myth, which reached its zenith in the pediments of the Parthenon, was yielding to a different system of observing and interpreting life. The intention of Euripides' plays is not always obvious, but that is because the mythical and realistic elements are not completely adjusted to one another and there is a conflict of temper and effect between them. The gap between them was to grow wider in common thought, and in the fourth century Plato, who liked myths, could use them only for emotional and religious purposes in the huge development of his arguments. Supremacy passed from image to argument, and in this process Euripides played a part. When he makes his characters rationalize their motives, he diminishes their mystery and appeals to something quite different. For a period the new intellectual movements had given strength to the old outlook, then come into conflict with it, and finally done much to destroy it. Euripides illustrated these stages, and in so doing speaks for his age.

This speculative, experimental outlook did not prevent Euripides from falling under the spell of Pericles and his ideal of Athens. We have seen how a chorus in the *Medea* sings of the spiritual and intellectual glory of Athens, as was indeed appropriate at a time when the Parthenon had just been finished. When war came, Euripides was much concerned with it and dramatized some of its salient issues. In 430, when Pericles was still alive, Euripides produced his *Sons of Heracles*. In a heroic setting it presents an essential Athens such as Pericles believed in. Its theme is the protection given by Athens to the sons of Heracles after their father's death. They are pursued by enemies from Argos, and Athens alone offers them protection, though she knows that it may mean war. The Argive herald tries to kidnap the children, but is rebuked by the king of Athens, who states the Athenian case. He wishes for peace with all other cities, but he will not offend the gods or betray the innocent. His city is free and takes no orders from outside, and so far from the children not being its business, its business is always to succour the oppressed. This is the Periclean doctrine, to which Euripides gives a new edge by making Athens assume responsibility for the oppressed, whatever their origin. To Spartans, whom he noticeably dislikes, this was typical of the interfering activities of Athens, but to Euripides it is right and noble, a way in which Athens increases her opportunities for doing good. Moreover, his Athens is true to Hellas and all that Hellas stands for, for the rule of law and of right, for democracy and constitutional government. The *Sons of Heracles* is a tract for the times in the sense that it presents an Athenian outlook in a dramatic form and makes use of current beliefs by setting them against their rivals and alternatives. When Euripides wrote, the war was still young, and we can detect the ideals for which Athenians believed themselves to be fighting.

This happy mood could not and did not last. Euripides changed his attitude and may have reflected a like change in the public as well as a sharpening of his own insight into the real character of war. About 424 Pericles had been dead for five years, and the most powerful influence in public affairs was wielded by the able, reckless, and brutal Cleon. No immediate end of the war was in sight, and neither side had a preponderant advantage. Euripides wrote the *Suppliant Women*. Its spirit is quite different from that of the *Sons of Heracles*; it contains very little action and much discussion, as if Euripides wanted to clear his mind on some fundamental issues and did so by a series of debates. He is again concerned with the treatment of suppliants, this time Argive mothers, whose sons have been killed and left unburied by the Thebans. This raises the point of expediency against principle. Theseus, who represents Athens, at first refuses to give help, on grounds of prudence, but his mother begs him to take action :

> You see your country, helpless and reviled,
> Lift up its glittering eye against all those
> Revilers. In its sorrow it finds strength.
> Cities, which work in twilight secretly,
> Have twilight looks, for all their careful plans.
> These dead men and these weeping women need
> Your help, my son. Will you not give it them?[14]

The contrast is between those cities who are afraid to adopt bold policies in the full light of day and Athens who is proud to do so. Athens is again portrayed as an ideal city. Though it has Theseus for king, he protests that it is a democracy. Athens is the champion of divine laws and the exponent of free speech. There is even a touch of religious enlightenment. When the dead bodies are brought in, they might be thought to be polluted and polluting, but the criticism is brushed aside, and we hear that no man should be repelled by the sufferings of another. Euripides is still faithful to his Periclean view of Athens, but he now knows more about war and its horrors. The play conveys nothing of its lure and much of its bestiality. But against this he sets an Athens which is still the champion of chivalry and honour. Euripides is in love with his city and as yet nothing has shaken his devotion. The eccentric misanthrope, as the comedians presented him, has this profound attachment which he shares with many of his countrymen. He clings to convictions which he held with Pericles and probably learned from him.

So long as Pericles was alive, Euripides knew what to think about the war, and he may have remained faithful until the peace of Nicias in 421 ended its first phase and gave a breathing space before new phases of violence began. The misfortune of Euripides was that, like Thucydides, he was so faithful to Pericles and his ideals that any policy which departed from them could only be a blow. The successors of Pericles were unable to pursue his policies at the same level, and lacked his moral authority. Euripides soon saw how war breeds brutality, but he may still have believed that good might come of it. The time came when he no longer believed even this, and no longer believed in Athens. Her prolonged agony touched him deeply, but she no longer inspired him by her way of life. In this he presents a marked contrast with Sophocles, whose life continued almost as long as his, but who never lost faith in Athens. Sophocles may indeed have marked some of the more disastrous wounds of war, notably in the corruption of public standards and the growth of vengeful passions, but tried to see beyond them, and at the very end saw Athens protected by indwelling divinities. Sophocles is more interested than Aeschylus in personal issues and interior conflicts, and his public concern is much less embracing. But it exists in the assurance of his opinions, and especially in his belief that there is a law above the state to which the state must conform. Pericles might wish to believe this, but he clearly had doubts and thought the state the best embodiment of law and order. He and Sophocles did not see eye to eye on all matters, but Sophocles' criticism of life was that of a man who sought to find in human order an image of divine order; when the one was broken so was the other.

Euripides' view of things was less bracing than that of either Sophocles or Pericles. It was also less consistent and less constant. He often changed his mind, and though he was moved by certain loyalties, such as to Athens, he did not base them on solid grounds. In him we see both the excitement of the Athenian heyday and the disillusioned reaction of its decline. In his changing moods and enthusiasms, his unremitting search for new solutions, we can see how the fifth century was touched by new movements, and how hard it was to adhere permanently to any single line. Pericles sought to give Athens a well-rounded character, and for a time succeeded in doing so. When this began to fail, it was not clear what character Athens should have, and among the least certain was Euripides. He presents the antithesis of the Periclean confidence. He could not find his own solution, and though for a time he accepted that of Pericles, he lost his trust in this also.

Greek tragedy had a longer life than Pericles and overlapped him at both ends. We know too little of its first plays to speak with any confidence about them, but what survives of Aeschylus comes from his mature years, and suggests a vaulting assurance and a bold sweep suited to the first years of Pericles. At the other end of the century the later plays of Sophocles and Euripides show how powerful the creative spirit still was but betray a growing bitterness. In the plays of the actual Periclean age there is a strong sense of human grandeur, of endurance and nobility in the harshest circumstances. The heroes and heroines are determined to be themselves and to shape their own destinies. Tragedy shows the individual and his claims honoured in the loftiest terms. This did not mean that the tragedians disregarded the claims of the state, but though they varied in their treatment of it, they recognized it as a setting which enables·the individual to flourish. If he comes into conflict with it, he gains in heroic stature, and that is what matters. Tragedy stressed the dangers to the individual from many quarters, and the state was one of them.

Tragedy provided a counterpoise to some of the stronger tendencies of the age. It displayed on an unexpected scale the courage of women and the worth of slaves. It showed little interest in the class squabbles which raged even in Athens and rent other cities to shreds. By placing its subjects in a heroic past it discredited many disguises and poses, which lost their meaning when exposed. On the other hand the ancient stories dramatized by the tragedians abated none of the horrifying elements which were theirs from the beginning. The tragedians deal with all manner of horror and violence, ranging from the murder of husbands and mothers and children at the one end to incest, madness, and burial alive at the other. Compared with this rich repertory the endless killings in the Homeric epics are simple and almost healthy. The tragedians did not attempt to dilute the horror of the tales which they inherited from a bloodthirsty past, and clung tenaciously to the more lurid among them. It is no accident that all three tragedians dramatize the vengeance taken by Orestes on his mother Clytaemnestra for killing his father. The tragedians accepted the view that life is always hard and often cruel, and they concentrated this into powerful examples drawn from legend. Through their education in such stories the Athenians were habituated to the notion of suffering, and this strengthened their toughness in action and their uncomplaining acceptance of disaster and death. Attic tragedy is an authentic creation of the Attic temper, and guides us to the centre of the Periclean age.

8

THE ATHENIAN OPPOSITION

In his later years Pericles, as Thucydides says, led the people, but in his earlier years he was faced by a formidable opposition, and even at the height of his power he did not lack virulent and unscrupulous critics. When he first emerged, to support Ephialtes in reforming the constitution, the opposition was fierce enough to murder Ephialtes, and Pericles must have been equally hated, not merely because he espoused a revolutionary cause but because he himself belonged to a social class which regarded such behaviour as rank treachery. At this period Cimon was a powerful figure in Athenian politics, and until he was ostracized in 461, Pericles had yet to establish himself. The immediate consequence of Cimon's fall was war with the Peloponnesians, and during it, opposition, though partly muted, was still at work. This is clear from what happened when Sparta moved into Boeotia and defeated Athens at Tanagra in 456. Athens at the time was building the Long Walls from the city to the Piraeus, and their purpose was to make the transport of food from the sea to the capital absolutely safe, while incidentally it heartened the seafaring folk on whom the democrats depended for many of their votes. It is therefore not surprising that the Spartans were privily aided in their movements by Athenians of the extreme aristocratic party which preferred Sparta to their own populace. They may even have forced a crisis at this dangerous time, but it is important to note that the dissentients can only have been a minority even in their own political world. For before the battle Cimon, who was still ostracized, appeared with a party of followers and asked to be allowed to fight on the Athenian side. The Athenian generals referred the matter to the Council at home, who forbade it, and Cimon took no part in the battle. His action shows how in a time of danger even solid conservatives would rally to their country's need. Cimon's offer furthered the annulment of his ostracism soon afterwards. Actions like this explain why during the war we find hardly anything that suggests a marked division into parties on political lines. This had existed in the preceding peace, and was to come again after the peace of 445.

The death of Cimon in 449 left the leadership of the conservatives vacant. For the moment this might not matter, but the peace of 445 gave new chances and new prospects to party politics. A leader was ready, and proved to be Pericles' most formidable opponent. Thucydides, son of Melesias, was for a time almost a match for him, and on their struggle much of the politics of the years of peace turned. Thucydides was born about 500 and was thus a few years younger than Cimon and a few years older than Pericles. He came from an aristocratic family, married Cimon's sister, and was possibly the grandfather of his namesake the great historian. In the next century Aristotle names him as a leader of the upper classes and adds of him and his like that 'practically everyone is agreed that they were not only fine gentlemen but also statesmen who treated the whole city as a nobleman treats his inheritance'.[1] His period of power and activity falls unfortunately in a period in the middle of the fifth century on which our information is lamentably scanty. Though he is not mentioned by his namesake, there is no doubt of his importance. He was an aristocrat of the old school, and it is agreeably characteristic of his class that his family was well known for its prowess in wrestling. His father, Melesias, was a famous trainer, and that this was socially acceptable is clear from his close association with noble families of Aegina in the sixties. This association, well known to Pindar, illustrates how international some Greek aristocrats were. In war between Athens and Aegina each party fought for its own side, but in peace they entertained one another and shared the same tastes. In view of his father's athletic reputation it is not surprising that the imagery of wrestling is more than once applied to Thucydides, especially with reference to his long struggle with Pericles, with whom he was said to be 'at close grips',[2] and of whose adroitness in debate similar metaphors were used. Thucydides was a characteristic member of the old aristocratic society and in this lay his strength; he disliked equally the growth of democracy in Athens and its imposition on the cities of the empire.

The opposition of Thucydides to Pericles was based on a total dissimilarity of temperament and outlook. Almost anything that Pericles did in peacetime was likely to horrify his opponents, if only because they disliked and feared him. With the declaration of peace Athens continued to exact tribute from the allies. She herself decided how it was to be spent, and a first call was the accumulation of unspent balances against future wars. This was conscientiously pursued and in due course proved of utmost value. With the surplus, which was considerable, Pericles, in a striking change of tactics, embarked on a resplendent building programme on the Acropolis at Athens and constructed the Parthenon, the Propylaea, which was the ceremonial entry to the Acropolis, and the Odeon or Hall of Music on its slopes. The first two of these buildings survive in ruins and are still unique in the world. They might seem to call for no apology, but Pericles had his own reasons for spending the payments of the allies on building instead of on even more armaments. He did not need the armaments, and money was plentiful. He might of course have reduced the tribute, but, since he might need it in the future, that was a dangerous step; once reduced, it would be difficult to restore.

Pericles could well have argued that, when the Greek states refused to combine in rebuilding the shrines destroyed by the Persians, somebody had to do it, and the Athenian League was the obvious body. It would be natural to start with Athens which led the league and had suffered the worst destruction. But though he may have used this argument, we do not know that he did. The case, as he put it forward, seems to survive in more or less his own words. They show his casuistical manner of argumentation, the characteristic weighing of the case for and the case against. He is answering attacks, and what he says is, within these limits, formidable:

Not a horse do the allies furnish, not a ship, not a hoplite, but simply money; and this belongs not to those that give it but to those that receive it, if they provide that for which they receive it; and it is but fitting that the city, when once she is sufficiently equipped with all that is necessary for war, should apply her surplus to such works as when completed will bring her everlasting glory, and will in process of completion bring that surplus into actual service, in that all sorts of activity and various demands arise, which wake every art and stir every hand and bring, as it were, the whole city under pay, so that she not only adorns but also supports herself from her own resources.[3]

The quotation has a Periclean smack. In the speeches which the historian Thucydides attributes to him, a like combination of abstract argument and practical prudence is infused with something more exalted and more exalting.

Pericles' first argument does not ring true. He might have claimed that since the allies paid with money, and the Athenians with their lives, the latter had a prior right to a decision on the use of the money. But this is not what he says. He claims that once the allies have paid their tribute, it belongs to Athens and they have no right to complain of its use. But they have paid it on an agreed understanding for a specific purpose. It is not enough to answer that this purpose has been met with part of the money; for the agreement was that all of it should be used for the same end. The allies could legitimately argue that they had been tricked. Yet probably Pericles did not mean this to be a neat bit of sophistry; it is rather an example of the thoughtless superiority with which Athens too often treated her allies and which was based on the assumption that since Athens bore the heaviest responsibilities and did most of the fighting, she was entitled to put her own interests first and to take the largest rewards. In effect Pericles means that since the allies have entrusted themselves to the care of Athens, she can do what she likes with them. He may even mean that, since Athens provides the machinery of war, which he describes factually, this is what really matters, and Athens almost alone is in control of it. This would conform to the common notion that it is the nature of the weak to be ruled by the strong, and here he applies this obliquely to prop up his equivocation.

Other, more realistic considerations follow. He stresses that Athens must have all that is necessary for war and he claims that she has got it. The claim was fully justified. When war came in 431, she was amply prepared and better equipped than her Peloponnesian opponents. Without this confidence Pericles would not have embarked on his bold building policy, for which he advances two very different reasons. The first is that the buildings which he has in mind will bring everlasting glory to Athens. A long lapse of years has not proved him wrong. Yet the historian Thucydides, who was fully awake to the lure of glory, knew that fine buildings are not always solid evidence for it and insists that the absence of them may not prove the lack of it. With remarkable prescience, he says:

Suppose, for example, that the city of Sparta was to become deserted and that only the temples and foundations of building remained, I think that future generations would, as time passed, find it very difficult to believe that the place had really been as powerful as it was represented to be.[4]

The remains of Sparta are so humble that it is hard to believe that this was the power which for many years challenged and finally conquered Athens. But Thucydides spoke for himself; Pericles did not share his doubts. Pericles was primarily concerned with the greatness of Athens and knew that fine buildings could not fail to impress other Greeks or to make the Athenians proud of their city. These buildings indicate not only the possession of money to build them but an incomparable skill in artists and craftsmen. It is true that in the Funeral Speech which Thucydides gives to Pericles, he says almost nothing about the building policy, though at this date the Parthenon was finished and the Propylaea more than half built. But in this speech Pericles is speaking less about a visible Athens than about the soaring spirit which is responsible for her greatness.

Pericles is avid for glory, and the essence of glory is that it endures through time. This was neither a new nor a specifically Athenian idea. For centuries the Greeks believed that death could somehow be defeated if a man acted worthily of his manhood and was celebrated for it in words or stone. It is hard to say how real this afterlife was thought to be, but though for some it was no more than a metaphor, for others it had a kind of reality which defied the usual gloomy forecasts of what happened after death. That is why in the short and touching epitaphs which were written in verse for those who fell in battle the point stressed is that they have won abiding glory, and this suggests, however vaguely, some posthumous prolongation of their existence. Pericles, with a fine practical sense, applied the notion to a visible monument like the Parthenon, which may survive even longer than songs and present a more powerful impression of heroic strength. But Pericles gives a new turn to the old belief when he transposes what used to be said of individuals or small groups to a whole city. He might be pressed to admit that, while Athens herself may not last forever, her glory will.

This far-reaching prescience is matched by prudential considerations for the present. The building programme demanded full attention; it would 'rouse every heart and stir every hand' and bring a large part of the population, which might become unemployed with the advent of peace, into the service of the state. This astonishingly socialistic project provided work for men who, when war came, were needed as soldiers and sailors, but in the meanwhile could be used to enhance the splendour of Athens. It was more profitable to keep them busy with skilful and healthy work than to leave them idle or to send them to found colonies overseas. Though the work done brought no financial return on the capital outlay, this need not trouble the Athenians because it was paid for by tribute from the allies. Pericles knew what he was saying. His policy of public works at this high level appealed to his sense of splendour and provided a living for that section of the population which gave him his strongest support. He might be accused of demagogy, and of course he was, but his way of conciliating the voters added incalculably to the lasting wealth of mankind.

Against this case which Pericles made for his policy, we must set that which his opponents made against it. This too is reported in words which look as if they were a more or less accurate record of what was said at the time. The theme seems to have taken a standard form in the debates in the Assembly:

The people has a bad name and is in ill repute because it has moved the public moneys of the Greeks from Delos into its own keeping, and against those that accuse it it has the most specious of excuses, that it took the moneys from Delos out of fear for the barbarians and was now guarding the common property in a safe place; of this Pericles has robbed it. Hellas seems to be insulted with a hideous insult and manifestly tyrannized over when she sees that with her enforced contributions to war we are gilding and making beautiful our city like a wanton woman when she decks herself with precious stones and costly statues and temples worth thousands of talents.[5]

This must be very much what Thucydides, son of Melesias, said against Pericles. It contains his sentiments, possibly some of his phrases. He accepts, or pretends to accept, the reason for the transference of the treasury from Delos to Athens; he blames not the Athenian Assembly, which has agreed to use the money for building, but Pericles, as if he did not have to go through the customary democratic procedure before getting anything done. He continues with accusations of tyrannizing over the allies and insulting them by a degrading waste of their money.

The accusation against Pericles is of behaving like a tyrant and acting from sheer arrogance. The second part of the charge goes back for centuries, at least to Solon who saw the rich nobles of Athens as driven by a like arrogance to oppress others. The notion was especially connected with tyrants, who despite their many good actions were thought to suffer from infatuate pride. In his imaginary discussion about different kinds of government Herodotus makes one of the Persian conspirators say: 'Pride grows in a tyrant because of all the good things that he has.'[6] Thucydides applied the doctrine not to Athens, as he might have, but personally to Pericles. He did not wish to alienate support in Athens and therefore put the blame on the man who in his view had bewitched the Athenian people. This he regarded as typical of a tyrant and grossly insulting to the allies. Now, as we have seen, Pericles might at times say that the empire was a tyranny, but Thucydides did not dare to say so. When he put all the blame on Pericles, he must have reflected the views of the Athenian rich and of their friends among the allies. He was wrong about Pericles, who held closely to the constitution and did not keep himself in power by armed force as tyrants did, but promoted his policy with the support of a majority in the Assembly. These words are propaganda, and may have had some effect, since Pericles was said to resemble in appearance and in some of his policies the Athenian tyrant Pisistratus. The great advocate of democratic liberty, who claimed that in Athens 'power is in the hands not of a minority but of the whole people',[7] is traduced as one who wants power only for himself, and that by a man who believes in government by fine gentlemen.

Thucydides then compares the beautification of Athens with

that of a wanton mistress who is covered with jewellery by her lover. We might be surprised that Thucydides speaks of his city in this way, but it is a backhanded hit at Pericles for saying that Athenians should be lovers of their city. This, says Thucydides, is what such lovers are. He takes a low view of Athens. His notion is that the new grandeur which Pericles confers on her is less truly grand than the simple dignity which she had in the past, though even then the temples, destroyed by the Persians and now being replaced, had an uncommon splendour. Moreover, the suggestion that Athens is kept by a rich master is Thucydides' way of saying that Pericles has bought the people by finding them work. Thucydides no doubt cherished the aristocratic belief that, since the poor deserve their poverty, it is not to their credit if they try to remedy it. Here again he goes against a central doctrine of Pericles:

As for poverty, no one need be ashamed to admit it: the real shame is in not taking practical measures to escape it.[8]

In this Pericles was ready to assist, and his opponents regarded his efforts with horror. Looking at it from a different angle we cannot but note the crudity with which Thucydides derides the temples and statues set up at the instigation of Pericles. For him they are mere extravagances, and that damns them. We hardly expect this from an Athenian aristocrat, and perhaps the speaker was disagreeably exceptional in his time, for Athenian nobles patronized architects and sculptors with imaginative generosity, unless we choose to think that this was merely a tyrannical whim indulged by Pisistratus and his sons to win popular favour. The most likely solution is that Thucydides is not honest about the arts. He may, for all we know, have liked them as most Athenians did. What he does is to deplore the waste of allied money on them when it might be used for armaments. This is a legitimate manoeuvre of controversy, though it is expressed with a crudity which indicates how hotly tempers could rise on this issue.

In championing the allies against Pericles his opponents were not indulging in controversy just for its own sake, though they did not disdain its sharper methods. They probably believed much of what they said and were moved by sympathy for the allies, or at least for those among them who belonged to their own class and disliked democratic policies. Rich Athenian families had many ties outside Attica, which would be easy enough in so small a land as Greece, where communications, at least by sea, were easy in the summer months. They had common interests in sports and games and would meet each other not only at the paramount games of Olympia and Delphi but at the many other athletic concourses which took place at regular intervals. Victory in the games was prized particularly by the well-to-do, who regarded it as a proof of their inherited breeding and descent from gods and heroes. When Pindar, who belonged to their class, celebrated their successes, he created a metaphysic of glory, which was very much to their taste. Athletes tended to come from this class, not merely because they could afford the quite considerable expenses, but because they believed in games as suitable to their origins. Victors came mostly from aristocratic circles, notably from Aegina, while very few came from Athens. Thucydides moved in these circles, not only through his father's athletic connections, but becaues he was probably an athlete himself. His family was welcome in Aegina, and we may surmise that he had friends in other places where Athens had not stifled the claims of eager aristocrats to name and fame. Even in the critical year 447–446 Aeginetans were not deterred from competing, and it was for a young wrestler that Pindar then wrote *Pythian* VIII. This international society of wealth and nobility found a voice in Thucydides and vented its grievances through him. He may even have thought that the buildings of Pericles were not only immoral but vulgarly ostentatious, glittering with newly cut marble and richly painted sculptures. History has decided otherwise.

Thucydides had ideas on the place that Athens should take in Hellenic affairs, and he saw it more as co-operation than as hegemony or domination. He was closely associated with the first stages of an unusual attempt by Athens to found in the west not a cleruchy but an authentic colony of the old-fashioned kind. The impulse came from without. Some time about 446 the inhabitants of old Sybaris, on the east coast of the toe of Italy, who had been thrown out by the men of Croton in 510, attempted to rebuild their city on the old site. They were again driven out by the men of Croton, and appealed to Athens and Sparta to join them in founding a new city. Sparta was not attracted by the suggestion and refused to take part, but Athens, who had long cherished ambitions in the west, saw possibilities in the offer and sent out a small company of Athenians and allies.

In this we can see Thucydides at work. The project at which he aimed was not exclusively Athenian but Panhellenic, and thought likely to placate the Peloponnesians. No doubt Thucydides also thought that to send out colonists was a better way to deal with the unemployed than to give them skilful and well paid work at home. The establishment of the colony could be interpreted as a conciliatory gesture by Athens to the rest of Greece and a presage of more friendly relations. When the project was accepted in 444–443, Thucydides was a general and well placed to start the scheme with a good chance of success. But things went wrong. The Sybarites quarrelled with the new settlers, claimed exclusive rights to the important offices of state, and treated the Athenians with contempt. War followed, and the Sybarites were again driven out. In the subsequent shortage of men the Athenian colonists applied to the mother city for reinforcements.

It was then decided to found a full, new colony on the neighbouring site of Thurii. In this Thucydides wished to play a leading part. He visited Sybaris, where he cut a prominent figure and was said later by Plato to have 'great power among the other Greeks'.[9] But again things went wrong. The failure of the first expedition still rankled in Athens; on the other side Corinth resented Athenian intrusion in the west and refused to share in the foundation, no doubt thinking that Athens would not take so active a part if the plan was really so innocent and so Panhellenic as she claimed. In the event there was a complete reversal of fortune. Pericles appropriated Thucydides' plans and used them not only to further his own interests but to discredit Thucydides. The latter may well have overplayed his part and excited the distrust of the Athenian public. When in the spring of 443 his year of office came to an end, he was prosecuted by Xenocritus, a supporter of Pericles, for the familiar faults of arrogance and peculation, though no doubt the charges were made in more specific forms. He may well have taken bribes or made promises which he did not carry out. The prosecution succeeded, and Thucydides was ostracized for ten years. In these manoeuvres Pericles completely outwitted his opponent and showed how strong he was by getting himself elected general for 443–442. In this remarkable change of fortunes the proposed colony played a large part. Thucydides intended it to be a Panhellenic venture, but Pericles insisted that this was against the interests of Athens and found a solution by getting Athens to take the lead and promote her own cause in the west.

In the event the new city of Thurii was founded in 443 near the site of old Sybaris. Athens gave the lead to volunteers from various parts, including Arcadia and Ionia. The foundation was conducted with correct ceremony. The seer Lampon, who was a friend of Pericles and connected with the worship of Demeter at Eleusis, obtained, as was proper, an oracle from Delphi, which described a site that was duly discovered at Thurii and settled. The new city was designed by the town planner Hippodamas, who had already laid out the Piraeus on a rectangular grid pattern. The constitution was a democracy, but the laws were not those of the Athenian Solon but of Zaleucus, who had been the lawgiver of Locri and was much admired in Greek Sicily and Italy. This was a concession to local feeling and perhaps a gesture to show that Athens did not always want things in her own way. Apollo, the god of Delphi, was honoured as the founder. Even after the Periclean victory Thurii was not quite free of its Panhellenic beginnings, and it was dramatically appropriate that it should play no important part afterwards in Athenian affairs.

Thurii was a fine gesture and attracted a measure of attention and support. In its early days it drew the philosophers Protagoras and Empedocles, the historian Herodotus, and the young orator Lysias. Economically and politically it flourished, and survived attacks from its jealous Dorian neighbour Taras. But if Pericles expected Thurii to become an outpost of Athenian dominion in the west, he was doomed to disappointment. The coins might be stamped with the head of Athene and an olive branch, but Thurii throve neither as an Athenian colony nor as an international settlement. It drifted quietly into the ambience of the Dorian states of southern Italy, largely because none of the colonizing elements other than the Athenian trusted Athens or believed that her Hellenism was anything but a disguise for imperial ambition. In the end Thurii did Athens little good and little harm. To Pericles it brought the solid advantages of getting rid of Thucydides for ten years.

From the ostracism of Thucydides in 443 to his own death in 429 Pericles remained continuously in office except for a few months in the last year of his life, when he was deprived of his office and then restored. Each year he was elected general, and this was the basis of his power, for it enabled him to exert his remarkable gift of getting the Assembly to do what he wished. The ostracism of Thucydides certainly reduced the strength of the opposition, but even before he returned in 433 there are signs that his followers were at work and busy with their old policy of attacking Pericles. In this second round they did not engage in open manoeuvre in the Assembly, for Pericles held it in such control that any adversary was doomed to defeat. Instead an ingenious strategy was followed of trying to discredit Pericles by prosecuting his more prominent friends on various unpleasant charges. Three such prosecutions took place in the years before the outbreak of war with Sparta in 431, and it was naturally said that Pericles went to war in order to divert attention from his own troubles. This is highly questionable; for none of these cases interfered with his control of the Assembly or with the trust that the majority of Athenians still put in him. In these attacks we can see first the work of the followers of Thucydides, and then of Thucydides himself. We are not sure in what order the prosecutions came, but they seem to have followed a steady succession as if their accumulated effect were intended to overwhelm and break Pericles.

We may first take the prosecution of the sculptor Phidias, which seems to have taken place in 437. In this we can see that Thucydides' followers agreed with him in complaining that Pericles spent public money on temples and statues. Phidias had made the great gold and ivory statue of Athene in the Parthenon; he was also an intimate friend of Pericles. It should be possible to attack him and through him to damage Pericles. Menon, an assistant of Phidias, was persuaded to take a suppliant's seat in the market-place and to demand immunity from punishment if he brought information and an accusation against Phidias. The proposal was accepted, and Phidias was accused of embezzling gold from that used for the statue. The attack failed completely; for Phidias, on the prudent advice of Pericles, had seen that the gold on the statue could all be taken off and weighed. It was now weighed, and nothing was found to be missing. But this was not enough for the attackers. They changed their ground and accused Phidias of impiety against the national goddess because on her shield he had carved a figure like himself and inserted another figure like Pericles fighting an Amazon. This was a natural enough thing to do, but the prosecution in this case must have been helped by some outbreak of superstition. Phidias left Athens for Elis to work on his statue of Zeus at Olympia, where his workshop has been discovered and in it some tiny chips of ivory and a small cup signed with his name. The informer Menon got the immunities for which he asked. Phidias' own end is told in several forms, but in one he was brought back to Athens and died there in prison before the charges against him could be heard.

A little later, after the return of Thucydides, an attack was launched against Anaxagoras, and Thucydides is said to have instigated it. Anaxagoras was charged under a recent law introduced by a religious fanatic called Diopeithes against 'those who do not acknowledge divine things or who give instruction about celestial phenomena'.[10] This was perfectly applicable to Anaxagoras, who thought that the sun was a mass of red-hot iron 'larger than the Peloponnese'[11] and knew that it is eclipsed by the interposition of the moon and that the moon shines with light reflected from it. He is also said to have been accused of Medism, that is, of favouring the Persians, but this can have had little meaning at the time and looks like a later invention. The trial involved the honour and prestige of Pericles. Pericles defended Anaxagoras, but did not get him acquitted. He was found guilty and fined five talents. The result was that he left Athens for Lampsacus, where he founded a school of philosophy. Once charges of this kind were made possible, it would be easy to prove almost anyone guilty of them; most Greeks, sharing an unorganized and undogmatic religion, developed idiosyncrasies of belief and enjoyed the tolerance afforded by polytheism, in which there are so many gods that they cannot afford to be jealous of one another. It is of course possible that Thucydides actually shared the spirit which inspired the decree of Diopeithes, but it is more likely that he took advantage of it and may even have supported it in the Assembly, seeing how useful a weapon it placed in his hands. It is also in character that the attacks were made on the most distinguished figures in Athens at the time, and that Thucydides saw nothing unbecoming in this and may even have taken pleasure in it.

A third line of attack was nasty in a different way, though its authors may have thought themselves very clever. It was aimed at Pericles' private life and struck him hard in it. Pericles' marriage to a kinswoman brought him two sons, but was not otherwise a success, and Pericles had it annulled. He had already fallen in love with Aspasia, an uncommonly gifted woman from Miletus. She may possibly have come to Athens with the famous town planner Hippodamas, who among his other activities imagined an ideal state which won some notice from Aristotle. In the early forties she met Pericles, who lived with her for the rest of his life. She bore him a son, who was illegitimate because of a law proposed by Pericles by which Athenian citizenship was limited to those with Athenian parents on both sides. Pericles later got the boy naturalized by a special act. Aspasia played a much larger part in the social life of Athens than any other woman of her time. This was due partly to her connection with Pericles but also to her remarkable character. Though gossip told appalling stories about her and she was accused of the usual aberrations attributed to the wives and mistresses of great men, she was a woman of dignity and intelligence. She was a friend of Socrates and kept a kind of salon at which, as in Plato's dialogues, current matters of general interest were discussed. Aspasia was said to have modelled herself on a famous Milesian woman called Thargelia, who was well informed on politics and married fourteen times, her last husband being king Antiochus of Thessaly, whose kingdom she ruled for many years after his death. Aspasia may have learned something from this capable countrywoman, and the parallel confirms her genuine interest in politics. There is no reason to think that she did not from time to time take an interest which might be construed as interference. The more scurrilous stories need not disturb us.

Aspasia was easy to attack. As a Milesian she could always be accused of insufficient loyalty to Athens, and there may have been passages in her past which could be brought up against her. She moved in a highly intelligent circle which would not have had much in common with the sporting friends of Thucydides. But above all she must have outraged the common Athenian sentiment that a woman's place was the home and her best duty to keep silence. This is said so often that, while it indicates a general desire to believe it, it must have been hard to maintain in practice, and we suspect that this view of what a woman ought to be was often disregarded in actual life. We have only to look at those magnified versions of Athenian women, the dominating heroines of tragedy and the boisterous termagants of comedy, to see of what wives and daughters were capable. Aspasia might not behave like either of these, but she had an unusual and much criticized prominence. It is therefore notable that in the Funeral Speech attributed to Pericles, we find towards the end words specially directed to the women of the fallen:

Your great glory is not to be inferior to what God has made you, and the greatest glory of a woman is to be least talked about by men, whether they are praising you or criticizing you.[12]

Whatever might be said about Aspasia, nobody could claim that she was not talked about. So these words are a little mysterious. If they are the correct record of what Pericles said, did he say them knowing about current gossip, and mean to defy it, claiming implicitly that Aspasia was in fact a quiet woman who kept to her home? Or are they an invention of the historian Thucydides who never mentions Aspasia by name or suggests that she played any part in politics, but may have thought it prudent to hint that he knew about her but did not believe that Pericles entrusted her with any intimate information? In either case Aspasia did not conform to Athenian ideals of womanhood, even if in practice she was not alone in her independence. She would naturally attract attention, envy, and misrepresentation, of which the rival Thucydides and his allies could take advantage.

Once again the attack was founded on an appeal to religious intolerance. Aspasia was accused of impiety by the comic poet Hermippus, who added for full measure that she procured freeborn women for the pleasure of Pericles. Impiety, however defined, was a natural enough charge since it was also made against Anaxagoras and Phidias, and it is possible that Pericles formed his own patriotic faith on a liberal interpretation of the divine nature. The second part of the charges was the result of endless slanders that had been in circulation for some time and must have been believed by some people. Pericles pleaded for Aspasia at her trial and was said to have wept copiously at it. The result was that she was acquitted, and though this caused by far the richest gossip of these trials, it was, from the point of view of Thucydides, the least successful. Pericles himself survived with undiminished authority, and Aspasia was acquitted of charges which might have excited harsh feelings against her. Perhaps the accusations were so trumpery that the jury saw their absurdity and rejected them. As for Thucydides, this was his last real fling. He lived on for a few years, but seems to have lost not only his prestige but his talents and become a pathetic old man. Our last glimpse of him is in 425 when in his *Acharnians* Aristophanes makes the Chorus lament the inability of Thucydides to stand up to the brutal glibness of a new generation of orators:

> O Thucydides to witness, bowed with age in sore distress,
> Feebly struggling in the clutches of that Scythian wilderness
> Fluent glib Cephisodemus – oh the sorrowful display!
> I myself was moved to pity, yea and wiped a tear away,
> Grieved at heart the gallant veteran by an archer mauled to
>   view,
> Him, who, were he, by Demeter, that Thucydides we knew,
> Would have stood no airs of nonsense from the Goddess
>   Travel-sore,
> Would have thrown, the mighty wrestler, ten Evathluses or
>   more,
> Shouted down three thousand archers with his accent of
>   command,
> Shot his own accuser's kinsman in his Scythian fatherland.[13]

Aristophanes pities the old Thucydides for being attacked by a new generation which is alien and unscrupulous. He gives him full credit for having been a powerful wrestler and indicates that he was also a soldier with resonant powers of command. Thucydides had outlived his time and ceased to count, but in his heyday he was someone to be reckoned with.

These trials all follow the same pattern and show how Thucydides set to work. Pericles himself was not attacked personally, no doubt because his opponents felt incapable of taking him on in the open. Instead he was assailed through those close to him who were less formidable. In this a new phenomenon is exploited, the religious intolerance which seems to have grown to ugly dimensions in reaction against recent philosophical and scientific speculation. It is hard to say why Athens had, with apparent suddenness, become so intolerant, and the explanation would be easier if we knew the exact date of the trials. It has been thought that they took place after the declaration of war, perhaps in 430 when the plague struck Athens and by its unforeseen horror undermined much traditional belief and piety. But this contradicts the talk that Pericles went to war to hide his own troubles, and the years before the declaration of war seem more likely. Athens and Sparta had already started a war of nerves which infected both sides and hastened the outbreak of hostilities. So long as Athens was at peace with herself, tolerance prevailed, but the prolonged frustration and fear caused by Spartan policy may well have induced a kind of hysteria in which unsophisticated people blamed all the trouble on those who neglected the gods. It would be easy to include Pericles among these, though in fact he was not this kind of doubter. Some of his friends perhaps were, and this made it easier to attack them. We may well believe that Thucydides and his agents worked up uneducated suspicions into hysterical outbursts and did so the more readily because they saw no other way to humiliate Pericles. In their main object they failed, but the exploitation of rumour is a nasty slur on the reputation of Athens. This vicious mood was all the worse because Pericles had been educating the Athenians for some years and had provided them with an exalted national religion. The decree of Diopeithes is a strange phenomenon in this setting, but once it had been passed, the task of the juries was to decide whether their cases fell under it or not. They judged each case on its merits and came to their conclusions. There is no reason to think that they were packed or bribed by Thucydides, though as a moneylender he had considerable financial resources behind him.

The attacks led or inspired by Thucydides, son of Melesias,

were the most dangerous that Pericles encountered. But throughout his career he was also the victim of a different kind of attack, less serious in intention but hardly less damaging in effect. Athenian ebullience found an outlet for its deflating and derisive spirit in its own brand of comedy. This was established as a national festival in 487 and maintained a lively career to the end of the fifth century. Comedy was not a drawing-room affair, but a mixture of farce, satire, ribaldry, obscenity, fantastic imagination and abundant poetry. Anything and anybody were food for it. It could say what it liked; its first aim was to provoke laughter. Comic poets were not going to leave Pericles alone, but there is no need to think that they served any special interest. They needed well-to-do patrons to pay for putting on a play, but such could be found among the friends of Pericles as well as among his enemies. The Old Oligarch, however, says that comic writers were forbidden to make fun of the popular elements:

That they themselves may not be ill spoken of, they do not allow anyone to make fun or speak evil of the people; for they well know that he who is made fun of is generally not of the people or the populace, but either rich or noble or powerful. But some few of the poor and the vulgar are made fun of, but not even these except for being busy-bodies and trying to get more than the people; so they are not annoyed when these are made fun of.[14]

This is entirely natural. The prominent are much better targets for comedy than the obscure. But so far as the democrats in politics were concerned, the Old Oligarch has got it wrong; for the popular party, including Pericles, was the butt of more than one comic writer, and there is no lopsided hostility towards the rich and the well-established. It is true that our full evidence does not begin until after the death of Pericles with the *Acharnians* of Aristophanes in 425. But there are substantial fragments of earlier plays, and Aristophanes himself is conscious of the tradition behind him and remains faithful to it. He assumes that he can say what he likes about anyone, and we cannot accuse him of extreme bias in any one direction. What is more surprising is that from 440 to 438 comedy was to some extent restricted. It was not stopped, for inscriptions prove that plays were still produced at the time. But it is possible that its licence in personal attacks on people by name and in their actual impersonation on the stage was forbidden. We do not know the reason for this, unless the revolt of Samos was sufficiently serious for unbridled freedom of speech to be thought dangerous. In that case the restrictions were made not by the enemies of Pericles but by Pericles himself. In any case they were soon abolished, perhaps because they had met an immediate, passing need and were no longer required. Pericles must have known that they contradicted his own principles of free speech.

Comic writers, in all times and climes, need something like an assured position from which they can fling their gibes and ribaldries with a ring of conviction. They must seem to be the only sane persons in a mad world, and for this they need a deadly air of infallibility. A common stance of the writers of Attic comedy was with neither the conservative right nor the radical left, but with some ideal Golden Age, which never existed, or, if it did, was not in the least what it was claimed to be. Some of them picked up such an age from poetry and used it to rail at the present. Cratinus (c.484–c.419) judged the Periclean age by such comparisons. In his *Chirons*, which took its name from the good centaur who trained Achilles in his boyhood, Cratinus glorified not primitive simplicity but primitive ease, because nature produced everything that man wanted without his having to exert himself. Or such Utopias could also be placed in the future. In the *Wild Beasts* of Crates, plates and dishes lay and wash themselves up, and fish cook themselves to a turn. Other poets found less fanciful but no less exhilarating ideals in more contemporary events of Athenian history, Teleclides using the time of Themistocles, Aristophanes the generation of Marathon. It is easier to make fun of the present when it is compared with a past of almost impossible felicity or heroic grandeur. The comic poets knew this and took advantage of it.

Cratinus has left enough fragments to give some idea of his treatment of Pericles. In 455, when Athens was at war with Sparta, the *Nemesis* indicates some pro-Spartan tendencies, which might suit Cratinus as a friend of Cimon and would show him to be an opponent of Pericles. In 443 the *Thracian Women* touches on events soon after the ostracism of Thucydides and refers to the recent building of the Odeon. Pericles himself seems to have escaped ostracism by a narrow margin, and Cratinus uses an imagery which suggests that it has been touch and go. The puns of the Greek in one place have been neatly caught in English by T. F. Higham:

> Here's Pericles, our own squill-headed Zeus.
> Where did he buy that hat? What, what excuse?
> It's new head-cover in *Odeon* style—
> Late storms of censure hardly left a tile.[15]

Cratinus, not for the first or the last time, compares Pericles with Zeus. This is harmless enough, and other comedians did the same. But Cratinus could be sharper than this and in the *Chirons* suggests that Pericles is best explained as a mythological monster:

> Strife and old father Cronus went together to bed
> And gave birth to the mightiest tyrant,
> Whom the gods call the Head-gatherer.[16]

The joke, such as it is, in 'Head-gatherer' is based on the traditional notion of Zeus as 'Cloud-gatherer'. It vaguely suggests Pericles' comic head but much more his ruthless treatment of enemies whose heads he makes roll like any head-hunter.

In the *Wealths*, which may have been written soon before the outbreak of war in 431, Cratinus used a myth to dramatize contemporary events. The gods of wealth belong to the old order of Cronus, who has been thrown out by his son Zeus, and they with him. Zeus of course is Pericles, and the implication is that by his rule he has impoverished the rich. Now however there seems to be a chance of the old order coming back, for Zeus has been defeated by the People, and the Wealths, who are Titans, have been liberated. They sing:

> Since he is robbed of his tyrant-rule
> And the People is master,
> We have hurried here to our near of kin,
> Our own brother; in his old age
> We search for him.[17]

The brother is Prometheus, the victim of Zeus and the friend of men, and we suspect that he is in fact Thucydides, son of Melesias, to whom the old-fashioned rich now look for help. The play may have been written just before the return of Thucydides from ostracism, and in accordance with comic practice the hopes of Cratinus and his friends are stated as accomplished facts because things will now be changed to suit them. By identifying Thucydides with Prometheus Cratinus makes him a benefactor and friend of the Athenian nobles, as indeed he wished to be thought. If he was returning from ostracism, he would be encouraged by this public support.

There is no reason to think that in this or any other play Cratinus was at all kind to Pericles. The identification with Zeus may have been made first by Cratinus, and it struck at the alleged ambition of Pericles to be a tyrant. This was a good theme for comedy and may have contained some spice of hatred. Almost any topic was good enough for an attack. When Pericles was building the Long Walls from Athens to the Piraeus, a measure of first importance to national safety, Cratinus mocked the slowness with which the work was done and claimed that the walls existed only in word. Many such shots must have gone home. The management of the empire provided rich material for the opposition to attack. Teleclides makes it a matter of Pericles' own responsibility and says that the Athenians have handed everything over to him:

> With the cities' assessments the cities themselves to bind or
>   release as he pleases,
> Their ramparts of stone to build up as he likes, and then to
>   pull them down straightway,
> Their treaties, their forces, their might, peace and richness,
>   and all the fair gifts of good fortune.[18]

We need not assume that Teleclides felt any real compassion for the allies, but the assumption of power by Pericles was too rich a topic to let pass. The comic poet was the court jester to the Athenian people. His task was to make fun, and often ill-natured fun, of anything that might earn disapproval.

If Pericles was Zeus, Aspasia was Hera, and Cratinus was particularly nasty about her:

> Lechery bore him Aspasia to be his Hera,
> A bitch-faced prostitute.[19]

Their son was treated with a like crudity. After Pericles' death Eupolis makes his spirit ask if his son is still alive and gets the answer from the spirit of the general Myrodines:

> He'd long ago have been a man
> If he were not ashamed of his harlot's birth.[20]

Since Aspasia came from Miletus, it was easy to say that when Pericles declared war on Samos in 440, he did so to please her. Samos and Miletus were already at war about the possession of Priene, and when Athens ordered them to stop, they would not obey. When Pericles took arms against them, he may well have pleased Aspasia, but he could hardly allow two allies to fight each other for the possession of a third. Add to this that Samos was governed by an oligarchy, and the picture is clear. But Cratinus could not miss so good a chance of throwing dirt at Pericles. Something similar happened in 432 just before the outbreak of the Peloponnesian War. Pericles imposed a blockade on Megara. There were nasty incidents and accusations against each country by the other. The whole thing was turned to farce by putting the blame on Aspasia and her alleged bawdyhouse. In 425 Aristophanes, writing in high spirits, analyses the origin of the war as he sees it:

> But some young tipsy cottabus-players went
> And stole from Megara-town the fair Simaetha.
> Then the Megarians, garlicked with the smart,
> Stole, in return, two of Aspasia's hussies.
> From these three wantons o'er the Hellenic race
> Burst forth the first beginnings of the war.
> For them, in wrath, the Olympian Pericles
> Thundered and lightened and confounded Hellas,
> Enacted laws that ran like drinking-songs,
> *That the Megarians presently depart*
> *From earth and sea, the mainland and the mart.*[21]

When this was written Pericles had been dead for four years, and though Aspasia was still alive, the joke that she kept a bawdyhouse was more than weather-worn. The comic poets acted on the principle that no jokes are so good as old jokes, and repeated stock themes without a qualm, for they were sure to raise a laugh.

It is hard to say how far Pericles was damaged by the crude

and unfriendly gibes of the comic poets. They certainly failed to unseat him, and he was probably wise enough to see that, however they might wound him and his family, they were a valuable safety valve. There is no assurance that he took legal proceedings against any poet as Cleon did later against Aristophanes for deriding the city before the allies with his *Babylonians* in 426. If Pericles had wished, he could have got his own back on the poets by some such procedures as Cleon's; for though Athens had no law of libel in the modern sense and though comedies were expected to be outspoken, it was possible to get around the rules. But Pericles did not try, and his example prevailed with a very few exceptions until the fall of Athens in 404. Cleon's successors seem to have left the whole thing well alone, except for a short-lived restriction on personal abuse in 414. It is a tremendous tribute to the tolerance and self-confidence of Athens that throughout the Peloponnesian War this liberty was preserved. The Athenian people refused to give up its right to criticize through comedy the defects and absurdities of its public men, whether generals or statesmen or poets or philosophers. It is true that when in 399 Socrates was accused of corrupting the young, he said in his defence that he had suffered from the comic poets, meaning the *Clouds* of Aristophanes, in which he had been mercilessly mocked, and this suggests that a man's reputation might suffer from derision before a very large audience. No doubt this happened often enough, but the Athenians were hardened to abuse and ridicule. The language used in their law courts was often intolerable by our thin-skinned standards, and in comedy likewise hard knocks were given and taken. Pericles may at one time have disliked the extreme licence of comedy and tried to limit it, but perhaps he felt that this was wrong, and certainly impracticable. So he left it alone and managed to survive it. We may contrast what he tolerated in it with his own idea of daily behaviour in Athens :

We do not get into a state with our next-door neighbour if he enjoys himself in his own way, nor do we give him the kind of black looks which, though they do no real harm, still do hurt people's feelings.[22]

9

THE INTELLECTUAL REVOLUTION

THE prodigious activity of Periclean Athens in politics and the arts was not equally matched in more severely intellectual pursuits. Far-ranging movements in science and philosophy had begun in Ionia early in the sixth century and maintained their momentum, but few of the new discoveries were made by indigenous Athenians. The only Athenian philosophers of any importance were Archelaus, a not very original pupil of Anaxagoras, and Socrates, who had in the long run an incalculable influence but who never wrote a book and was renowned more for his personal ascendancy than for his philosophical theories. The most famous mathematician of the time was the Athenian Meton, who won his name by town planning and reforming the calendar. Mathematics seem to have been honoured as a useful rather than an abstract pursuit, and we can see a delicate by-product of them in the skill with which the lines of the Parthenon are calculated to look straight by not being so. Athens, however, welcomed thinkers from other cities, though not always to their satisfaction, for one of the greatest, Democritus of Abdera, the father of atomic physics, complained: 'I came to Athens, and no one knew me',[1] but he won disciples who popularized his views.

Pericles, as a friend of Anaxagoras, welcomed the new knowledge but seems to have had doubts about its place in public life. It looks as if he approved of it so long as something practical could come of it but resisted the idea that a thinker should cut himself off from his fellow men. His famous words 'We are lovers of wisdom without effeminacy'[2] indicate his attitude. For him effeminacy meant abstention from public life. This he condemned, while he welcomed the application of thought to anything that helped the city. This may seem a narrow, unimaginative attitude, but it was prompted by a healthy caution. When Greek science developed in later centuries, it almost insisted on being pursued for its own sake and having no useful purpose. In the long run this contempt for mechanical inventions did inestimable harm to scientific thought itself. Pericles cannot have foreseen this, but his instinct was right.

Intellectual activity at Athens operated at several levels. At the top were men, not often Athenians, who had new, bold ideas and gave them expression in concise and memorable form. Below these were popularizers, who may sometimes have had ideas of their own, but on the whole flourished by borrowing from others. Then came the mass of intelligent people, not by our standards well educated but eager for ideas and able to discuss them in their own undebased language. They had for the most part been trained in the old curriculum of song, dance, and poetry. They knew the Homeric poems, and their minds were stocked with dramatic and imaginative legends. But they were able to absorb new notions because these rose out of their actual lives, from their practical and practised knowledge of agriculture and sailing, their uncertain approach to whimsical and wilful gods, their capacity to form embracing theories for such pastimes as athletics and conversation. Their curiosity was sharpened by new prospects which were continually being opened to them, largely from their advantageous exploitation of the sea whether for trade or for battle. What they saw tickled their interest and made them ask questions. This eager, questing spirit found its generous incarnation in Herodotus. He was not an Athenian but he relished Athens as a place where there was always something new to learn. He himself pursued information by long travels, notably in Egypt and Scythia, and assimilated the lore of Greeks and barbarians alike. He presents it without pretence and without fuss. He makes no claims to be a learned man, but he was immensely well informed on the Mediterranean world. He took it all with a happy tolerance, a conviction that all things are possible and that, though one may be surprised, one should not be shocked when Indians eat their parents or Africans eat lice. He was in Athens just after the middle of the century and mixed in the circle of Sophocles. He embodies what Athenian enlightenment meant to a highly intelligent man who was occupied with conducting a *historiê* or inquiry into the Persian Wars and found that all manner of scientific or quasi-scientific matters were relevant to his theme, even if only as footnotes and appendices.

The growth of the new knowledge could not fail to affect religious beliefs, but it need not provoke any violent conflict with them. Herodotus combines quite happily an unquestioning trust in oracles and in divine envy of human success with bold speculations about what can happen in nature over long tracts of time. He thinks it quite fair to say that a gorge in Thessaly was made by Poseidon, because after all Poseidon is the god of earthquakes. Herodotus equivocates from politeness but does not dissimulate. He was not at all sure what demarcation there was between what was done by gods and what by natural causes. Nor was there any need for him to distinguish between them in a world where all things were full of gods. Neither he nor anyone else had a notion of the uniformity of nature which excluded the gods from active participation in physical events. This was to come later when Epicurus (342–271), following in the steps of Democritus (c.460–c.376), developed his theory of universal causation in atoms and relegated the gods to a quiet haven of non-interference. The scientific spirit did not claim to explain everything but made exploratory reconnaissances in various directions with no overall strategy.

In the heyday of the fifth century the two most prominent and energetic lines of inquiry were first in medicine and second in politics. Both had a decisive influence on the historian Thucydides, and just because we see so much of the fifth century through his eyes, we may overestimate their importance. But though physics and anatomy were on the move, medicine and politics touched others than Thucydides and made a special impact. The first made man aware of his physical being; the second tried heroically to find guiding principles for political behaviour. In an age fully conscious of unrealized powers these two fields of study gave encouragement and warning, and were for both reasons treated with respect and thought worthy of effort.

Medicine, as a serious scientific pursuit, began in Ionia, but had long played a part in Greek life if only because some elementary knowledge was needed to tend wounds on the battlefield or to mend limbs broken on the sports ground. For these purposes anatomical theory was as yet not much in demand, and in its early years Greek medicine was pragmatic and experimental. Hippocrates of Cos (496–399) followed good Ionian precedents in basing his studies on observed phenomena. The first thing was to diagnose what the trouble was, and this could be done only by the most careful description of symptoms. His disciples, taught by him to do this, laid the foundations of scientific medicine. When the ailments had been analysed, it was possible to consider the cure. This practical procedure matched a practical frame of mind. Though the Hippocratic doctors did not believe in the magic which had traditionally been thought necessary for any cure, the doctors were not discredited. There was no influential priesthood to denounce them, and even when the public had come to accept them, old methods of sleeping in holy places and the like continued to attract many adherents. The scientific and the theological approaches to sickness existed contentedly side by side. There was no need to force a conflict between them, and the discoveries by the doctors could be left to reinforce the teaching of the priests. The ways of the gods were strange, but it was quite proper that men should try to extend their understanding of them.

These studies did much to shape the advanced thinking of the fifth century. The early Hippocratic writings show how seriously doctors took their work and how carefully they studied it, sparing nothing in the application of system and method. The Hippocratic Oath, which still binds the medical profession, began its existence at this time, and though it has received various adjustments, its temper and main substance remain unchanged today. Medicine burst its old limits and in its study of disease examined climates and living conditions. The spirit in which it worked may be seen from the tract *On the Sacred Disease*, which deals deftly with the place of religion in medicine as concerned with epilepsy:

This disease has the same cause as others that come and go from the body – cold, sun, and changing restlessness of winds. These are divine. No need to put this disease in a special class as more divine than others; all are divine and all human. Each has its own nature and power.[3]

This detached attitude could be applied to other matters than medicine. In Thucydides we see how much a powerful intellect gained from it and its application to large issues. When the plague fell on Athens in 430, Thucydides suffered from it but survived. In his History he gives a dry, careful account of its possible place of origin, its symptoms and effects and its general influence on society. We do not know what the plague was, opinions vary from measles to typhus, but there is no need to doubt Thucydides' description just because we know of no plague exactly like his. More importantly, the study of medicine had a formative influence on his view of history. He set out to diagnose what went wrong with Periclean democracy and found his answer in the irresponsibility of certain demagogues and a lowering of intellectual standards by the war. He did not suggest a cure.

Medicine sharpened the scientific temper and cleared away accumulations of superstition. We need not assume that all prominent Athenians knew as much about it as Thucydides, but others were fascinated by the knowledge of the human system which it revealed. Euripides, with his taste for new discoveries, sought to dramatize madness on the stage, not only in the prophetess Cassandra, who is possessed by Apollo and combines manic meanderings with flashes of terrible insight, but in the great hero Heracles, who kills his wife and children in a fit of murderous fury laid on him by Hera. Medicine made both historians and dramatists more conscious of the physical side of man. To this extent it diminished belief in the omnipresent influence of the gods and asked questions to which rational answers were expected. Even in the political orators and pamphleteers there are traces of this diagnostic spirit, an assumption of wishing to establish the facts. When the lawyers worked out certain rules of probability for human behaviour and based forensic arguments on them, they were working on the same lines as doctors who predicted the course of an illness.

Parallel with this strict discipline grew something else, no less urgent and obsessing but less easily reduced to order and method. The Greeks had long discussed politics and generalized about it. The abolition of the old monarchies and the attacks on the land-owning aristocracies had been occasions for argument and moral judgements but not provocative of abstract theories. We do not know how Clisthenes justified his revolutionary introduction of democracy, but we may suspect that, like Solon before him, he used tags of proverbial wisdom. These were still common form in the fifth century. When Herodotus dramatizes his discussion on the merits and demerits of tyranny, oligarchy, and democracy, he builds each on more or less familiar notions. These were the stuff of current controversy and propaganda and have an unsophisticated look, though they are not without a good measure of common sense. If we compare this passage with any political discussion in Thucydides, they seem worlds apart, and yet there need not be many years between them. The fact is that Herodotus was not touched by the new technique of applying to politics the kind of argument and discussion which may have come from Greek colonies in Sicily and certainly owed much to the demands of debate in the law courts and the Assembly. It was assumed that argument must be met by argument and that in the end the better case won. This kind of controversy was taught by professional teachers to young men who wished to make a mark in law or politics, and for this reason it developed idiosyncrasies. Fine points were answered by points even finer, and much of the argument was conducted on abstractions and generalities which had a semi-philosophical flavour. This manner is to be seen in the formal speeches of Antiphon (480–411) and in Thucydides himself. This was the way in which he and his generation were educated, and amid much else it testified to the seriousness with which they treated politics. Once it came into fashion it had an extensive career and set a mark on the time.

This method took some of the drama and the humanity out of political debate but did not lesson its acrimony. Indeed the fictitious assumption of detachment and of cold analysis adds strength to the passions which lurk behind it. It was usual to disguise strong feelings by pretending to see the other side of an argument and show some sympathy for it. This is characteristic of the Old Oligarch, who was anti-democratic, anti-imperialist and implicitly anti-Periclean, though Pericles was probably dead when he wrote. He does not pretend that he is not all these things, but he adopts a pose of understanding his opponents and granting them certain abilities. His argument is that, if we believe in democratic control, as he himself most assuredly does not, we must admit that the Athenian democracy is consistent in its actions. This realistic, professionally detached spirit reflects the Greek habit of working out an appropriate technique for any activity. The great thing was to conduct controversy with an air of not being deceived and a proclaimed refusal to shirk the truth. Politics might in some cases be an art but its conduct called for rules defined and clarified. Each particular action must be explained on a general basis. This meant that for the moment other considerations were laid aside. So long as the politician was doing his own special business, he must not let his mind stray into other spheres. Nor was there any doubt what his special business was; it was to get his way for his country or his party or himself. Our pamphleteer admires the Athenian democrats while he disapproves of them. He disapproves of them because they are plebeian and therefore base; he admires them because they are good at their job and know how to get what they want. His admiration is that of one professional for another, even if they are rivals and competitors. This separation of politics from other interests and this concentration on politics for its own sake are typical of the fifth century. It did not make politics a game but made it more exclusive and more savage, since these qualities were needed for success. If all that mattered was to outwit opponents and get one's own way, there was no need to introduce other considerations such as men would observe in personal relations. Politics had its own place and developed according to the claims of power.

This technique gave a special character to political discussions. Alike in tragedy and in history, in Euripides and in Thucydides, arguments on large issues are put forward in a curiously abstract way. Powerful emotions lurk in the background but do not often break through. The actual debate moves through a series of fine points and is not above splitting hairs. This comes from the desire to find the essence of a matter. If calculation led to pure mathematics, practical politics led to abstract considerations of advantage and disadvantage. Conducted in this manner, political arguments neglect other issues and concentrate on expediency. Something of the kind is to be found in most circles whose task is to conduct policies for a country, and it is natural to subordinate other considerations to the attainment of success. But the Athenian manner has a special character, to which more than one factor has contributed. First, politics has the appearance of an applied science. It has rules which insure success; it demands and deserves precise analysis; it treats human feelings in an apparently inhuman way. Secondly, such discussions reflect the manner of argument which came into fashion in the middle of the fifth century and owed much to the law courts with their manufactured psychology and their arguments from probability. Thirdly, though emotional and ethical considerations are sometimes admitted, they are of a limited kind and used mainly for expedient ends. It is thus quite common for a maltreated city to cite its nobility in the past and to hope for better treatment because of it, but this is not a moral or an emotional argument. It means simply that a city which was reliable in the past is likely to be reliable in the present, or even that nothing is to be gained by making an enemy of a harmless neutral. For these reasons discussions on politics have an almost professional character, and seem to be divorced from much that must have carried weight with the ordinary Athenian. But behind this parade of calculation is the solid foundation of conviction which dictates the ends for which these means are employed. The ends are power and glory, and though Athens made a special cult of these, she was not alone in doing so.

All this was a product of Periclean Athens. We have only to set a passage of political argument from Thucydides beside one from Herodotus to see how complicated and loaded it is in comparison with the Ionian lucidity. It owed something to the law courts, which, after they had been made democratic, gave fine openings to men who liked dispute and speechmaking and developed both in the art of rhetoric. Our earliest examples are three actual speeches and three sets of model speeches by the professional advocate Antiphon, who was greatly admired by Thucydides for his intelligence and especially for the speech which, as quite an old man, he made in defence of his life in 411. In him the new manner is at work. He uses *a priori* arguments and provides examples of speeches on both sides of a case. Without much effort to coin striking phrases he has considerable attack and drive, and carefully does not talk above the heads of the jurors but tries to conciliate them. He is a good example of Attic legalism at work, and we can see what it aims at. Even the worst case can be given a plausible air if the right arguments are found for it, and this was the aim of Attic forensic oratory. The art practised in the law courts was equally useful in the Assembly, where appeals to the emotions reinforced dry exposition, and the simplicity and strength of an older generation changed into a more complex and more devious art. Pericles' own manner owed something to this. He was as capable of speaking in a law court as in the Assembly. The legal outlook emerges in his public speeches, especially when he tends to discuss a national issue with juristic agility. Though his emotional appeals reach far beyond any personal controversy, they are held in control by the grave language and the desire to give point to his formulations. If sometimes he may seem to be making too much ado about nothing, that is all part of the technique. The orators of the time were upbraided for being too clever, but they were proud of it. This too, like their manner of expression, arose partly from the new importance of the law courts, but it was also influenced by a phenomenon special to the time.

The emergence of rhetoric and the popular passion for it gave a new direction to intellectual activities. Its aim was not to find the truth but to win a case by persuading the jury or the populace that such and such a cause was what they liked. This received a new, strong impetus from the Sophists, a class of men who acted as public educators in return for fees. The word is of Greek origin but has certain associations in English which it does not quite have in Greek. At first it could be applied to any thinker or scientist, as Herodotus applies it to the great musician and mathematician Pythagoras. The Sophists taught all manner of subjects, and among them were serious mathematicians, like Hippias of Elis, who discovered the curve called *quadratrix*. But what they had in common was that most of their teaching was intended to be useful, to produce practical results, and was therefore of much relevance to politics. In this they differed from the great thinkers of the sixth century, who had sought truth for its own sake and made astonishing discoveries in physics and mathematics. The usefulness admired by the Sophists was not practical in the sense that it produced engineers or skilled workmen. What they claimed to teach was *aretê*, or the full life, in which a man's natural gifts were properly realized. This all too easily became a study of worldly success. This the Sophists offered, and it coincided nicely with the new taste for rhetoric. Two of the most famous Sophists, Protagoras of Abdera and Gorgias of Leontini, were teachers of politics and of rhetoric. Protagoras was the older and more serious of the two and made a great mark on his generation. It was this care for social activity that changed the intellectual atmosphere of Athens. Science was not widely exploited; much more effort was given to politics. To entertain and support Sophists was socially fashionable, and though some were charlatans, others were men of original talent, who had something to say about the society which had sprung into existence at Athens.

Such inquirers could not neglect the gods, and some were sceptical about them. This was neither new nor very revolutionary. In the late sixth century Xenophanes of Colophon had denounced the old stories of divine misbehaviour and settled for a single divine being, solid and spherical. In the generation of the first Sophists Pindar, who was an Olympian mystic, refused to accept some stories of the gods, notably that Demeter ate the shoulder of the boy Pelops when his father served him up as a dish for the gods, or that Heracles fought against Apollo, Poseidon, and Hades. Greek religion, which had no organized priesthood and no sacred books, could afford to dispense with dogma, and, like most polytheistic religions, was by nature tolerant. But this easy attitude on details was not the same as denying the existence of the gods. It is true that Protagoras and Anaxagoras did not quite do this, but they came near to it. Protagoras was at least some sort of agnostic:

With regard to the gods I cannot feel that they are or that they are not, nor what they are like in figure; for there are many things that hinder sure knowledge, the obscurity of the subject and the shortness of human life.[4]

Anaxagoras, by contrast, is a reforming deist, who in giving the leading part to Mind regards it as divine and says nothing, so far as we know, about gods. Such theories do not seem to have attracted organized bodies of supporters, but they helped to shake the rather battered fabric of Olympian belief. Cults and ceremonies kept the gods in people's minds, and anyone who cared for them could interpret them as he pleased. But while Pericles made use of them to strengthen that love of country which was his private and public devotion, others sought for other solutions. There were varieties of modernism, among which it was possible to treat the gods as powers of nature or the human mind. Euripides presents several versions of reformed or remodelled religion at work, while he himself may have oscillated from one novelty to another, to come to the conclusion that the gods indeed existed but were beyond good and evil, cruel and unpredictable, and worthy of awe and fear. Once the old fabric began to dissolve, it was not easy to find something new and coherent to take its place.

It was of course theoretically possible to jettison the whole Olympian system and to put in its place something shaped in accord with the latest discoveries of science or philosophy. This was what Anaxagoras did. He postulated Mind as a supreme force which set everything in motion and kept it moving. The process is continually at work and the sphere in which Mind operates is always growing. At the same time when Mind has started something, that something is able to continue on its own strength. This is a scientific system which has little appeal for the religious spirit, and though Anaxagoras may have identified Mind with God, he could not persuade Socrates that the identification was valid. Indeed his chief interests were scientific, and his personal religion lay in the search for truth. This was too exacting for the average Athenian, and we may doubt whether it had much vogue. Yet Anaxagoras was an intimate friend of Pericles and it is hard to think that there was no intellectual interchange between the two. No doubt Anaxagoras' notion of Mind was too abstract for Pericles, but possibly the bold idea that it is forever extending its realm appealed to the statesman who saw Athens doing much the same thing in the actual world. The sense of an inborn force at work would suit his ideal of Athens as a divinely inspired power. But in general Pericles was not much interested in speculations of this kind, and preferred those which concerned immediate affairs or threw a glorifying light on Athens. Nor would such ideas appeal to the serious critics of Athenian civilization. In reducing the gods to Mind Anaxagoras seems to have left no place for morality or for those distinctions between good and evil which troubled restless Athenian curiosity. Religion might show cracks, but its place could not be taken by a purely abstract philosophy, which tried to explain everything in terms of physics and had little appeal for the ordinary man.

In this confusion the Sophists found their opportunity, and the better among them sought to build up a new scheme of things from a fresh start. Contemporary thought provided them with a useful distinction which they could accept and elucidate and apply to their problems. This distinction was between *physis*, nature, and *nomos*, custom or law. The first was not so much the whole physical world as the forces of growth and action in it; the second was made by man and ranged from strict legal enactments enforced by penalties to anything that could be called custom or habit or convention. Older thinkers thought that nature embodied an immanent law which lay behind all human laws, but this did not suit a generation which was busy changing society by changing its laws. It was clear that law and nature were not the same. The distinction was made by the Athenian philosopher, Archelaus, who is said to have taught Socrates. His theory was that law and morals were not a primal gift of nature to man but were acquired by him through the passage of time; that though men had at first much in common with the beasts, they began to show their differences when they set up their own rulers and developed laws, arts, and cities. For him this was the result not simply of possessing intelligence but of possessing more intelligence than the animals, who are incapable of rising to the same level. In this we can see some resemblance to Anaxagoras' view of Mind and its place in the scheme of things but, whereas Anaxagoras thinks that Mind is continually extending its control, Archelaus seems to treat its victories as already won and not a source of constant change. Both however give a primary place to Mind in the advance of mankind, and Archelaus may have been the first to propose that man differs from the beasts by his greater share of it. Law follows because it is needed to help progress. This theory adds dignity and authority to law and custom and has much in common with the various notions of human development propounded by Aeschylus and Sophocles. It was perhaps the standard view of a subject which was to become highly controversial and lead to some formidable conclusions.

The gap, so revealed, between nature and law grew progressively wider and more difficult to cross. Protagoras saw the dangers of allowing nature to be the final arbiter in all matters of conduct, especially in a society which had never been fully convinced that the gods cared about right and wrong, and was now developing new doubts about them. He therefore laid a powerful stress on law and claimed that goodness was taught by the laws of the state and by public opinion, and that such teaching begins with childhood and shapes a man's character. The more sceptical Protagoras became about the gods, the more firmly he clung to his belief in law. It was his buttress against nihilistic scepticism and his hope for the growth of civilized societies. This was one solution of a difficult problem, and it had some appeal for Pericles, who knew how indispensable laws were for the preservation of Athens. What Protagoras did not answer was the question of what authority the laws had: if they could be evaded, was there any reason why they should not be?

At the same time the distinction between nature and law might be pressed to a very different conclusion. Nature had been there from the beginning, and if anything was divine, surely nature was. It followed that man could fulfil himself by falling in with her dictates which were powerfully at work in his own appetites, and by treating laws and customs, which were merely his own creation, very much as he pleased without too much respect. If Protagoras preferred law to nature, that was his lookout, but it was perfectly open to others to prefer nature to law and to claim it as their justification when they found laws inhibiting them from getting what they wanted. This antinomian spirit was compatible with the Athenian quest for empire, which was a strong response to natural ambitions for power. It had too other appeals for Athens. The new importance of the law courts and the uncertainty about what judgements would be given made men sceptical about the existence of ideal justice. The free development of individual citizens had as an obverse to its many virtues the weakness that it encouraged less worthy men to think themselves important and entitled to have their own way. This is common at any time, but it grew stronger as the vetoes and taboos of the Olympian religion grew weaker. In the old days some men would refrain from certain acts of violence or breaches of faith simply because they feared the gods; now that the gods were becoming dimmer, arrogant questions were asked about how much was permissible.

If nature was accepted as having a right to assert herself through men and their actions, it was largely a question of deciding what was in accordance with her will, what was truly natural and therefore right. The question could be posed for public and international affairs and particularly for the relations between one city and another. War illustrated the case that could be made for nature against law. Not everyone would agree with Heraclitus of Ephesus (flor. 500) in saying that 'War is the father of all things and the king of all things; some it shows to be gods, some to be men; some it makes slaves, and some free.'[5] This is a fair enough account of war as nature practises it, but it does not necessarily follow that this is how men should behave. But this was what the new emphasis on nature tended or tried to do. If war was always at work in nature, why in human society was it not natural for the weak to be ruled by the strong? This idea was common in the fifth century and accepted both by Pericles and by his opponents. For Pericles nature might be much the same as Anaxagoras' Mind, a living and life-giving principle, but for other, less civilized people nature stood for their own rougher appetites and self-assertive ambitions. As such she could easily be put in the place of the gods and given the authority which had recently been theirs. Some fourteen years after the death of Pericles this notion had hardened and taken a crueller shape. When the Melians tried to persuade the Athenians that they trusted the gods to protect them from the wicked threats of the Athenians, the latter are said to have answered:

Our aims and our actions are perfectly consistent with the beliefs men hold about the gods and with the principles which govern their own conduct. Our opinion of the gods and our knowledge of men lead us to conclude that it is a general and necessary law of nature to rule wherever one can.[6]

This is totally cynical but has its own cruel logic. The Athenians pretend to follow the gods and argue that divine behaviour is natural and that it is absurd to dispute it. This attitude informed Athenian imperialism in its later years and must have been at work in Periclean times, though not with Pericles himself, who expressed related ideas in a less brutal way.

In recounting the events that led to the outbreak of war in 431 Thucydides reports a speech made at Sparta by anonymous Athenian envoys who are there for some other purpose but rise to the occasion and speak for Athens. They say quite firmly that they will not relinquish their power and add:

It has always been a rule that the weak should be subject to the strong; and besides, we consider that we are worthy of our power. Up till the present moment you, too, used to think that we were; but now, after calculating your own interest, you are beginning to talk in terms of right and wrong. Considerations of this kind have never yet turned people aside from the opportunities of aggrandizement offered by superior strength. Those who really deserve praise are the people who, while human enough to enjoy power, nevertheless pay more attention to Justice than they are compelled to do by their situation.[7]

This may be regarded as the more or less official Periclean view just before the Peloponnesian War. It accepts the 'natural' view of power but tempers it with certain humane considerations, though at the same time it insists on the irrelevance or hypocrisy of moral qualms. It may be both natural and right to conquer other cities, but there are proper ways of doing this which temper nature with law. Natural zest is itself admirable and leads to adventurous actions, but it gains by some admixture of man-made rules and limitations. This was what the fifth century at its zenith was prepared to accept, and it was not until nature was exalted at the expense of law that an ugly crack began to show in the moral structure of habit and thought. If nature was as important as she was said to be, why should she not dictate behaviour and encourage men to follow their instincts, no matter how unsocial?

This attitude might be thought appropriate enough for international relations in which the desire for power was the guiding spirit but inappropriate for personal relations. Such seems to have been the position of the historian Thucydides, who expected Athens to be ruthless in her treatment of other cities but to maintain high ethical standards at home. This has always been a common position, and the contradictions in it are too familiar to call for notice. But in Athens the case for nature intruded into private affairs and much troubled Plato in the next century when he looked back on the failure of Periclean Athens and tried to find its cause. As a young man he saw this 'natural' spirit at work but later, as he sought to imagine an ideal Athens with none of its old faults, he regarded the exaltation of nature at the expense of law as the main perversion of the time. He attributes it to the Sophist Thrasymachus of Chalcedon, who was busy in Athens before the death of Pericles. Thrasymachus advanced the notion that 'justice is the interest of the stronger'[8] and regarded it as simply a matter of success, with no implication that justice should be desired for its own sake. The idea appealed to clever young men, and one, Callicles, portrayed by Plato and surely taken straight from life, held that might, not right, is what really matters. He is willing to deceive the populace in his own interests and regards it as a proper and natural thing to do. He probably belongs to a later generation than Thrasymachus, and his amorality has a certain dash and high spirits. He is bored by old-fashioned conventions and admires those who circumvent them. This version of the view that might is right owed its popularity to the Sophists, who saw that it appealed to the sons of rich families not wholly at home with the democracy and willing to try other forms of government in which they would be more handsomely treated. It was basically a transference from the theory of public affairs, as it was now known in the Athenian empire, to private life, and it was bound to cause havoc. The paradox is that it did not cause more. But it is nonetheless a symptom of change in Periclean Athens, and something that Pericles himself could not fully control and for which he was partly responsible. If power made the city glorious, why should it not do the same for the individual citizen?

The undermining of established values and the pursuit of nature at the expense of law was laid to the discredit of the Sophists. The best of them, like Protagoras, were well aware of the dangers and did their best to counteract them, but they too were thought to be partly responsible, not because they advocated the claims of nature but because they had ruined the assurance of knowledge by their scepticism. Protagoras went as far as he could when he said that 'Man is the measure of all things'[9] and substituted a precarious solipsism for an objective view of reality, and Gorgias, who was a much less serious thinker, denied any certainty at all in our thought. Once the foundations of knowledge had been sapped, it was natural to follow those fiercer and less rational impulses which had been kept theoretically in control. Such forces are more persuasive than arguments, and the pupils of the Sophists could claim that the passions have their reasons which they cannot explain. It was therefore legitimate to blame the Sophists, as in the fourth century Plato did, for insisting on the opposition between nature and law and thereby abolishing the distinction between right and wrong. Of this he says in the *Laws*:

In the first place, my dear friend, these people would say that the gods exist not by nature but by art, and that there are different gods in different places, according to the conventions of the legislators; and that the honourable is one thing by nature and another thing by law, and that the principles of justice have no existence at all in nature, but that mankind are always disputing about them and altering them; and that the alterations which are made by art and by law have no basis in nature, but are of authority for the moment and at the time at which they are made.[10]

This is a *post mortem* verdict. When Plato passed it upon 'these people', who are the Sophists, they had already ceased to count, and the brevity of their heyday is an indication that they seemed to be more influential than they were. There were cracks and holes in the old system of beliefs, and the Sophists for a time drew notice to them, but, though they answered some needs in the existing structure of thought, they did not answer every need, and were in some respects countered by other tendencies which appealed to the Athenians. Much of the more controversial side of the Sophistic movement comes from the last quarter of the fifth century when Pericles was dead and the long strain of war corrupted standards which were difficult to maintain in frustration and failure. The Sophists show that something was wrong, but this was not the whole picture.

The most powerful counterattack on the scepticism of the Sophists was the authoritative assertion of the importance of truth and its pursuit. Anaxagoras was said to have set up an altar to it, and it is quite likely that he did, for the Greeks tended to exalt to divinity what we might think to be mere abstractions, but which for them evoked awe and a profound devotion. The search for truth was inherited from the Ionian scientists and philosophers, and Athens was the chief place for the exchange of ideas on their subjects. Euripides, always sensitive to new notions, caught their appeal when he wrote:

> Happy is he who has knowledge
> That comes from inquiry. No evil he stirs
> For his townsmen, nor gives himself
> To unjust doings,
> But surveys the unageing order
> Of deathless nature, of what it is made,
> And whence and how.
> In men of this kind the study
> Of base acts never finds a home.[11]

This suggests that Euripides was by no means content with his normal way of life but caught the infection of learning and discovery and attributed unexpected virtues to it. For him knowledge is, after all, a social activity, which adds something much needed to society. What he praises is not contemplation but inquiry, which takes him out of his transitory activities to the deathless order of nature. This is characteristic of the Greeks. They were always seeking for an unchanging order behind phenomena and found it most satisfyingly in mathematics; they sought it not as an escape but as a fulfilment, and when they found it, they felt more at home in the world. In spite of all the restless activities of Periclean Athens it had time to extend itself in this direction also and to add something positive to its negative findings.

The special significance which some of the Sophists gave to nature as an uncontrolled force met with considerable opposition, not merely from adherents of the old religion but from thoughtful poets who were impressed by the upward advance of man and sought to explain it not by actual history but by some illuminating myth. One class of explanations insisted that, after being given a tremendous start, man made his own way. In the *Prometheus Bound* Aeschylus makes Prometheus the benefactor of mankind when he teaches it the essential needs of life, such as building houses, planting crops and fruits, writing, taming animals, driving chariots, and sailing ships. He does not suggest that all this happened at once, but Prometheus gets the credit. In a surviving fragment of the *Nauplius* of Sophocles the credit goes to Palamedes. He is made responsible for the invention of weights, numbers and measures, military tactics and devices, and the meaning of the stars. Euripides follows precedent when in his *Suppliant Women* he makes Theseus speak of someone, possibly Palamedes, who taught men how to speak, cultivate the earth, protect themselves against the weather, and sail on the sea. In each case the pattern is the same and may go back to a common source. This provided a myth through which more serious persons could speculate how man had moved from the state of the beasts to his present state. A medical author says quietly that man's present ways of living have been found by him 'over a long time', and this was what the first scientists thought. Xenophanes had already said: 'The gods have not revealed everything to men from the beginning, but men by searching out find out better in time.'[12] This was the view of educated men in Athens. They had enough understanding of history to see that human progress could not have come otherwise. The inspired single benefactor, who belongs to myth, gives place to the upward struggle by mankind to better itself, and the struggle is against a brutal disorder.

It is here that Protagoras made his most powerful impact. He saw that the current myth of human progress did not mention law and morality. His own myth made good this lack. In their first stage men are helped by gods to the elementary knowledge needed for survival. Then, as they mature and find themselves faced by discord and violence, the gods intervene and save them. Zeus sends Hermes to earth with instructions: 'Further, make a law by my order, that he who has no part in reverence and justice shall be put to death, for he is a plague to the state.'[13] This doctrine was the answer to those who claimed to live according to nature, and it is based on the assumption, which Protagoras must have found difficult to make, that in some ways the gods look after men. A like assumption lies behind a famous choral song of Sophocles. In his *Antigone* the Chorus sings of the surprising nature of man, who crosses the sea and ploughs the earth, tames animals and fends off disease. This is the normal account at the time, the natural history of man. But Sophocles goes further and agrees with Protagoras in seeing that this could not have happened if man were not a social animal who has learned to protect himself with law :

> With cunning beyond belief,
> In subtle inventions of art,
> He goes his way now to evil, now to good
> When he keeps the laws of the land
> And the gods' rule which he has sworn to uphold,
> High in his city. No city has he
> Who in rash effrontery
> Makes wrong-doing his fellow.[14]

This is the opposite view of that of the antinomian Sophists. What helps man in his progress is the rule of law, and it is this that makes and keeps a city great. The alternative preached by some Sophists means in the end the destruction of city life. Sophocles wrote this about 441, when Athens was at the height of her power, and it is the final answer to those who advocate the survival of the fittest. What saves a city and makes her great is not a mere exhibition of might but a structure of law and order.

Periclean Athens had defences against the undermining theories of the Sophists, and though some of these were specifically Periclean, others were simply Athenian, the heritage from a tradition of public service and self-respect. The new thought was no doubt exciting but it was of rather a low grade, and did not really matter until the political fabric of Athens was damaged by unforeseen forces which facilitated discontent and unqualified ambition. This happened soon after the outbreak of war in 431. The historian Thucydides describes the effect of the plague which devastated Athens in 430 and again in 427 and caused the death of Pericles. Thucydides insists that it undermined both religion and morality, since people, knowing that death was in the offing, threw aside restraint and lived for pleasure:

> No fear of god or law of man had a restraining influence. As for the gods, it seemed to be the same thing whether one worshipped them or not, when one saw the good and the bad dying indiscriminately. As for offences against human law, no one expected to live long enough to be brought to trial and punished.[15]

It is curious that Thucydides, who elsewhere shows almost no interest in religion, should here regard loss of belief as a grave fault, but the chances are that, though he was a sceptic, he thought religious belief necessary to restrain the conduct of men. This is a common enough notion and suits his realistic politics. That the appalling catastrophe of the plague meant a growth of lawlessness is natural enough, but it may have been in part due to a lack of men to enforce the law. People who normally avoided crime for fear of punishment were less scrupulous when they saw that many crimes passed unpunished. This is not a collapse of old values but the exploitation of an anarchic situation. Naturally in the middle of a war such a situation had dangerous possibilities, but in itself it reflects little discredit on the Athenians, and we may suspect that Thucydides, writing from after-knowledge, has exaggerated its effects, though not its actual horrors at the time. At least Athens survived and continued to fight with almost unabated energy, and democratic processes survived with her.

The Sophists cannot be blamed for the demoralization brought by the plague. But Thucydides analyses and describes another, more terrifying case of demoralization, for which an external cause like the plague cannot be made responsible. In 426 civil war broke out in Corcyra and lasted for at least two years, and Thucydides insists that this was by no means the only place where such things happened and that, though this was the first case, other cases followed elsewhere. He describes the situation with an astonishing insight, and what he says of Corcyra is familiar from Europe in our own time. War brutalizes those who are caught in it:

> War is a stern teacher; in depriving them of the power of easily satisfying their daily wants, it brings most people's minds down to the level of their actual circumstances.[16]

He analyses the growth of violence and dishonesty, especially the process by which the vocabulary of decent actions is perverted to suit the immediate interests of a gang:

What used to be described as a thoughtless act of aggression was now regarded as the courage one would expect to find in a party-member; to think of the future and wait was merely another way of saying one was a coward; any idea of moderation was just an attempt to disguise one's unmanly character; ability to understand a question from all sides meant that one was totally unfitted for action.[17]

Every word in this rings true, and its relevance at least to Corcyra is confirmed by the discord there which prevented her from taking a part in Hellenic politics consonant with her wealth and population. Pericles had encouraged the democratic party in Corcyra, and the aristocratic party tried to seize power from them. The result was appalling atrocities committed by both parties—fathers killed by their sons, men dragged from temples or butchered on altars, walled up in the temple of Dionysus and left there to die. Both sides stuck at nothing, and though in the end the democrats got the better of it, it brought them little advantage. This is what happens in war, and nothing is gained by minimizing its horrors, but they were not the fault of the Sophists. A deeper cause was the struggle between rich and poor in most Greek cities, and shortages and suffering brought this savagely to the surface.

The fifth century in Athens was a time of intellectual ferment, change, and achievement. The Sophists contributed to the ferment and did much for such new branches of knowledge as political theory, rhetoric, and logic but did not produce a central philosophy. Aristophanes saw their seamy side and attacked it in his not entirely false caricature of Socrates, and his debate between Right and Wrong in the *Clouds*. In the next century Plato assailed them because he thought they had undermined knowledge and morality. He saw their good points and was more strongly attracted to them than he admitted even to himself. He suggested antidotes to their errors, but we may doubt whether the Sophists were in fact as influential as he thought. The decay which followed the fall of Athens in 404 was due to defeat and to the exhaustion which preceded it. If the Sophists had any role in this, it was rather as victims than instigators.

The great figures of the fifth century are as remarkable for their truthfulness as for their intellectual grasp and creative vigour, and they undeniably exerted a large influence over their countrymen. They might do this through intellectual analysis, as Thucydides and Socrates did; or they might use the resources of a noble art, as the tragedians and sculptors did. But in either case what counts is the powerful effort to grasp reality as it is, not to shrink from its complexities or be content with easy answers. Of course only the greatest rise to this level, but even inferior creatures like the Old Oligarch tried in their way to see the facts as they were. This respect paid to truth was largely the result of Ionian thought in science and philosophy. If it superseded some of the respect for the gods, it was not any less exalted or serious or responsible.

10

THE INCONCLUSIVE WAR

FROM 446–445 to 431 Athens was at peace with the Peloponnesians. She had her own problems, notably the revolts of Byzantium and Samos in 440–439, which were troublesome to subdue but did not bring any serious setback to her prosperity. These were her paramount years in the arts of peace. The Parthenon was begun in 447, and the gold and ivory statue of Athene by Phidias was set up in 438. This was the age of Sophocles' *Antigone* and Euripides' *Medea*; about 445 Herodotus was in Athens reciting portions of his History; the Old Comedy, personified in Cratinus, spat flame and fury and ribaldry at all manner of men. Athens had not neglected the arts even during war, but in peace she found the full range of her many-sided genius and was powerfully set to become the school of Hellas. Her multifarious gifts fell into a pattern in which each complemented and illuminated the others. She seemed likely to continue this creative career for many years, and to some degree did so. That she did not do even more was the fault of Hellenic politics. Political strains and rivalries forbade any lasting security, and once again war devoured energies which might have enhanced the living scene.

The Peace between Athens and Sparta in 446–445 solved no problems but left both sides suspicious and resentful. Athens, who in 458 had entered war with prospects of establishing an ascendancy over Greece, had failed to do so. The land empire had been lost; hopes for a new base of power in Egypt had been annihilated; Athens had lost the strategic point of Megara, and Pericles himself must have seen that Athens could not maintain an empire on land as well as on sea. The division of Greece into two camps, Athenian and Spartan, was hardly even a compromise; it was an uneasy acceptance of a situation with little prospect of lasting peace. Both sides might feel that if Greece were to realize all her potentialities, she must be somehow united; otherwise her dispersed energies would never find the fulfilment of which they were capable. Naturally each side thought that it alone could provide the right kind of union. In these circumstances peace was never secure, and though most Greeks might accept this as inherent in the order of things, it was a disagreeable handicap to enterprise and invention. The prospect was darker because the division of Greece into two large alliances meant that, when war came, it would not be a local affair but would before long involve almost all Greek states. The situation in Greece at this time was not unlike that in Europe in 1914. Alliances were so carefully woven that a single pair of combatants might drag a number of others after them into war, although its issues might mean very little to them.

The central, unsolved problem was the balance of power. Must Greece always be divided between two main groups? Or could either Sparta or Athens defeat the other and control the whole country? No possibility was completely convincing. The existing balance could of course be maintained, but this was almost an argument of despair, desired by neither side, since Sparta was frightened of what effect Athenian propaganda and example might have on Helots and Messenians, and Athens regarded Sparta as the denial of all that her own free society stood for. To remain as at present meant that each side acquiesced in the perpetuation of a political system which it hated. Yet though this solution had no appeal for the more sincere spirits in either camp, it was not inconceivable. Even Pericles seems for a time to have dallied with a modified version of it. When after the loss of Boeotia in 447 he realized that Athens could not be a land power and must make some sort of accommodation with Sparta, he decided that the Greek cities should act together more closely, and for this there was the precedent of cooperation against Persia. This seems to have been already in his mind when about 449 he introduced a bill in the Assembly by which all Greeks in Europe and Asia were to be invited to send deputies to a council at Athens. The first objective would be to discuss the restoration of the shrines and temples burned by the Persians and the fulfilment of vows about sacrifices. But a second objective was to discuss the freedom of the seas in the sense of the right to sail anywhere and the duty to keep peace. The object of all this was to find some means by which the Greek cities might restore their broken unity and mark their kinship with one another not merely in religion but in politics. Athenian envoys were sent to the different cities with the purpose of deliberating 'for the peace and common welfare of Hellas'.[1]

We do not know what impelled Pericles to take this unexpected action, or how seriously he treated it. He may of course have decided that since he could not defeat Sparta in war, he must come to terms with her in some coalition. This looks suspiciously like a return to the policy of Cimon, but Pericles may have thought that such a coalition could be controlled by Athens. If it was to keep the freedom of the seas, no power but Athens had the ships to do so. Yet it is hard to believe that Pericles would acquiesce in so defeatist a policy when his two main assets were not only intact but increasing – a large navy and a large balance from the tribute. Each year strengthened his position, and if he treated this new policy seriously, it was surely as a stopgap until he was ready to take the offensive. The whole thing failed. The smaller cities outside the two alliances were unwilling to agree because Sparta was hostile, and Sparta was hostile because she feared that a diplomatic success on such a scale for Athens could only increase her power. She may also, with some reason, have suspected that Pericles was playing from weakness, that the recent reverses suffered by Athens had made him more ready to compromise, and that now was not the time to give in to him. Pericles must have foreseen this and known that, though his proposals had failed, he could use his failure to show how unreasonable Sparta was and how unwilling to enter into any agreement for the general good of Greece.

This failure, if failure it really was, stiffened Pericles in his conviction that Athens could not rule the whole of Greece by cooperating with Sparta but must instead consolidate her existing empire and extend it where she could. Such considerations lay behind his manipulation of the Thurii project in 443 and the foundation of Amphipolis on the Tracian seaboard in 436. About this time he took a large naval expedition to the Black Sea, established friendly relations with Greek settlements on its coast and gave an impressive display of naval power to show that Athens was fully capable of keeping guard over the corn supply from the north. He seems in general to have cast his eyes on the fringes of the familiar Greek world to the north and the west. So far as we can infer a policy from his actions, he was prepared to accept, anyhow for the present, Sparta as dominating a large part of the mainland, but he was not prepared to make concessions or to be bullied by her. At the same time he looked around for room for expansion and perhaps thought that if Athens added sufficiently to her strength, she might in the end overwhelm Sparta and her allies. This policy lacked glamour and was no more than a second best. Pericles had digested the lessons of the recent war against Sparta. At its start he may have felt that Athens might actually win; at the end he knew that she had not won and might never do so. He then tried conciliation, but found that also useless. The only policy left was to keep Athens strong and to look out for trouble so that she could defend herself advantageously when it came. Athens may have lost her first fine confidence but she remained resolute and formidable.

The deadlock which arose from the even balance of Athens and Sparta meant that in the long run Greece was never sufficiently united to become a world power except for a few years under Alexander, and Alexander, in spite of his Hellenic aspirations and his powerful genius, was not an embodiment of Periclean ideals. Greece, we feel, could surely have been united under Athens as Italy was under Rome; then indeed the destinies of the Mediterranean world would have been different. The various peoples of Italy whom Rome brought into her dominion were linguistically and culturally far more unlike each other than were the different city-states of Greece, all of whom spoke a common language and shared common traditions. No doubt geography made the unification of Greece more difficult than that of Italy, where mountain ranges were less obstructive, but the real cause of failure was the insoluble antithesis of Sparta and Athens at the time when Athens was in her heyday and ready to assume new burdens. The Greeks were aware of a need for unity and in the next century found an eloquent spokesman for it in Isocrates (436–338), who urged them to settle their quarrels and join in a common campaign against Persia. When he made his plea, it was too late, for Philip of Macedon was preparing to impose upon Greece the unity it refused to impose upon itself. Union under Athens remained a dream. Her differences from the Peloponnesian states were too great to allow any working agreement with them, and any division of power would have been a perpetual source of quarrels. Not all the other states would have been equally recalcitrant. Even Corinth had moments, inspired by prudence or realism, when she relaxed her hatred for Athens, though she had good enough reason for it, since Athens was always encroaching on her commercial outposts. Nor was Athens likely to prove an easy or reasonable partner. She insisted that she control her present allies, and her behaviour was often arrogant and harsh. Any new allies might expect to be treated in the same way. Even if she had been able to conquer her enemies, it is hard to see how she could have kept them in subjection without expending most of her manhood and resources in doing so, and then unity would have been bought at too high a price.

The peace between the two wars took the form of a cold war, in which each side endeavoured to annoy, frustrate, and humiliate the other. Such conflicts often end in open violence because they make the prospect of it so familiar that everyone takes it for granted and is almost relieved when it comes. Pericles wished to maintain an armed neutrality with Sparta, to leave her alone in her own sphere of influence, to confine Athenian expansion to regions outside it. Sparta could complain that he was interfering with her, but he was not prepared to make concessions to Spartan arrogance or the jealous fears of her allies. It was from the latter of these that the crash eventually came, and it came appropriately in outlying areas of the Greek world, in the north-west and the north-east. In both Corinth was deeply involved as the injured and complaining party, and this was right, for alone of Sparta's allies she had a powerful fleet which she used to protect her trade in the west with Sicily and southern Italy.

The trouble began with obscure events in an obscure corner of the Greek world. Epidamnus, on the coast of what is now Albania, was a colony of Corcyra, which was itself a colony of Corinth. Epidamnus was in trouble with some exiled aristocrats, and appealed to Corcyra for help. Corcyra refused, and Epidamnus appealed to Corinth, who sent ships. This meant that Corcyra and Corinth were soon at war; Corcyra defeated Corinth at sea, and regained Epidamnus. Corcyra, not Corinth, was now in command of the Ionian Sea. The conflict was a family affair, involving three generations of cities, and so far nobody else had entered it. Corcyra was for the moment in the ascendant, and the humiliation of Corinth was a blow to the Spartan League of which she was a leading member. The trouble grew when it was clear that Athens was not uninterested. This part of the world was far from the centre of Greek politics, and Athens, seeing that it lay on the way to the west, had been advancing her connections there. When Corinth prepared for vengeance by building new ships, Corcyra took fright. She had no allies and was likely to be defeated by a fully armed Corinth. Her solution was to ask Athens for an alliance. Envoys from both Corcyra and Corinth came to Athens and put their cases to the Assembly. The historian Thucydides, who was probably present, describes in his own words what was said. The Corcyreans, who speak first, assume that war between Athens and the Peloponnesians is going to come soon, for the Spartans are afraid of the Athenians and listen to the bellicose promptings of the Corinthians. It is in the interest of both Corcyra and Athens to forestall attack. In this light the alliance looks attractive. Corcyra lies on the way to the west; if the Corinthians get hold of the Corcyrean fleet, Athens will be faced by a far larger navy. Anyone at Athens who was concerned for the jealous fears of Corinth and Sparta would see the Corcyrean offer as an unforeseen blessing at a dark moment.

The Corinthian answer to the Corcyreans is inevitably rather ineffective. They appeal to past services rendered to Athens, but these were outweighed by disservices. More realistically, the Corinthians point out that by allying herself with Corcyra Athens will in effect violate the Thirty Years' Peace with Sparta. The result was that Athens accepted the alliance but confined it to defensive purposes; Athens would help Corcyra if the latter was threatened. In this we may see the restraining hand of Pericles, who did not wish to hurry into war with Sparta but knew that Sparta might force war on him, and in that case he must be ready for it. The Corcyrean navy looked a promising asset against a Peloponnesian coalition in which Corinth was a leading member. Ten ships were sent as a token force to Corcyra with orders not to fight unless Corcyra was attacked. A conflict soon followed, and Athens sent more ships. The battle of Sybota, fought in 433, two years before war fully broke out, showed how quick Athens was to put her decisions into effect and how powerful even a small squadron of Athenian ships could be; for it frightened the Corinthians into retreat home.

At almost the same time as this crisis in the north-west, Athens and Corinth came into conflict also in the north-east, in the Chalcidic peninsula. The city of Potidaea lay in an admirably strategic position. It straddled the very narrow waist of the westernmost prong and prospered in its possession of fertile land. It was a Corinthian foundation and received annual magistrates from Corinth, which was more than Corcyra did. But it was also a tribute-paying ally of Athens. In view of these dangerous ties with Corinth, Athens, immediately after the battle of Sybota, demanded that the Potidaeans should pull down their city walls on the south side, where they were not needed for protection against Macedon, and cease taking annual magistrates from Corinth. For the Athenians these were prudent precautions. Corinth was more than a potential enemy; Athenian ships had fought Corinthian at Sybota. A fortified place in this area might well be a source of trouble. The Potidaeans, strengthened by the promise of Sparta to invade Attica if Athens attacked Potidaea, refused. This was the first time that Sparta had come with such an offer against Athens, and Corinth must have wrung it out of her. The situation was serious for Athens, and became more serious when Perdiccas, king of Macedon, who had quarrelled with her for defending his brothers against him, began to organize a general revolt of Chalcidice against Athens, persuading the inhabitants to pull down their cities on the coast and concentrate their forces in the inland town of Olynthus. Another tribe, the Bottiaeans, joined them, and Athens was faced by a revolt on a large scale.

Again the Athenian response was immediate. A force advanced against Potidaea and defeated the Corinthian general. Three gravestones for the Athenian fallen survive, each with an elegiac quatrain in the traditional manner, but each with its own character as if three different poets had composed them.

One makes its point by contrasting the Athenians and their opponents:

> The sky received their souls, the earth their bodies;
>   They died by Potidaea's city-gates.
> Some of their foes are in the grave, and others
>   Found in a wall the surest hope of life.[2]

The last line refers to the flight of the enemy into the city, which the Athenians then captured, proving that 'the surest hope of life' was illusory. The Corinthians saw that unaided they could not withstand Athens and invited the Spartans to declare war against her. Pericles, who saw that an attack was coming, retorted with a hard economic blow. Because Megara had assisted Corinth at Sybota, the Athenians excluded the Megarians from the Athenian market and from the ports of the empire. This meant ruin for Megara and struck at the whole Peloponnesian League, of which Megara was economically an important member. The Megarian decree was not the real cause of the war to come but it was the active occasion of it, a response to Peloponnesian behaviour at Corcyra and Potidaea. Looking back on it some seven years later Aristophanes might with some excuse claim that Pericles started a fearful conflagration:

> So before misfortune reached him, he contrived a flame to raise
> By his Megara-enactment setting all the world ablaze.
> Such a bitter smoke ascended while the flames of war he blew
> That from every eye in Hellas everywhere the tears it drew.[3]

The decree was the culmination of a series of events. After it war was inevitable. It could be argued that both Athens and Sparta had broken the peace—Athens by fighting at Sybota, Sparta by promising to invade Attica. In all this we see Corinth working to keep her power intact from Athenian interference and persuading Sparta of the dangers of Athenian policy. But even this was not final. As Thucydides saw:

> The real reason why the Spartans went to war, though it was not one that they spoke of in public, was the fear which had been caused in them by the growth of Athenian power.[4]

If this was the real force at work, war could not have been avoided.

What this fear meant to the Spartans is dramatized by Thucydides in the debates which precede the outbreak of war and give a hardheaded assessment of the situation. The most conclusive takes place at Sparta at a conference of the Peloponnesian allies. The general feeling is that war should be declared against Athens, and the Corinthians have helped this by sending their own ambassadors to all the allies urging them to vote for war. Since Sparta has already declared war on Athens, the Corinthians have an easy task, which is to persuade the allies to go with them, and their most forceful argument is that Athens, if left unchecked, will dominate trade routes and stop commerce all over Greece. To this they add the threat of the horrors that Athenian domination will bring:

And let us be sure that defeat, terrible as it may sound, could mean nothing else but total slavery.[5]

They advance reasons for thinking that victory is possible and reach their climax when they say:

As for that dictator city which has been established in Hellas, let us make up our minds that it is there to dominate all alike and is planning to subdue what has not been subdued already.[6]

This was not true but it was commonly believed. Athens was not planning to subdue the rest of Greece, for she knew that she was incapable of doing so. But this was what Corinthian propaganda needed as a theme, and it appealed to Spartan fears.

Having decided on war, Sparta proceeded to send a succession of embassies to Athens, each with a different ultimatum. Such manoeuvres are common before wars start, and we must not conclude that they were meant to do more than give Sparta a little more time to get ready and to disarm criticism by pretending, not very convincingly, to act reasonably. They certainly do not imply that there was an anti-war party at Sparta or that king Archidamus, who had counselled caution in the earlier discussions, had not accepted the decision for war. Each embassy came with a different demand. Athens must drive out the curse of a goddess which lay on the family of the Alcmaeonids. Since Pericles was connected with them, this was a stab at him, skilfully timed for the religious hysteria which had recently broken out and had already been exploited against him by his political opponents. The Athenians replied that Sparta must purify the Brazen House of Athene where Pausanias had been starved to death. Next the Spartans demanded that Athens should abandon the siege of Potidaea and give independence to Aegina, and added that war could be avoided if Athens would revoke the Megarian decree. Finally came an ultimatum: 'Sparta wants peace. Peace is still possible if you will give the Hellenes their freedom.'⁷ With each demand the Spartans stepped up their claims, as if they were gaining confidence and felt better prepared for war. We need not believe that the demands were serious; for even if, inconceivably, Athens had given in to the last and surrendered her empire, she would have been thought so feeble that an attack would at once have been launched on her. The result could have been foretold. Pericles had no intention of making concessions and was ready with his unqualified negatives for them. In these ghoulish exchanges Sparta and her allies were the aggressors, and Athens, for good reasons, made no pretence to humour them or offer the least semblance of conciliation. The time had come when everyone knew what had long been suspected, that the two groups were ready for a violent confrontation, and if anyone had doubts, they seem to have been suppressed. In this hostile policy Corinth played a leading part, and her motives were largely economic. Her wealth came from her maritime trade, and Athens was a more than serious menace. But such arguments can have had little appeal for the Spartans with their agricultural economy or for others of the Peloponnesian allies. With them the real cause was the fear of Athenian democracy with its sense of mission and its contempt for the old aristocracies. This would be equally powerful in Corinth where the ruling class was highly select and class-conscious and quite as frightened of losing its hold on the populace as of losing its profits from commerce. Most Greeks, then as now, wished to extend their trade, but the determined efforts to humble Athens were directed more by hatred than by greed. Men do not get quite so hysterical as this in a purely commercial struggle, and in the first speech which he gives to the

Corinthians Thucydides indicates how deeply they loathe and fear the Athenians as upsetting their notion of what Greece ought to be. Some of the words which he gives them are perhaps too admiring to be genuine, but at least they show an admiration born of hatred and envy:

If they aim at something and do not get it, they think that they have been deprived of what belonged to them already; whereas, if their enterprise is successful, they regard that success as nothing compared with what they will do next. Suppose they fail in some undertaking; they make good the loss immediately by setting their hopes in some other direction.[8]

The comfortable merchant princes of Corinth were made uneasy by this people always on the move and upsetting the dignified calm which was the alleged ideal of Greek aristocrats. In the end it was too much for them, and their fears and irritations could find no outlet except in war.

In reply to this Pericles made clear to his own people that for the past ten years or so he had been entirely consistent in his policy:

Athenians, my views are the same as ever: I am against making any concessions to the Peloponnesians.[9]

He is sure that the Peloponnesians are the aggressors and that Athens is in the right and must go through with it. Though he has kept on the defensive for years, he has abated nothing in his love for his country or his confidence in it. He has given much thought to the strategy of the coming war and made up his mind what it ought to be. First, he claims that the Peloponnesians, living on their lands and confined to them, will be handicapped by lack of money. Secondly, they have little experience of seafaring and will find it difficult to acquire. On the other hand, the Athenians have large accumulations of money and a long and varied experience at sea. Because she is rich, Athens is better able to sustain a long war than Sparta, and because she has a large navy, she can attack the enemy at any point that she chooses as well as enforce a blockade. Pericles admits that Sparta is strong by land but, not very convincingly, suggests that Athens is equally strong. But he gives away his position when he lays down a fundamental rule of his strategy:

> As it is we must try to think of ourselves as islanders; we must abandon our land and our houses, and safeguard the sea and the city. We must not, through anger at losing land and homes, join battle with the greatly superior forces of the Peloponnesians.[10]

In other words, Pericles advocates a defensive strategy by land and an offensive strategy by sea. This was consistent with his peacetime policy after the loss of Boeotia. It was carefully thought out, observing the advantages and the limitations of Athenian power.

This dual strategy did not promise any decisive result. The only hope lay in some happy accident which would set the enemy at some real disadvantage and allow Athens to exploit the occasion with her fleet. In general the policy of Pericles was to turn the city of Athens, the area within the Long Walls, and the Piraeus, into a fortress, into which the country people of Attica were to come for protection when their lands and homes were devastated by the Spartans. And, exactly as he expected, the Spartans invaded the country annually, doing all the harm that they could. Some was easily reparable, but the destruction of olive trees, which would take many years to replace, was a savage blow. Meanwhile food came safely by sea to the Piraeus and between the Long Walls to Athens, but it can never have been plentiful, and some families must have found it a starvation diet. But worse than this was the hideous overcrowding in the city, which led to results which Pericles did not and could not foresee. Such conditions made Athens an easy victim for contagious diseases, and inflicted on her more fearful and more lasting damage than any military campaign.

In 430 Athens was ravaged by a plague, which lasted for about two years and reappeared for a short spell in 427–426. Its origin and nature are unknown, but it must certainly have been greatly aggravated by the crowded conditions of life in the city. Filth, lack of hygiene, lice, bad food, shortage of fresh water combined to spread the contagion and to increase the number of deaths. Infection was often fatal, and to a besieged city the daily toll of dead and the presence of unburied bodies in the streets added hideously to a demoralizing situation. It is very hard even to guess how great the destruction of life was, but it seems likely that when the plague came to an end one third of Athenian first-line troops had died of it and many others were maimed, while the numbers of civilian casualties are not known. Athens never regained the advantage in numbers which she had at the start of the war, and this was the more serious if she was to conduct large-scale operations by land as well as by sea.

The plague did more than this. Thucydides, who was one of its victims and watched it with sharp eyes, suggests that, gruesome though its physical effects were, its psychological effects were equally horrifying. The Athenians, who built so much of their life on personal honour and found in it a whole system of values, ceased, according to Thucydides, to believe in it:

As for what is called honour, no one showed himself willing to abide by its laws, so doubtful was it whether one would survive to enjoy the name for it.[11]

We need not press this too far, but it is relevant to the military situation. The policy of defence and of little but defence has special dangers for ardent soldiers, who soon get bored and demoralized by a routine which offers neither adventure nor glory. They may know that they are safe, but that has its risks since it discourages attempts to leave the defences for battle in the open field. The only available remedy was for the Athenians to devise small expeditions by sea, for these would at least do something to maintain morale and might avoid the deadly contagion of the plague.

The navy kept Athens alive by securing her supplies. It also enabled trade to continue and helped to pay for imported goods as well as for food. Strategically, it did more. When the large island of Lesbos revolted in 428, the dispatch of ships brought it to order. This was not like sending a battleship or even a gunboat in recent times. Greek ships could not fire broadsides or indeed do more than transport troops. If one fleet was faced by another it could engage it in battle by ramming and by bringing its ships alongside, grappling and boarding, but this was all it could do. The main use of the Athenian navy was to transport troops for offensive purposes, and for this it was admirably suited. It could also ravage and blockade the coast of the Peloponnese by regular patrols. This caused trouble to the enemy by stopping imports of food, though this was not very serious for an agricultural region, and of materials of war, especially weapons and arms or the metals needed for them. Such a blockade could never be complete, but it might be a considerable nuisance. These are the normal uses of a navy in war, and Athens could make the most of them. They provided a lively alternative to the grim tedium of waiting in a beleaguered city. Yet though Pericles defended his dual policy, it did not appeal to all Athenians, and the plague added to the common discontent. In 430 he was deposed from the office of general, fined, and then reinstated. Pericles' temporary unpopularity may have risen from the citizens' sense of frustration, from resentment that the policy which demanded such sacrifices did not give anything worth while in return.

The plague may account for a somewhat mysterious expedition which Pericles conducted in 430. It looks as if it were more than a mere raid or reconnaissance or demonstration in force. With his fleet he attacked the coast of Argolis, especially Epidaurus, Trozen, Hermione, and Halieis. With it went four thousand spearmen and three hundred cavalry. This was a formidable force which might create the impression that Athens was by no means broken by the plague but capable of taking the offensive almost in the middle of it. The time was well chosen, for the Epidaurian troops were away with their Spartan allies invading Attica. Epidaurus, if captured, would have been an excellent base for harassing Corinth and Megara, for worrying Spartan armies from the flank, and perhaps for luring Argos into an alliance. But something went wrong. Epidaurus was not captured, and Pericles returned home with little to show for his efforts. Thucydides is curiously reticent about the whole campaign, and we inevitably suspect that he is shielding Pericles from the charge of failure. Indeed the failure was the more noticeable because Athens was faced not by Sparta but by a minor city of little importance. It suggests at least that Athens had not yet learned how to conduct amphibious warfare on any scale and that the plague had done more damage than Pericles' fine gesture could conceal. Perhaps the explanation is simpler. In this war the technique of besieging cities was unexpectedly backward. The defence was usually stronger than the attack and able to keep it at bay for long periods, just as in 1914–1918 the system of fortified trenches made an offensive almost impossible except at a fantastic cost of life. The Spartans took two years to take the small town of Plataea; the Athenians failed altogether to take Syracuse. Towns might be taken by surprise or treachery, but open, prolonged assault was seldom successful, until blockade and starvation did what siege engines failed to do. In dealing with recalcitrant allies Athens might be able to seize a city, but it was because she had friends in it. In the cruder processes of war she was less successful, and even at this early point of the conflict it was clear that she would not win by trying to subdue the enemy on his own terrain.

This military failure may be contrasted with the remarkable skill of the Athenian navy as shown in the next year, 429. Athens kept a flotilla in the Corinthian Gulf, where it had a good, well-protected base at Naupactus and could do excellent work in hampering the transport of Peloponnesians across the gulf and the passage of Corinthian ships to the west. In 429 the Corinthians put to sea westwards but ran into the Athenian admiral Phormio with twenty ships against her forty-seven. Phormio let the enemy sail into the open sea as this suited better his methods of attack. There he formed his own ships into file and sailed around and around the Corinthians, crowding them into an ever narrowing space until they collided into each other and suffered serious damage. When they were in thorough confusion, the Athenians went in for the kill and gained a complete victory. The Spartans were horrified at this result and could not understand how a smaller force could defeat a greater. They did not give up the struggle but tried new tactics, placing a fleet on the south side of the Gulf, while Phormio was at Rhion on the north side. The Peloponnesians hoped to lure him to battle in the narrow strait, where his skill would count for less than in the open sea. At first they did well and, by attacking the Athenians as they moved towards Naupactus in single file, grounded some of them. Then the Athenians sank a leading Peloponnesian ship, and the course of battle changed. The front Peloponnesians dropped oars and waited for the others to come up. The Athenians, who had reached Naupactus, immediately turned around, bore down on them, and again won a complete victory. For some obscure reason Phormio was not employed after this, but in these brief episodes he proved how skilful and inventive the Athenians were at sea. Unfortunately this was not the element in which the war could be decided.

Soon afterwards Pericles died from the plague, and for the historian Thucydides this was a terrible blow to Athens. At first his successors kept the main lines of his strategy. Athens was in full command of the sea, but seemed unable to face a full Spartan army on land. The problem for each side was to find suitable country where it could engage the other side and inflict a decisive defeat on it. Though Athenian morale was damaged by the first Spartan invasions, it soon recovered. In these years Athens continued to strengthen her periphery, especially on the sea routes to the west. She took the island of Cephallenia in 430, Minoa, off the harbour of Megara, in 427, Oeniadae to the north-west of the Corinthian Gulf and Cythera off the south-eastern Peloponnese in 424. None of these moves was sensational or decisive, but they helped to contain Sparta by sea. In 424 Athens brought off a bigger stroke when she occupied Nisaea with the Long Walls from Megara to the Saronic Gulf. These successes helped to sustain Athenian spirits and improve her position at sea, but they still left her far from final victory.

If Athens could not take on Sparta in open battle, she might still strike at her through her allies, and of these Boeotia was an obvious choice, both because she shared a frontier with Attica and because she was reputed to be militarily not in the first class. The enterprising general Demosthenes formed a plan to attack Boeotia from the rear, by marching over the mountainous country on the northern side of the Corinthian Gulf. Here Athens had friends in Acarnania, Locris, and Phocis, who might be strong enough to hold up the Spartans from Doris and Heraclea. Transport over the Gulf was easy because Athens held Naupactus. But there were difficulties. The Aetolians were hostile. The rough country was ill suited to the heavily armed Athenian hoplites. The 'back door' to Boeotia was protected by large mountains. In the first stage of the campaign Demosthenes failed. His infantry was ravaged by the Aetolian javelin men. He had to retreat before them and saved Naupactus only just in time from a Spartan incursion from Heraclea. But in the following winter he retrieved his failure by advancing farther into the north-west and defeating the Spartans at Olpae on the Gulf of Ambracia. The Spartans tried to betray their allies, but these found it out in time and inflicted a heavy slaughter on the traitors. This was a grave blow to Sparta, but with it no more was heard for the present about an attack on Boeotia. It was probably thought that any further advance into Boeotia was too risky to be worth trying. If Athens had reached Boeotia with a tired and reduced army, she might well have suffered a reverse, especially as the Boeotians were less negligible in battle than the Athenians liked to think.

This divagation from Periclean strategy was not a failure, but neither was it a decisive success. This meant that the Athenian generals still thought of attacking Boeotia, but in the meanwhile something happened which seemed to be just what Pericles had had in mind. Chance gave Athens an opportunity which might have led to an end of hostilities. Militarily she made the most of it, politically almost nothing. In 425 Demosthenes, sailing to the north, dropped in with a force at Pylos in the south-western Peloponnese and was delayed there by rough weather. Largely to keep his men busy he set them to fortify the place, which lay across a narrow strait to the north of the long barren island of Sphacteria. The Spartans sent a small force to deal with him. They succeeded in blockading the Athenians, but gained nothing because an Athenian squadron arrived, defeated the Spartan ships in the bay, and in turn blockaded the Spartans on Sphacteria. The Spartan authorities did not wish to lose these men, who came from good families and were regarded as picked troops. They sent an embassy to Athens offering terms of peace. The Assembly, seeing that their country was at last in a strong position, turned these down. In the Assembly Cleon was vigorous in pressing on the war, but did not wish to be put in command of the new expedition to Pylos. However, he was appointed, and to the surprise of everyone and the disappointment of many, he won a complete victory. The Spartans on Sphacteria were blinded by a fire in the scrub, lost their discipline and sense of direction, and surrendered. The credit for the victory largely belonged to Demosthenes, but Cleon claimed it for himself, not entirely without excuse. He had seen an opportunity and made use of it.

Pylos was the justification of Periclean strategy, which recognized that the centralization of Spartan power was such that a damaging blow at a tender part might disorganize or demoralize the whole. Luck gave the chance and the Athenian generals, supported by the Assembly, took able military advantage of it. Politically Athens failed to pursue a peace she might have made to her advantage.

If on the whole Athens avoided hazardous enterprises, Sparta on her part failed to force Athens into a full-scale fight on land. Even Sparta's annual invasion of Attica was made on the assumption that Athens itself was impregnable and that the Athenian army had no intention of going out to fight. The Spartans probably overvalued the fighting worth of the Athenians, who might do well in small skirmishes on difficult terrain but whose lack of professional training made them no match for the Spartans in a head-on encounter. Sparta may also have feared the loss of too many of her best troops who formed the core of her army and kept it up to its high level. In any case the policy which she pursued in the first years led her nowhere. The yearly invasions yielded diminishing returns, and no serious battle was engaged. Slowly she began to change her strategy. First, she was persuaded by Thebes to attack the city of Plataea which lay on the frontier of Attica and Boeotia and was hated by Thebes for her loyalty to Athens. The Spartans laid siege in the autumn of 429 and were kept at it until the summer of 427. In the winter of 428 some Plataeans escaped by night and got away safely, but the rest of the inhabitants were driven to surrender in the following summer. The Spartans behaved with brutal harshness, executed 200 Plataeans, and razed the city to the ground. No doubt the Thebans, who cherished old resentments, urged this savagery, but it was the first of a series that darkened the later years of the war. What is surprising is that Athens did nothing to help Plataea. Perhaps she had too much on her hands to equip an adequate expedition; perhaps she was nervous of facing even a small Spartan force in open country. In either case her behaviour confirms the view that on land at this date Athens was cautious to the point of ineffectiveness.

The failure at Plataea however seems to have stung the Athenians into deciding that they must do something. They had conquered Boeotia in the not too distant past, and surely they could impose their will on her again. This was a reversal of Pericles' mature policy, and the result showed that he was right. The plan for invading Boeotia in 424 was at least ingenious, but broke down almost at the start, first from failure to synchronize the arrival of a land army under Hippocrates with that of a seaborne force under Demosthenes; secondly, by bad security, which meant that the scheme was betrayed by a Phocian to the Boeotian commanders, who went into action and held up Demosthenes after his landing. Hippocrates, basing himself on Delium, put up a good fight, but his troops were defeated and he himself was killed. Delium confirmed that Athens could not run Boeotia or this time even conquer it. Her army, trained on small raids, lacked the experience for full-scale battles and Boeotia also had Spartan advice and assistance. There had been a time when Pericles thought that Athens gained by her lack of professionalism:

There are certain advantages, I think, in our way of meeting danger voluntarily, with an easy mind, instead of with a laborious training, with natural rather than with state-induced courage.[12]

This may have seemed true before the war, but by 424, when Pericles had been dead for five years, it was no longer true in any useful sense. If the Boeotians could save their country from Athens, other peoples might do likewise.

After her victory at Pylos in 425 Athens had had a chance of making a tolerable peace. She might even have persuaded Sparta to let her keep the substantial gains she had made in the war. But peace did not come. Sparta's allies, especially Corinth, wanted war to a finish, a complete humiliation of Athens. On the Athenian side the new generation of popular leaders wished to gain glory and power by new victories. Their appetite had been whetted by the success at Sphacteria. They would not believe that they could not repeat this on a larger scale elsewhere, though Delium should have taught them that they were unlikely to do so. But the ambitious war parties on both sides dismissed any suggestions of peace and, looking round for new possibilities, they changed the general character of the war itself.

Eventually this change brought Athens and Sparta into open

conflict with each other, not simply through allies, though not yet on a full scale. It was due to the initiative of Sparta. In the northern Aegean the Athenian position looked secure, but it was here that Sparta struck, in a campaign of dashing originality. Few Spartan leaders seem to have had unusual personalities, but in Brasidas Sparta produced a skilful soldier with a flair for diplomacy and politics. At the invitation of the king of Macedon he was sent north, overland, with a small body of troops among whom were no full-blooded Spartans. On arriving in Macedon he set to work to persuade the Athenian allies to revolt from Athens. This bold policy brought immediate rewards. He proclaimed himself the protector of the liberties of Hellas against Athens, and the local oligarchic parties rallied to him. After winning over Acanthus and the small towns of Stagira and Argilus by diplomacy, he made himself master of Amphipolis, which was by far the most important Athenian city in these parts. He took it by surprise and offered generous terms which were promptly accepted by the inhabitants. They had previously sent a message for help to Thucydides, the historian, who was in charge of seven men-of-war at Thasos. He moved at once, but arrived on the evening after the surrender. For this he was cashiered and exiled, and in his enforced leisure he collected materials for his history and began to write it. Brasidas continued his progress unimpeded, capturing the city of Torone on a hill by the sea and treating the inhabitants with his customary chivalry.

This reversal of Spartan strategy was brilliantly successful, largely because Brasidas was quite unlike most Spartan commanders. But though he did serious damage to the interests of Athens, he did not deal her any crippling blow. He could not strike at the centre of her power or even at any important lifeline. The Athenians, none too soon, saw the dangers of the situation in Thrace and in the summer of 422 sent thirty ships with twelve hundred hoplites and three hundred cavalry. In command was Cleon who, since the death of Pericles, was the most successful speaker in the Assembly, and had recently shown courage and ability at Sphacteria. He made a good beginning by taking Torone with its Spartan governor. He then moved to Eion on the mouth of the Strymon to wait for reinforcements. Brasidas got to work, and Cleon, troubled by the clamour of his inexperienced troops for action, led them to the top of a ridge near Amphipolis. Caught between the small force of Brasidas and another force which emerged from the city, the Athenians put up a good resistance, but Cleon was mortally hit by a javelin, it was said, while running away. Brasidas won, but he too had received a deadly wound and died after being carried into the city. His death robbed Sparta of its only commander who might have secured a substantial victory, while the death of Cleon robbed Athens of its main obstacle to peace.

The peace negotiations for Athens were conducted by Nicias, who was a man of the centre. Peace was signed in 421, and it was clear that Athens would have done better if she had signed immediately after Sphacteria. For both sides the peace was an attempt to restore Greece to the *status quo* of 431. Each agreed to return most of the places they had occupied during the war, to keep peace for fifty years, and to give back all prisoners. For both sides the war had proved unnecessary because it did not alter the main situation to the advantage of either. The Spartans had dealt no death blow to Athens; even Brasidas' sensational successes were of no importance. Sparta could not defeat Athens until she vanquished her at sea. For Athens it was clear that her land army was not capable of any prolonged or extended campaign and that on the field it was inferior not only to the Spartans but to the Boeotians. Fears for the loyalty of the allies were not so justified as many had anticipated. The only serious revolt was that of Lesbos, and that was put down without too prolonged an effort. Though some cities joined Brasidas of their own accord, it was more probably from prudence than from hatred of Athens, and after the peace they returned to their old allegiance. The war proved that the danger from the allies was much less disloyalty than civil strife between rich and poor, which was accentuated by the Athenian support of the poor. (The Old Oligarch, who greatly disliked this policy, may not be far from the truth when he says that the Athenians hate the aristocrats and 'that is why they disfranchise the aristocrats, take away their money, expel and kill them'.[13]) After the death of Pericles his successors sometimes diverged from his policy, and when they did so, as at Delium, suffered defeat. Otherwise they did not at first do very badly. The victory at Sphacteria was a real victory; it was entirely consistent to defend the allies from Brasidas in Thrace. The empire remained more or less intact. The insoluble deadlock maintained during the war persisted after it. So long as Athens was content with her sea empire and did not wish to extend her dominion on the mainland, the Periclean policy suited her capacities.

The war lasted too long, largely because Athens wanted another success like Sphacteria. Instead she gave Sparta a chance to improve her position, which she did through Brasidas. At the start the war had not been unpopular in Athens, and all through it the Athenians fought with admirable courage, if not with adequate skill. But it looks as if in the last years there was a slackening of discipline which would account for the carelessness that allowed Brasidas to walk unopposed into Amphipolis. Moreover in these years there was a party which, while not eager to appease the enemy, thought it unnecessary to harass him too much. It was led by the rich Nicias, who was generally liked. His opponent Cleon kept the war going in the unrealized hope of winning more successes, and because of it was killed in battle, in what may not have been personally glorious circumstances. His bellicose spirit won him many enemies, including Thucydides and Aristophanes, but he still had a substantial following. Though Aristophanes wrote five of his surviving comedies during the war, we must not treat too literally his attacks on it. Of course he disliked it, denounced its privations, its blustering generals, its sneaking informers, and the brutality of Cleon, but he was writing to get laughs, and we must not assume that he was always entirely serious, still less that he was some sort of pacifist. His blistering comments on the war and his luxurious dreams of peace and plenty after it are the normal comments and dreams of all soldiers who surmount the horror of their dismal and dangerous present by denouncing politicians and generals and indulging in rich fantasies of self-indulgence when they are demobilized. Aristophanes was much closer to Nicias than to Cleon, and when peace came he celebrated it with a play by that name. Yet though we must not press doctrines on him, he hints that the war has always been pointless and hopes that it is really finished. This fits his view almost at the start, even when Euripides flared with fine patriotism. Later when Euripides took things more sourly, Aristophanes could still joke at them, but the jokes were sometimes deadly. The trouble with the war was that it left things not as they were, but worse. Both sides had spent lives and money and effort, and had nothing substantial to show for it. The reason for this was that the balance of power was such that neither side could defeat the other. Until this balance could be broken Greece would continue as before, but the two camps into which it was divided would view one another with undiminished suspicion and hatred.

In our taste for might-have-beens we may well wish that Athens had been able to unite Greece. Nor is this merely a desire for neatness. It is because Athens was the most creative of all Greek cities that we regret her failure to share her gifts with them. She, who was the 'Hellas of Hellas', did not realize her full potentialities because of an incompatibility of temperament with Sparta. A united Greece under Athenian leadership would have enhanced the common brilliance of Hellenism. To this full achievement the high morale of the Periclean age was indispensable, and though in later centuries Athens was unquestionably the intellectual and artistic centre of Greece, she never regained the first rapture which carried her through the crowded years of the fifth century. She was so grimly tested by the long war with Sparta that she lost something forever, and the rest of Greece shared in her loss. Great as Greek achievement was in succeeding centuries, notably in philosophy, mathematics, and science, it was not spread over a wide field and lacked the range and strength of the fifth century. The existence of a permanent division between two blocks of Greek states and the failure of each block to end it may well have been decisive in the political decline of the Greek world. Nor did Alexander's conquests and the long period of half-Greek monarchies which he inaugurated atone for the failure of the Greeks to make a unity of themselves. For a short time in the fifth century it looked as if this were possible. Pericles may even have hoped for it when war came in 458; he may still have cherished modified hopes for some sort of Athenian predominance when war came again in 431, but by then he had learned some harsh lessons and was content to plan for honourable survival in the hope that it might lead to something more. The divisions among the Greek states and the failure of any one of them to establish a lasting hegemony over the rest weakened Greece, first against Philip and Alexander, then, even more disastrously, against Rome. It is ironic perhaps that Rome, in her day weaker than Athens, nevertheless succeeded where Athens failed, building a world empire which safeguarded the Roman peace.

II

AFTERMATH AND AFTERTHOUGHTS

THE Peace of Nicias, to which Aristophanes gave an exuberant welcome, was never fully implemented. Though Sparta desired peace and needed it to bring her restless allies under control, the allies themselves felt that they had been betrayed and refused to observe the clauses that concerned them. The Chalcidians would not give up Amphipolis, and this provoked the Athenians into holding on to Pylos and Cythera. The situation in the Peloponnese was worse for Sparta because her long peace with Argos was running out, and there was a danger that soon she would have an enemy on her north-eastern frontier. For the moment it looked as if the Periclean strategy had after all succeeded, as if Sparta had been sufficiently weakened to lose some of her hold on her allies and thus be unable to resume the offensive. She was certainly uneasy, and moderate Athenians like Nicias might reasonably conclude that when the various points of dispute in the peace treaty had been resolved, Athens and Sparta might settle down amicably in a Greece dispirited by a surfeit of war.

Nothing of the kind happened. In Athens the party of Nicias was overruled by the democratic imperialists, led at first by Hyperbolus, who was made of the same stuff as Cleon. Of more significance was the young Alcibiades, the ward of Pericles and a member of his clan. Handsome, rich, extravagant, clever, and capable, Alcibiades for a time looked like the heaven-sent heir of Pericles, who might revive his manner of leadership with a renewed zest and a fresh imagination. Alcibiades had indeed some remarkable qualities. The high confidence, which Pericles fostered in the Athenians, filled the being of Alcibiades. He had fought at Delium and understood the art of war as perhaps no other Athenian of the time did. He was a highly effective speaker in the Assembly and able to make it accept his proposals. More ambiguous was his relation to the Sophists and their teaching. He was a friend of Socrates and admired him enormously, but did not share his respect for the laws or his moral integrity. In practice Alcibiades resembled those young men in Plato who argue for self-interest and are more concerned for themselves than for their country. He awoke admiration and amazement, but not trust. Though he had many of the qualities which made Athens great, he had others which might bring her to ruin. In 420, in the general disappointment at the failure of the peace, he was elected general, no doubt because he promised to get something done, to break the deadlock which the peace had confirmed as the normal condition of the Greek powers, and to devise a policy in which Athens could exert herself more fully and more gloriously than she had in the last years of the war.

Alcibiades believed that Sparta must be defeated, and he decided that this was possible and not even very difficult if sufficient force was pitted against her. In 418 he thought that he would get what he wanted not through a large concentration of Athenian arms but through the acquisition of allies in the Peloponnese, especially Argos, whose peace with Sparta was now at an end. Sparta saw the danger and sent a force under King Agis into the Argolid. But in one of the strange whirligigs of Greek history the two generals, to the fierce dissatisfaction of their troops, made a truce for four months. Alcibiades was soon afterwards present at Argos on an embassy. He persuaded the Argives to break the truce and renew the war with some Athenian help. But things did not go as he planned. At the battle of Mantinea in 418 the Spartans won a resounding victory, more complete than any won by either side in the preceding war and fully deserved by their strict discipline and fighting spirit. Thucydides describes a small but characteristic detail of the battle:

The Spartans came on slowly and to the music of many flute-players in their ranks. This custom of theirs has nothing to do with religion; it is designed so as to make them keep in step and move forward steadily without breaking their ranks, as large armies often do when they are just about to join battle.[1]

Spartan drill won the day. Though the Mantineans on the Spartan left were routed, the rest of the line held, and the Athenian contingent would have been surrounded if Agis had not been distracted by having to send help to his left wing. Sparta, whose reputation had sunk, was rehabilitated, and Argos exchanged friendship with Athens for friendship with Sparta. Spartan power in the Peloponnese was restored, and Athenian attempts to defeat it on land were again proved to be futile.

Alcibiades had brought Athens a serious setback. It was true that, as he boasted, he had built up a coalition against Sparta. But it was not strong enough to defeat her. When he claimed that Athens, seeming to be worn out by war, had asserted her strength, it was false; for neither by diplomacy nor on the battlefield did she secure any gain. Anyone who had thought that she was Sparta's equal would now know that she was not. The result was inevitable. Athens made no further attempt to engage Sparta on the mainland or to decrease her influence by seducing her allies. On this point Periclean caution had been justified.

If the mainland was ruled out, an alternative might be found in Sicily and southern Italy; and this Alcibiades now advocated. Athens might have been wiser to do nothing and let her manhood and her finances recover. But this did not appeal to Alcibiades or even to the average Athenian, who felt that his efforts had been insufficiently rewarded and that with new exertions he might secure some prodigious gain. Pericles would have approved of the use of sea power to extend the dominion of Athens, as Alcibiades now advocated. But Athens was now shifting her attention from Sparta to vaguer and vaster goals. No doubt it was believed that if she made large conquests in the west, she would be strong enough to defeat Sparta without difficulty. In the meanwhile Sparta, somewhat improvidently, would be left to look after herself. Alcibiades had a soaring vision of the conquest of Syracuse by Athens and the foundation of a new empire in the west which would conquer Carthage and rule the Sicilian seas from this strong outpost in Africa. He carried the Athenian people with him, and large preparations were approved. The armada sailed in the highest spirits in 415; in the early autumn of 413 the whole expedition, both men and ships, was annihilated by the Syracusans in Sicily. This was the end of Athenian expansion, and the historical conclusion of Athens' imperial mission. She held on for almost ten years but could launch no new offensive on a substantial scale.

The Athenian campaign in Sicily is recorded in all its disastrous failures by Thucydides, who passes his verdict on it:

> In this case the mistake was not so much an error of judgement with regard to the opposition to be expected as a failure on the part of those who were at home to give proper support to their forces overseas.[2]

In his view the politicians in Athens hampered a full prosecution of the war. Yet at the start they equipped the expedition most liberally and later sent men and money in large supply. No doubt he is right in thinking that the scheme was practicable, though in retrospect we can see the extent of its failure. In some respects it repeated what happened in Egypt in 454, when large reinforcements arrived too late and were destroyed soon after their arrival. The Sicilian expedition, like the British expedition to the Dardanelles in 1915, was conceived with vaulting hopes which seemed to be frustrated by a malignant doom. Nicias, who opposed it in the Assembly, was elected general, and throughout proved himself disastrously hesitant and incompetent. Of his two colleagues, Alcibiades was recalled almost at once on a charge of impiety unrelated to the war, and the able general Lamachus was killed in the first fighting. Alcibiades deserted to Sparta and gave excellent advice on how to defeat the Athenians. Athens had been cheated at the start about the state of affairs in Sicily, giving the Syracusans invaluable time to strengthen their defences. The navy deteriorated as it lay idle in the harbour of Syracuse, and in the end its officers were so demoralized that they were outmanoeuvred by the quite simple devices of the Syracusans. Nothing went right, and in the last weeks the morale of the Athenian forces sank to a fatally low ebb. Athens failed at Syracuse not because the task was beyond her powers, but because she made too many mistakes.

The failure of the Athenians in Sicily has often been ascribed to their democratic system of government, and this gets some support from Thucydides. It is an easy explanation but, apart from the recall of Alcibiades, it is not final or even fair. A Greek democracy might make mistakes like any other government, but it might equally win successes, as Athens had for fifty years. It was not the democracy as such that failed but certain policies and personalities. The Assembly was of course much influenced by prominent figures who are dismissed as demagogues and were in fact generals. Alcibiades put the case for the expedition, Nicias the case against, and both were elected to supreme command. This was not done frivolously. Hitherto Nicias had been lucky in war, and his much lauded caution and moderation were regarded as a useful foil to the headstrong wilfulness of Alcibiades. It would be hard to foresee that Nicias would develop a disease of the kidneys which would ruin his powers of command. No less serious was the public behaviour towards Alcibiades, who was first acclaimed as general and then summoned home on a charge of impiety in connection with the mutilation of statues of Hermes. While some Athenians believed in Alcibiades, others hated him and wished him out of the way. An outburst of irreligious behaviour provided an excuse, but the fact that this was treated seriously is not specifically democratic; it might equally happen in an oligarchy. No doubt, if Pericles had been alive, he would have tried to curb the popular hysteria against Alcibiades, but that does not mean that he would have succeeded. None of the mistakes in the Syracusan expedition was peculiarly a fault of democracy. They were rather the faults of a society which had for long over-exerted itself and now, when it undertook a huge new task, was not sufficiently rich in the right men for it.

Athens was also an empire, and this is very relevant to its Sicilian ambitions. Athens had become so accustomed to expansion and the acquisition of power that she could not hold back. She had no just quarrel with Syracuse and attacked her merely because she was rich and lay in a position well suited for fresh enterprises. That one state should attack another in this cold-blooded way may have caused qualms among some Greeks, but it happened as often with them as with us. It is remarkable that Thucydides says nothing about this aspect of the matter but confines himself to judging that the plan was feasible. Syracuse was a rich prey, and Athens did not even offer the excuse that she wished her to pay tribute. It was not alliance that she sought but conquest. The Syracusans had no illusions on this point and saw from the start what Athenian intentions were. Athens had lost all restraint. In such circumstances the Syracusans could not think of coming to any agreement or yielding to any demands. Their leader Hermocrates is made by Thucydides to unmask the Athenian plans and say to the people of Camarina:

The fact is that just as they won an empire in Hellas, so they are trying to win another one here, and by exactly the same methods.[3]

To Syracuse Athens offered nothing but servitude, and this shows how her imperial ambitions had hardened and become more ruthless. There was no pretence of combining to fight a common enemy, though Carthage was not far away and could well have been named as a likely danger in the near future. The Syracusans hated the Athenians for trying to enslave them, and there was no division between classes on this issue. That was why, when the Athenians retreated from Syracuse and were routed at the river Asinarus, no mercy was shown, and the generals, Nicias and Demosthenes, were put brutally to death. If democracy under Athenian tutelage had no appeal for the Syracusans, Athenian imperialism aroused virulent hatred, and every effort was called forth to defeat it. Athens had been transformed into a great power by the establishment of democracy; in the end she was ruined by the hatred which her desire for dominion brought upon her. She held on until 404, and even then her fall was almost accidental; for her fleet was destroyed when the crews were out foraging. Without her fleet she must starve or surrender, and she decided to surrender. Her greatness lasted as long as her fleet, and when that went, she was finished.

Athens had reason to think that surrender would bring vengeance in full flood to her but in fact Sparta imposed less extreme penalties than many must have expected. Her cruellest action was to set up a government of Thirty Tyrants, who committed every outrage and defied every sanctity, but were soon defeated and ejected in spite of Sparta. In the fourth century Athens survived, with many changes, but at least she survived. She even restored some pieces of her empire and showed that she had learned from her former mistakes not to impose her will too crudely on her allies. But the surrender of

404 was the funeral of the Periclean ideal. It had begun to wither before this, and perhaps it was never the same after the disappointments of the Peace of Nicias. Yet from 421 to 404 the Periclean system remained more or less intact, and Athens held it together. Men fought for their city with the same ardour, and the same vigour was at work in the arts and letters. But by 404 the notion of Athens as a leading power in Greece, founded on democracy and guided by her native genius, had outlived its day. The superb vitality which had inspired so many elements in Athenian life was much impaired, and she was no longer united by a single life-giving ideal. A great chapter was closed because the prodigious expense of spirit which had carried Athens through nearly a century could not be maintained in circumstances which were both materially and spiritually impoverished. Instead of vast attempts to create an all-sufficient state from an actual city, efforts were now turned by Plato to discover by hard thought what an ideal city ought to be. It was to combine a judicious selection of Spartan and Athenian virtues, and it is not surprising that it was never translated into reality. The prodigious Athenian experiment came to an end, but that does not mean that it had failed. What counted was what Athens did in the years of her proud ascendancy, and it is by these that she should be judged.

In the speech which Thucydides ascribes to Pericles in the Assembly in the last year of his life, Pericles tries to stiffen resistance to Sparta by claiming that his countrymen have won

... the greatest power that has ever existed in history, such a power that will be remembered for ever by posterity.[4]

It is a strong claim and at first sight not fully justified. Even if Pericles does not look beyond the Greek world and omits not only Persia but the rapidly growing empire of Carthage, his words are not pre-eminently true of Athens. She had had her great triumphs in the Persian Wars, and Marathon and Salamis were indeed remembered. But even these victories were no greater than Sparta's at Plataea. In the middle years of the fifth century Athens had certainly displayed power on a formidable scale, when she subdued Aegina, Euboea, and parts of Cyprus and held a land empire in Boeotia and Megara. But she lost the land empire; she surrendered Cyprus to Persia, and Euboea was after all a voluntary ally who had revolted. Attempts to found an empire outside Greek waters failed catastrophically in Egypt, as later they were to fail in Sicily. If the greatness of political power is to be judged by military success, Athens is not very obviously superior to other Greek states. No doubt Pericles means more than this, and if he judges power by the fear and resentment that it arouses, there is something in what he says, since for the main part of the fifth century Athens was feared by a large part of Greece. Pericles is speaking at a time before Athens had begun to fail, and he echoes from the Athenian side what would be said with hostility from the Spartan. He is proud that the Athenians should be feared and wishes them to realize how important it is.

Pericles sought Athenian power as something intrinsically desirable and an undeniable testimony to his country's worth. In the sharp rivalries of Greek city-states such ambition was inevitable, and the recognition of its claims was necessary to survival. The interest of this policy lies in its incidental consequences, in the ideas which it fostered, and their practical results. In Periclean Athens we cannot dissociate Athenian power from the whole question of uniting Greece under a single authority. This need not mean the tyranny of a single state, since some kind of confederacy would be possible, and better than the existing rivalries. By creating an empire Athens made her contribution to a solution of this problem. It did not succeed, because even at its height the Athenian empire, based largely on sea power, could not overthrow the Spartan League, based largely on land power. We do not know how far Pericles thought that he could defeat Sparta decisively enough to force her to surrender much of her power to Athens. It was not unimaginable that this might happen, but it was never a strong possibility. Of course if Spartan power were curtailed, she might have been more ready to cooperate with Athens, and this would have been a step of some sort towards a united Greece. Pericles may have thought of such results, but even then he might prize them mainly for the honour which they would bring to Athens. His belief in glory was the centre of his system, and from it important consequences followed.

Pericles' conception of glory embraced both his city and her individual citizens. The special strength of the Athenian way of life under his leadership was that it applied the old Greek sense of honour in a new direction. A man still lived for his own dignity and found in this a code more exacting than most codes of morality, but he also identified himself with his city and its honour with his own. The heroic Achilles lived for himself alone, for his own glory and self-respect, but Periclean man believed that he must maintain his personal standard in order to win honour for his city. Inevitably, but not exclusively, this came through war, for war was the most decisive way in which one city could show its superiority to others. Pericles made many other claims for the superiority of Athens and was conscious that she could and should boast of more than success in war, but this was nonetheless fundamental, for on it other kinds of success depended. By making Athenians believe in their city, Pericles made them believe in themselves. He explained why they were right to do so, and, when he based this on the strength and power of Athens, he had reason on his side. For without the safety guaranteed by military and naval predominance and without the self-confidence engendered by successes over other states Athens could not have sustained the high morale which inspired her well-being, though this would not in fact have been incompatible with a more generous treatment of the allies.

This unrivalled self-confidence had begun with the establishment of democracy by Clisthenes. No doubt it owed something to the liberation from the tyrants, who in their later years had ceased to be beneficent autocrats and assumed the harsh methods of despots. But it was greatly enhanced when the mass of Athenians saw that they were now the political equals of their old masters and could enforce their own policies. In the exuberance of high spirits they attacked their neighbours and extended Athenian territories, partly because this was their instinctive response to liberation, partly because their opponents stood for oligarchic systems of government which kept the populace in subjection. This new self-confidence was largely responsible for the victory at Marathon and was strengthened and sustained by it. It persisted through the first years of the league with its handsome victories over the Persians. The Athenians believed in their own prowess, and this made them powerful adversaries. But they also had opponents at home. The new spirit which democracy gave to Athens was not likely to lie idle, failing to claim more power for the people. When it did move, it struck the established rich who thought that enough had been done for the people and that its powers should be curbed. It was this conflict which gave Pericles his chance when he came into power and renewed policies which had been discredited with the fall of Themistocles. The mark of the truly Periclean age is the enormous energy which Athens displayed in all departments of life, and this was the direct consequence of her democratic system, which encouraged everyone to make the most of his opportunities. The expenditure of this energy was not actually directed from on high, but received encouragement and approval. In this way democratic Athens responded to the ideals presented to it.

To later generations, and indeed to ourselves, perhaps the most striking feature of Periclean Athens is this inspired confidence with which it approached many kinds of activity. Every endeavour of her citizens seems to have been carried out to the full stretch of their powers, and though they must at times have produced inferior work, the remains of their visual arts suggest that this was not common. It is true that their painted pottery, which at the beginning of the century was often the work of great masters, loses some of its distinction as the century proceeds, but this may be due simply to over-production. It is also true that both sculpture and architecture in the last quarter of the century became less grand and more pretty, but they have lost nothing of their accomplishment or their originality. Such changes in the visual arts are natural. A mature art which has to alter its style if it is not to decay is likely to become more subtle and less noble as it leaves its high achievements to explore new complexities. If we apply similar tests to politics, it is clear that Athenian democracy was kept going by the ardent enthusiasm of the Athenian democrats. Their opponents made no serious inroad until near the end, and even then failed. So far from being bored by legal or administrative chores, the Athenians positively enjoyed them and saw in them the safeguard of their liberties. The same was true of attendance at the Assembly. It too might have become tedious, and the public might have left decisions to a few professionals who enjoyed this kind of thing. But nothing of the sort happened. Debates in the Assembly were fully attended to the last, and serious matters were seriously discussed. It was easy for later generations to decry the influence of demagogues, but it only means that issues were treated with passionate commitment, and if bad arguments were put forward, they did not always prevail, or Athens would have fallen much sooner than it did. The first and most striking features of Athens through the fifth century are the zest and zeal with which public activities were pursued. It was the result of a high confidence, and this in its turn was the result of a conscious and eager democracy.

The Athenian ideal of manhood was not attained without considerable struggle and cost. To make democracy worthy of its claims, the aristocratic class had to be reduced in wealth and power. The Old Oligarch deplores this but regards it as a natural policy for democrats both in Athens and in allied cities. But in this Pericles did not go too far, and it is notable that in all these years Athens was not stricken by bloodthirsty feuds between rich and poor such as ravaged Corcyra. In the long run Athens was the gainer, for the democrats absorbed many of the tastes and manners of the aristocrats and tempered their vaulting self-regard with a certain responsibility and refinement. Athens of course had her political divisions, and aristocrats, like Thucydides, son of Melesias, were prepared to go a long way in pursuing their aims but seldom to actual bloodshed. Democracy grew in spite of dangerous opposition. It was never entirely safe but had to keep watch for attempts to disestablish it. This meant that the Athenians must in the end fight for it, and this was the central theme in their struggles against Sparta and oligarchic dependents like Corinth. The self-respect which liberty brought to Athens meant that every man saw himself a champion and was happy to prove his manhood on the battlefield. No doubt he gained by the acquisition of land, by the opening of new seas to his ships, by the beautification of his city at the cost of the allies. But this was only part of the story. Equally important was the belief that success in battle, or glorious defeat in it, was an end in itself and indissolubly tied to personal dignity. The glory which Athens won from such success was shared by all her citizens. From it they drew solid profits and an enrichment of experience. Athenian democracy was tested at the start of war and poised for war through its career. The Athenians conformed to the rule that if people really believe in something, they will be ready to fight for it. Since they believed in their way of life and its advantages, they were ready to fight, not merely to preserve it but to make it available for Hellas. It is useless to say that they believed in it too strongly; for without it they would have been nowhere.

No Greek would condemn all war as such, and most Greeks would think that wars fought by their own countries were right. Personal prowess in battle was much esteemed because it called for strength of limb, quickness of eye, rapidity of decision, and indifference to danger. Combat in battle set a man's whole being to work. It resembled an athletic contest but was fought for much higher stakes and provided even more absorbing excitement. War, not being mechanized, gave every man a chance to prove himself in full view of his companions and of the enemy. There was no question of operating invisible weapons over long distances. Moreover, war played a large part in the development of small units of government into larger. The Athenian confederacy was born from fear of Persian attack; the Spartan League was enforced on its members by bellicose action or threats of it by Sparta. The smaller unit was swallowed in the larger, and the pity is that this was not merged into something larger still. The evils of war were recognized and often deplored, but it was regarded as an inescapable element in human life and much preferable to dishonourable inactivity or surrender. Distinctions were made between just and unjust wars, and usually each side was persuaded that its cause was just while that of its antagonists was not. The distinction may have been useful in influencing public opinion outside the belligerent states, but it probably did little to prevent them from pursuing their own advantage. Most states, and certainly Athens, believed that once they were at war it was the duty of their citizens to defend them. What counted was the readiness to do this. A city known to be likely to defend its claims by arms got its way more effectively than one which shrank from putting issues to the test. Pericles knew that Athens, with her unwillingness to submit to any affront or slight, was acting as a proud city should. It was a sign of the spirit which kept her at work and inspired all her activities.

This does not mean that war was controlled by international regulations or even by decency and restraints. As the Peloponnesian war went on, it prompted increasingly hideous atrocities. Fear provoked fury and bloodshed. Even at the start the Spartans killed all foreign merchants found within their boundaries. When in 428 Mytilene revolted from Athens, the Assembly, excited to violent revenge by Cleon, decided to kill all the male population and to enslave the women and children. This was a far more savage punishment than Athens had hitherto exacted from a rebellious ally, and it was largely dictated by the fear that other allies would revolt if Athens did not deter them by a murderous example. However, this proved too much for some Athenians, and the next day the decision was reversed, not from any motives of humanity but because it was inexpedient. A ship was sent in haste to the Athenian generals at Mytilene, and instead of the whole male population one thousand prisoners, thought to be the leaders of the revolt, were killed. Worse was to come. In 427 the small city of Plataea, after withstanding a long siege by the Spartans, surrendered. Prompted by the Thebans the Spartans killed all Plataeans who had not helped Sparta or her allies. In 423 Scione, who had revolted like Mytilene, was treated as Mytilene so easily might have been, by the slaughter of men and the enslavement of women. This too was advocated by Cleon, who repeated the second half of the formula when in 422 Torone, which had gone over to Brasidas, came back to Athens. In the winter of 416–415 the Athenians, having captured the neutral island of Melos for purely strategic reasons, inflicted the same vengeance on the inhabitants, who were quite innocent of revolt or betrayal. The occasion horrified Euripides, who in the following spring made the treatment of the conquered in war the main theme of his *Trojan Women*. In the autumn of 413 the Athenians who surrendered at Syracuse were killed either at once on the spot or slowly by hideous conditions of captivity in the stone quarries, except for those few who won some alleviations by being able to recite Euripides to their conquerors. One atrocity bred another, and as each side became less sure of itself and its chances of victory, it extended the scope of its savagery. War became as fearful for civilians as for soldiers, perhaps even more, since it became a matter of policy to exterminate whole male populations.

This decline in civilized behaviour did not pass unnoticed, and though most Athenians accepted it as necessary to their continued existence, some at least were disgusted by it, notably Euripides, who fell out of love with Athens and left her to spend his last years in Macedonia. The behavioural change is an ugly flaw in a great achievement, but the achievement remains. The final claim of Periclean Athens is that she brought to a climax and combined in a single society various powerful tendencies. When most states were held by entrenched oligarchies, Athens created democracy, but did not lower her standards of culture and taste. This democracy was wedded to imperial aims, which inspired and strengthened it. In this way the Athenian heyday marked the end of a long period of experiment and development in most parts of Greece. Athens broke through the barrier which seemed to hold other cities from further advance. In this process Pericles was both a bold inventor and a reverent traditionalist. His idea of a heroic Athens had its roots in the beginnings of Greek history and a lost world of warrior-kings; his ideal of empire was partly shaped by the scientific thought of his time. Athens was never again to attain so rich a range of performance, and though she remained the foremost city of Greece, she had lost the ability to deal with political matters at the highest level. Where she fell short, other cities fell shorter, and none of them succeeded in taking her place as 'the eye of Greece'. The various forces which Pericles united in Athens were the common heritage of Greece, but his special claim was that he gave a new meaning and a new life to much that seemed to be on the way out. The strain was enormous, and what Athens did in the fifth century might well be ruinous for any single city. Yet, though she lost the war and with it a large part of her confidence and creative zest, she still had enough strength in reserve to achieve much of lasting worth. Above all she left a memory of much more than the military triumphs which Pericles admired so greatly. In action and in thought about action, in the pursuit of truth and its presentation in imaginative forms, she set an example which was hardly ever again equalled.

The greatness of Athens depended largely on her being a democracy and thereby engaging the full and willing service of her citizens. The democracy was not seriously challenged until the summer of 411, when a Council of Four Hundred was put into power, but survived for only a few weeks. Even at this perilous time the Athenians were unwilling to shirk their responsibilities or to hand over decisions to a few men of alleged social superiority. The strength of Athenian democracy was that it was truly democratic. Unlike modern representative democracies, the government was not in the hands of elected agents but of the whole people, which had the last word on all decisions of any importance. This has been repeated at rare intervals in history where a state has been small enough for all its citizens to be able to meet in a single place, as it could in Athens. Direct democracy of this kind has its own faults. When decisions rest with the whole body of citizens, it is difficult to follow a consistent policy and for the voters not to be flustered or frightened into hasty decisions of which they soon repent. This happened at Athens in the decision to kill all the male Mytilenaeans, but fortunately the Assembly changed its mind. In other cases there was no change of mind, and unjustified atrocities were committed. They were usually inspired by politicians who knew that they could inflame the people by playing on its vanity and its fears. But the paradox of the Athenian democracy was that it seldom made gross miscalculations and on the whole maintained a consistent policy.

We know the demagogues who came to power after Pericles through the ribald gibes of Aristophanes and the aristocratic disapproval of Thucydides. But there must have been better men than Cleon whose names are lost to us but who were capable of observing a coherent policy. In any case the Athenian democracy made fewer mistakes than the Spartan oligarchs, even when the latter had everything in their hands.

With these considerations in mind it is not absurd to ask what would have happened if Pericles had been defeated and ostracized by his opponent Thucydides, son of Melesias. There was a real chance of this in 443, but Pericles turned the tables, and Thucydides was ostracized in his place. If the views of the Old Oligarch are typical of the Athenian opposition, the triumphant aristocrats would have been delighted to overturn the democracy both in Athens and among the allies. In the second case we can see from the events in Corcyra how harshly each side would treat the other and how difficult it would be to come to a peaceful conclusion; in the first case any attempt to limit the number of enfranchised citizens would have led to cruelty and chaos. The class to suffer most would be that which manned the navy, and without it Athens would have soon been starved and defeated. The victors might well have looked to Sparta for support, but what Sparta was likely to do can be deduced from her installation of the Thirty Tyrants in Athens after her surrender in 404. This was a total failure because all Athenians were against them, and they soon came to suitably disastrous ends. Democracy was the inspiring force of Athens in the fifth century, and without it she would never have done so much as she did. Even her sculptors and architects would not have shown the full range of their powers, since the great buildings on the Acropolis would never have been begun. Nor is it likely that either tragedy or comedy would have attained their special splendours. The first would have had no spur to raise fundamental questions on the capacities and limitations of the state; the second would not have been allowed to make fun of the exclusive gentlemen who sought to run the city. Democracy was now bred into the Athenian character, and when alternative systems were chosen or imposed, they began badly and ended worse. In the fourth century, when Athens began to revive, she preferred a modified democracy to any more restrictive system. We may doubt whether later admirers of Athenian democracy understood how anomalous it was, and how unlike later systems, but the memory of it survived when much else was forgotten.

Most of us know Athens mainly from her works of art and her literature. Though only a small proportion of these has survived, it is enough to cast a special enchantment and to bring home the strength of Athenian genius. If she had nothing else, these would be remembered and prized, but they might not in themselves justify the almost unequalled tributes which we pay to Athens. Their appeal is greatly enhanced because they are part of a complex whole, of a living society in which they played a serious but by no means preponderant part. Quite as important as these is the influence which Athens had on later thought and on the transformation of thought into action. Distant and different though modern democracy is from Periclean, there is a real connection between them. The Athenian conception of democracy has disappeared for centuries on end and been superseded by other conceptions of government based on quite different assumptions. But it has been kept alive by unexpected allies, by Stoic philosophers and Christian theologians, by the thinkers of the Enlightenment and the founding fathers of the American republic. Whenever men have thought seriously about just government, they have had at the back of their minds recollections, not necessarily friendly, of the Athenian discovery that the first task of government is to treat men as ends in themselves. Bloodthirsty and bestial systems of modern times have made this the target for their destructive hate, and that shows how fundamental it is. Behind respect for democratic government lies respect for the individual, and this is the great Athenian contribution to the world. It has often been lost, often submerged; it has never been wholehearted or complete, and it was not so even in Athens. But once such an ideal has been brought to life it cannot be entirely eliminated. It lingers in small matters when it is lost in great; it becomes a matter for religion and morals when politics will have nothing to do with it. It was the inspiring centre of the Athenian achievement in its most vigorous days, and from it came the unparalleled vitality and creative zest, the belief of Athenians in their city and themselves. They made mistakes; they did not always see how much they had undertaken; the strain of events was often too strong for them, but even when we allow for their failures in humanity and in prudence, the prodigious achievement remains, not indeed quite as Pericles imagined it, but in some ways wider and richer and more lasting. Under his guidance the ideal of the 'four-square man', dear to earlier, more aristocratic generations, remained intact, but its elements were developed with a new vigour and a new purpose. Periclean Athens set an example of what can be done if human faculties are released from unnecessary restraints and inspired to follow their special bent. Athens expected her sons to work for her, but she was content if this work was something which they chose for themselves and practised for its own sake as well as for its benefit to their city.

CHRONOLOGICAL TABLE

B.C.

528	Hippias succeeds his father Pisistratus as tyrant of Athens.
514	Hipparchus, brother of Hippias, is murdered by Harmodius and Aristogiton.
510	Hippias is expelled from Athens by the Alcmaeonids with Spartan support.
508	Constitutional reforms of Clisthenes in Athens.
508–506	Athenians defeat attempts of Spartans, Boeotians, and Chalcidians to intervene in Athenian affairs.
499–494	Revolt of Ionians against Persia, and subsequent failure.
490	Persian invasion of Greece, defeated by Athenians at Marathon.
487	Ostracism first used at Athens.
483–482	Discovery of new vein of silver in mines at Laurium.
482–480	Building of large Athenian fleet at instigation of Themistocles.
480	Athens recalls ostracized citizens.
	August: Xerxes enters Greece. Battles of Artemisium and Thermopylae.
	September: battle of Salamis.
479	Persian army defeated at Plataea, and Persian navy at Mycale.
478–476	Athenian walls rebuilt.
478	Pausanias in Cyprus and Byzantium.
	Formation of Delian League under Athenian leadership.
476–475	Cimon captures Eion.
472	The *Persians* of Aeschylus, paid for by Pericles.
471	Naxos tries to secede from the League but is brought back by force.
470	Ostracism of Themistocles. He goes to Argos.
469	Victory of Cimon over Persians on the Eurymedon.
466–465	Condemnation of Themistocles. His flight to the north-west; then to Persia.
465–463	Revolt of Thasos from League crushed.
464	Earthquake at Sparta and revolt of Messenians.
?–463	The *Suppliants* of Aeschylus.

463–462	Cimon takes force to help repression of Messenians but is dismissed by the Spartans.
	Ephialtes and Pericles in power at Athens. Reduction of authority of the Areopagus.
461	Ostracism of Cimon.
	Murder of Ephialtes.
460–445	War between Athens and Sparta (First Peloponnesian War).
459–454	Athenian expedition to Egypt, ending in disaster.
459	Athens defends Megara, who has already joined her.
459–458	Battles of Halieis and Cecryphalea.
458	*Oresteia* of Aeschylus.
	Battle of Aegina.
	Building of Long Walls from Athens to Piraeus.
457	Spartan victory at Tanagra.
	Autumn: Athenian victory at Oenophyta and conquest of Boeotia.
457–456	Athenian conquest of Aegina.
454	Treasury of League transferred from Delos to Athens.
453–446	Parts of Achaea included in Athenian empire.
451	Five Years' Truce between Athens and Sparta.
451–450	Law of citizenship in Athens.
450	Death of Cimon in Cyprus.
449–448	Athens invites Greeks to restore temples, and to join in peace pact.
447	Parthenon begun.
	Athens defeated at Coronea, and loss of Boeotia. Cleruchies sent to the Chersonnese and Euboea.
447–446	Revolt and reduction of Euboea. Athens loses Megara.
446–445	Thirty Years' Peace between Athens and Sparta. Foundation of New Sybaris.
443	Foundation of Thuria.
	Ostracism of Thucydides, son of Melesias.
c.441	*Antigone* of Sophocles.
440–439	Revolt and reduction of Samos and Byzantium.
438	Statue of Athene Parthenos set up in Parthenon.
437	Prosecution of Phidias.
436	Foundation of Amphipolis.
c.435	Pericles' expedition to the Black Sea.
436–435	Trouble at Epidamnus.
435	Spring: sea victory of Corcyra over Corinth.

c.432	Defensive alliance of Athens with Corcyra.
	Battle of Sybota.
432–431	Assemblies at Sparta decide on war.
431	First year of Peloponnesian War.
	March: Theban attack on Plataea.
	May: Peloponnesian invasion of Attica.
	Athens expels Aeginetans from Aegina.
430	Outbreak of plague at Athens.
	Second invasion of Attica.
	Expedition of Pericles to Argolis, and failure at Epidaurus.
	Pericles deposed from office of general, tried, fined and reappointed.
	Surrender of Potidaea.
429	Peloponnesians besiege Plataea.
	Sea victories of Phormio.
	Death of Pericles.
428	Third invasion of Attica.
	Revolt of Mytilene.
427	Fourth invasion of Attica.
	Surrender of Mytilene to Athens.
	Surrender of Plataea to Sparta.
	Civil strife in Corcyra.
	Athens captures Minoa.
426	Demosthenes operates in Aetolia.
425	Fifth invasion of Attica.
	Occupation of Pylos and surrender of Spartans at Sphacteria.
	Acharnians of Aristophanes.
424	Athens captures Nisaea, with the Long Walls of Megara and Cythera.
	Athenian invasion of Boeotia, and defeat at Delion.
	Brasidas in Thrace.
	Banishment of Thucydides, the historian.
	Knights of Aristophanes.
423	*Clouds* of Aristophanes.
422	Battle of Amphipolis, deaths of Brasidas and Cleon.
	Wasps of Aristophanes.
421	Peace of Nicias.
	Peace of Aristophanes.
420	Intrigues of Alcibiades in Peloponnese, leading to alliance of Athens and Argos.

418   Sparta defeats Argos and her allies at Mantinea.
416–415   Athenians sack Melos.
415   *Trojan Women* of Euripides.
           Athenian expedition to Sicily.
           Alcibiades recalled, and seeks asylum in Sparta.
414   Siege of Syracuse.
413   Athenian reinforcements sent to Sicily.
           Defeat of Athenians in Syracuse Harbour.
           Destruction of Athenian forces.
411   Oligarchic revolution in Athens, succeeded by more moderate oligarchy.
410   Restoration of full democracy.
405   Athenian fleet destroyed at Aegospotami.
404   Surrender of Athens.
           Establishment of the Thirty by Sparta in Athens.
403   Restoration of democracy and general amnesty.

REFERENCES

2 ATHENIAN DEMOCRACY BEFORE PERICLES

1   Herodotus 5.66.2.
2   Idem 5.66.1.
3   Aeschylus, epigram 3.
4   Aristophanes, *Acharnians* 180–81, translated by B. B. Rogers.
5   Timocreon, fragment 1.5–8.
6   Thucydides 1.138.3, translated by Rex Warner.
7   Aeschylus, *Persians* 353–354, translated by G. M. Cookson.
8   Aeschylus, *Seven against Thebes*, 592–594.
9   Hiller von Gaertringen, *Historische griechische Epigramme*, no. 42.
10 Eupolis, fragment 208.
11 Cratinus, fragment 1.
12 Aristophanes, *Frogs* 1021–2, translated by B. B. Rogers.
13 Plutarch, *Cimon* 16.9.

3 THE GREAT REVERSAL

1   Plutarch, *Cimon* 16.9.
2   Pindar, *Olympian* 8.54–5.
3   Pindar, *Nemean* 8.32–4.
4   Thucydides 2.41.4, translated by Rex Warner.
5   *Inscriptiones Graecae* I² 909.
6   Aeschylus, *Eumenides* 292–8, translated by George Thomson.
7   Pindar, *Isthmian* 7.26–37.
8   'Xenophon', *Athenian Constitution* 3.11.
9   Aristotle, *Politics* 1302b 25.
10 Thucydides 1.69.4, translated by Rex Warner.
11 Thucydides 1.70.3, translated by Rex Warner.
12 'Xenophon', *Athenian Constitution* 2.1.

4 PERICLEAN DEMOCRACY

1   Xenophon, *Memorabilia* 1.2.46.
2   Aristotle, *Eudemian Ethics* 1215b 7.

3 Plato, *Phaedrus* 268 e.
4 Plutarch, *Pericles* 8.8.
5 Aristotle, *Rhetoric* 1411a 16.
6 ibid. 1407a 5.
7 ibid. 1365a 32.
8 Aristophanes, *Frogs* 530–31, translated by B. B. Rogers.
9 Eupolis, fragment 94, translated by T. F. Higham.
10 Plutarch, *Pericles* 8.5.
11 Thucydides 2.65.5–10, translated by Rex Warner.
12 Plato, *Laws* 694a–701d.
13 'Xenophon', *Athenian Constitution* 1.10.
14 ibid. 1.2.
15 Herodotus 3.81.1–3.
16 Thucydides 2.65.8, translated by Rex Warner.

5 THE NEW IMPERIALISM

1 Thucydides 2.39.1, translated by Rex Warner.
2 ibid. 2.8.2.
3 ibid. 2.11.2.
4 ibid. 3.37.2.
5 ibid. 5.99.1.
6 ibid. 2.63.2.
7 'Xenophon', *Athenian Constitution* 1.14.
8 Thucydides 1.144.1; 2.43.3; 2.63.1.
9 Thucydides 2.62.2, translated by Rex Warner.
10 ibid. 2.36.2–3.
11 ibid. 2.64.3.
12 Aristophanes, *Knights* 1111–14, translated by B. B. Rogers.

6 THE PHILOSOPHY OF EMPIRE

1 Thucydides 1.128.7.
2 Euripides, *Suppliant Women* 576–7.
3 Thucydides 1.70.9, translated by Rex Warner.
4 Pindar, fragment 64.
5 Plutarch, *Pericles* 8.9.
6 Thucydides 2.40.1, translated by Rex Warner.
7 ibid. 2.41.1.
8 ibid. 2.43.1.

9   Aeschylus, *Eumenides* 913–915, translated by George Thomson.

10 Sopohocles, *Ajax* 1217–23.

11 Euripedes, *Medea* 824–45.

12 Thucydides 2.37.3, translated by Rex Warner.

13 Xenophon, *Memorabilia* 1.2.42.

14 Thucydides 2.38.1, translated by Rex Warner.

15 ibid. 2.41.1.

16 ibid. 2.41.3.

17 ibid. 2.61.1.

18 Plutarch, *Pericles* 38.4.

19 Thucydides 2.40.2, translated by Rex Warner.

20 Aristotle, *Politics* 1253b 27.

21 Thucydides 2.40.3, translated by Rex Warner.

22 ibid. 2.40.4.

23 Aeschylus *Eumenides* 976–87, translated by George Thomson.

24 Thucydides 2.60.3, translated by Rex Warner.

25 ibid. 2.64.5.

26 Pindar, *Pythian* 1.85.

27 Pindar, fragment 64.

28 Pindar, *Isthmian* 7.43–8.

29 Pindar, *Pythian* 11.36–7.

30 ibid. 8.8–12.

31 ibid. 98–100.

7 POETRY AND POLITICS

1   Thucydides 2.41.4, translated by Rex Warner.

2   ibid. 2.61.4.

3   Aeschylus, *Persians* 241–2.

4   ibid. 401–4, translated by G. M. Cookson.

5   Aristophanes, *Frogs* 1020–22, translated by B. B. Rogers.

6   Thucydides 2.42.4, translated by Rex Warner.

7   ibid. 2.40.4.

8   Aeschylus, *Eumenides* 707–9, translated by George Thomson.

9   ibid. 861–4.

10 Thucydides 2.43.2, translated by Rex Warner.

11 *Athenische Mitteilungen* lvii (1932), 142.

12 Sophocles, *King Oedipus* 906–10, translated by R. Whitelaw.

13 Sophocles, *Antigone* 450–60.

14 Euripides, *Suppliant Women* 321–7.

8 THE ATHENIAN OPPOSITION

1 Aristotle, *Constitution of Athens* 28.5.
2 Plutarch, *Pericles* 11.1.
3 ibid. 12.3–4.
4 Thucydides 1.10.2, translated by Rex Warner.
5 Plutarch, *Pericles* 12.2.
6 Herodotus 3.80.3.
7 Thucydides 2.37.1, translated by Rex Warner.
8 ibid. 2.40.1.
9 Plato, *Meno* 94 d.
10 Plutarch, *Pericles* 32.2.
11 Diogenes Laertius 1.8.
12 Thucydides 2.46.1, translated by Rex Warner.
13 Aristophanes, *Acharnians* 703–12, translated by B. B. Rogers.
14 'Xenophon', *Athenian Constitution* 2.18.
15 Cratinus, fragment 71, translated by T. F. Higham.
16 Idem, fragment 240.
17 D. L. Page, *Greek Literary Papyri* I p. 198.
18 Teleclides, fragment 42, translated by B. B. Rogers.
19 Cratinus, fragment 241.
20 Eupolis, fragment 98.
21 Aristophanes, *Acharnians* 524–34, translated by B. B. Rogers.
22 Thucydides 2.37.2, translated by Rex Warner.

9 THE INTELLECTUAL REVOLUTION

1 Democritus, fr. 116.
2 Thucydides 2.40.1.
3 'Hippocrates', *On the Sacred Disease* 1.
4 Protagoras, fragment 4.
5 Heraclitus, fragment 53.
6 Thucydides 5.105.1–2, translated by Rex Warner.
7 ibid. 1.76.2.
8 Plato, *Republic* 338 c.
9 Protagoras, fragment 1.
10 Plato, *Laws* 10.889 a.
11 Euripides, fragment 910.
12 Xenophanes, fragment 18.
13 Plato, *Protagoras* 322 d.

REFERENCES

14 Sophocles, *Antigone* 365–75.
15 Thucydides, 2.53.4, translated by Rex Warner.
16 ibid. 3.82.3.
17 ibid. 3.82.3–4.

10 THE INCONCLUSIVE WAR

1   Plutarch, *Pericles* 17.3.
2   F. Hiller von Gaertringen, *Historische griechische Epigramme*, no. 53.
3   Aristophanes, *Peace* 608–11, translated by B. B. Rogers.
4   Thucydides 1.23.6.
5   Thucydides 1.122.2, translated by Rex Warner.
6   ibid. 1.124.3.
7   ibid. 1.139.3.
8   ibid. 1.70.7.
9   ibid. 1.140.1.
10 ibid. 1.143.5.
11 ibid. 2.53.4.
12 ibid. 2.39.4.
13 'Xenophon', *Athenian Constitution* 1.14.

11 AFTERMATH AND AFTERTHOUGHTS

1   Thucydides 5.70, translated by Rex Warner.
2   ibid. 2.65.11.
3   ibid. 6.76.2.
4   ibid. 2.64.3.

INDEX

MORE ABOUT PENGUINS
AND PELICANS

Penguinews, which appears every month, contains details of all the new books issued by Penguins as they are published. From time to time it is supplemented by *Penguins in Print*, which is a complete list of all available books published by Penguins. (There are well over four thousand of these.)

A specimen copy of *Penguinews* will be sent to you free on request. For a year's issues (including the complete lists) please send 30p if you live in the United Kingdom, or 60p if you live elsewhere. Just write to Dept EP, Penguin Books Ltd, Harmondsworth, Middlesex, enclosing a cheque or postal order, and your name will be added to the mailing list.

Note: *Penguinews* and *Penguins in Print* are not available in the U.S.A. or Canada

Penguin Classics

THUCYDIDES

THE PELOPONNESIAN WAR

Translated by Rex Warner
With an Introduction and Notes by M. I. Finley

'My work is not a piece of writing designed to meet the taste of an immediate public, but was done to last for ever.'

Written four hundred years before the birth of Christ, this detailed contemporary account of the long life-and-death struggle between Athens and Sparta stands an excellent chance of fulfilling its author's ambitious claim. Thucydides himself (c. 460–400 B.C.) was an Athenian and achieved the rank of general in the earlier stages of the war. He applied thereafter a passion for accuracy and a contempt for myth and romance in compiling this factual record of a disastrous conflict.

GREEK LITERATURE IN TRANSLATION

Edited by Michael Grant

Greek literature provides powerful evidence in support of Sophocles' statement that language is what raises mankind above the animals. Not only did Greek provide the earliest literature in the western world, but it maintained a flow of masterpieces for a thousand years, well into Roman imperial times; and today (because of the Greek writer's faculty for reaching to the heart of his subject) this literature still possesses significance.

In this companion volume to his *Roman Readings* Michael Grant displays, as far as possible, the whole range of Greek poetry and prose, from Homer and Hesiod to the Hellenistic poets and the works of Ptolemy, Galen and Plotinus. His selection vividly demonstrates the extraordinary extent of Greek achievement in every literary field – in epics, lyrics and drama, in history, biography and oratory, in philosophy, criticism and satire, and in works of fundamental scientific thought.

Moreover, Michael Grant's choice of English versions serves to show how the mounting waves of modern translations now challenges the splendid output of the Elizabethans.

THE GREEK MYTHS

(IN TWO VOLUMES)

Robert Graves

Few modern writers are better qualified than Robert Graves to retell the Greek legends of gods and heroes for a modern audience. In the two volumes of *The Greek Myths*, with a dazzling display of relevant knowledge, he provides a complete 'mythology' to replace Smith's *Dictionary of Classical Mythology* of the nineteenth century. Graves's work covers, in nearly two hundred sections, the creation myths, the legends of the birth and lives of the great Olympians, the Theseus, Oedipus, and Heracles cycles, the Argonaut voyage, the tale of Troy, and much else.

All the scattered elements of each myth have been assembled into a harmonious narrative, and many variants are recorded which may help to determine its ritual or historical meaning. Full references to the classical sources, and copious indexes, make the book as valuable to the scholar as to the general reader; and a full commentary on each myth explains and interprets the classical version in the light of today's archaeological and anthropological knowledge.

GREEK SOCIETY

Antony Andrewes

'Highly readable and remarkable' – *Economist*

'It would be hard to imagine a more comprehensive and readable modern account of the subject ... it is also a remarkable act of creative evocation which will stand unchallenged for many years' – *The Times Literary Supplement*

The civilization which fought off the Persian invasion of 480 B.C., tore itself apart in the long Peloponnesian war between Athens and Sparta in the late fifth century and was overpowered by Macedon in the latter part of the fourth century is the subject of *Greek Society*. In this exciting study Professor Andrewes defines the basic and distinctive features of Greek Society during the late archaic and classical eras. His central chapters are devoted to a survey of the Greek world according to its functional and occupational categories, and he examines in turn the tribes, landowners, peasants, colonists, traders, craftsmen, slaves, soldiers and sailors who composed one of the greatest civilizations in history.

THE GREEKS

H. D. F. Kitto

This is a study of the character and history of an ancient civilization, and of the people who created it. Since its first publication as a Pelican, *The Greeks* has sold 1,400,000 copies.

The critics have said of it:

'The best introduction I have ever read to Ancient Greece. The author's liveliness of mind and style has enabled him to make a mass of information appetizing and digestible' – Raymond Mortimer in the *Sunday Times*

'Very easy to read ... a triumph of balance and condensation' – Harold Nicolson in the *Observer*

'Professor Kitto is a model historian – lively, accurate, and fully acquainted with the latest developments in the subject ... never vague ... often witty and always full of vigour' – *The Times Educational Supplement*

THE PELICAN HISTORY OF GREECE

A. R. Burn

There are few histories of Greece and still fewer designed for the general reader.

The Pelican History of Greece presents the whole story of Hellas in one volume and addresses itself principally to the adult reader with little or no knowledge of classical literature. Its narrative is readable, its scholarship modern, its enthusiasm infectious, and its judgements notably fair.

From the days of Mycene and the Heroic Age to the splendour of Athens and the conquests of Alexander, Mr Burns invests with new significance the works and words of an astonishing people.